GRAPHING JANE AUSTEN

Cognitive Studies in Literature and Performance

Literature, Science, and a New Humanities
Jonathan Gottschall

Engaging Audiences
Bruce McConachie

The Public Intellectualism of Ralph Waldo Emerson and W.E.B. Du Bois
Ryan Schneider

Performance, Cognitive Theory, and Devotional Culture
Jill Stevenson

Shakespearean Neuroplay
Amy Cook

Evolving Hamlet
Angus Fletcher

Cognition in the Globe
Evelyn B. Tribble

Toward a General Theory of Acting
John Lutterbie

Trusting Performance
Naomi Rokotnitz

Graphing Jane Austen
Joseph Carroll, Jonathan Gottschall, John A. Johnson, and Daniel J. Kruger

Graphing Jane Austen

The Evolutionary Basis of Literary Meaning

Joseph Carroll
Jonathan Gottschall
John A. Johnson
Daniel J. Kruger

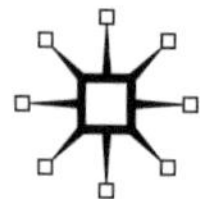

GRAPHING JANE AUSTEN

First published in 2012 by
PALGRAVE MACMILLAN®
in the United States—a division of St. Martin's Press LLC,
175 Fifth Avenue, New York, NY 10010.

Where this book is distributed in the UK, Europe and the rest of the world, this is by Palgrave Macmillan, a division of Macmillan Publishers Limited, registered in England, company number 785998, of Houndmills, Basingstoke, Hampshire RG21 6XS.

Palgrave Macmillan is the global academic imprint of the above companies and has companies and representatives throughout the world.

Palgrave® and Macmillan® are registered trademarks in the United States, the United Kingdom, Europe and other countries.

ISBN: 978–1–137–00240–2

Library of Congress Cataloging-in-Publication Data

Graphing Jane Austen : the evolutionary basis of literary meaning / Joseph Carroll . . . [et al.].
p. cm.—(Cognitive studies in literature and performance)
Includes bibliographical references.
ISBN 978–1–137–00240–2
1. Characters and characteristics in literature—Statistics. 2. English fiction—19th century—History and criticism. 3. English fiction—20th century—History and criticism. 4. Austen, Jane, 1775–1817—Characters. 5. Hardy, Thomas, 1840–1928—Characters. 6. Human behavior in literature 7. Reader-response criticism. I. Carroll, Joseph, 1949– II. Title: Evolutionary basis of literary meaning.

PR878.C47G73 2012
823′.80927—dc23 201104231

A catalogue record of the book is available from the British Library.

Design by Newgen Imaging Systems (P) Ltd., Chennai, India.

First edition: May 2012

10 9 8 7 6 5 4 3 2 1

Printed in the United States of America.

Contents

Figures and Tables

Figures

Tables

Acknowledgments

Several people have contributed helpful comments on part or all of this book while it was in progress, notably Brian Boyd, Gwendolyn Carroll, Paula Carroll, Mark Collard, Ellen Dissanayake, Denis Dutton, Harold Fromm, John Knapp, Richard Kopley, Matthew McAdam, Jessica McKee, Gary Saul Morson, and Michael Ryan. David Michelson went through the whole manuscript twice, at different stages. All these readers made constructive criticisms and offered welcome encouragement, but of course none is responsible for the contentions in the book.

Introduction

The Purpose of this Study

The research described in this book is designed to help bridge the gap between science and literary scholarship. Building on findings in the evolutionary human sciences, we constructed a model of human nature and used it to illuminate the evolved psychology that shapes the organization of characters in nineteenth-century British novels (Austen to Forster). Using categories from the model, we created a web-based survey and induced hundreds of readers to give numerical ratings to the attributes of hundreds of characters. Participants also rated their own emotional responses to the characters. Our findings enable us to draw conclusions on several issues of general interest to literary scholars—especially the determinacy of literary meaning, the interaction between gendered power relations and the ethos of community, and the evolutionary basis for telling stories and listening to them. The data on novels of the whole period provide an interpretive base line against which we graph the distinctive features of the novels in two case studies: all the novels of Jane Austen, and Thomas Hardy's *The Mayor of Casterbridge.*

This kind of research crosses several boundaries not usually crossed in literary study. Readers might thus reasonably wonder what to make of it—why we did it, and how we hope it might influence the whole field of literary study. To answer such questions, in the next section of the introduction, we locate our effort in a historical and theoretical context that includes the development of modern empirical methods, the conflict between "the two cultures," the decline of the humanities, the growth of the evolutionary human sciences, and the emergence of "literary Darwinism" as a distinct school of literary theory—part of a "third culture" that integrates research in the life sciences, the social sciences, and the humanities. In the conclusion to the book, we compare the research in *Graphing Jane Austen* with work in other schools of literary theory that take up similar subjects, engage similar themes, adopt similar ideas, or use similar methods.

Moving Past the Two Cultures

Steven Weinberg, a Nobel Laureate in Physics, makes a compelling case that the most important development in knowledge since ancient Greek philosophy consists of deploying empirical methods.[1] Those methods include formulating testable hypotheses, producing quantitative evidence, and using that evidence to falsify or confirm hypotheses. Researchers began to rely on empirical methods first in the Renaissance, roughly at the same time that humanists began both to recuperate ancient literature and to develop a distinctively modern form of literary culture. In some ways, science and the humanities have since then influenced each other. Scientific questions have emerged out of large imaginative and philosophical paradigms. And the humanities have absorbed information from science, adjusting their imaginative vision to the changing world picture produced by scientific discovery. Nonetheless, in method science and the humanities have remained fundamentally distinct.

In contrast to the culture of modern science, scholarship in the humanities progresses, if at all, by way of argument and rhetoric. More often than not, humanists believe that rhetoric operates within a qualitative realm radically incompatible with quantitative forms of evidence. In its most scholarly guise, traditional literary study aims at producing objective textual and historical information. Scholars weigh alternative explanations against the evidence. In the hands of a judicious scholar, this method can produce valuable results. Still, it has two serious deficiencies: (1) it contains no means for combating "confirmation bias"—the selective use of evidence to confirm favored hypotheses; and (2) it contains no means for settling differences between two or more plausible but incompatible hypotheses. In *The Two Cultures and the Scientific Revolution* (1959), C. P. Snow charged literary scholars with ignorance of scientific facts, but the absence of neutral, objective methods for assessing the validity of ideas is a deeper, more serious problem than the ignorance of particular facts.

All efforts at interpreting evidence are encompassed within larger theoretical paradigms.[2] In literary scholarship, those paradigms have often been speculative and rhetorical in character. During roughly the first two-thirds of the twentieth century, the most common interpretive frameworks available to literary study included quasi-scientific systems of thought drawn from outside the realm of humanistic culture—most prominently from Marxism (sociology and economics), Freudianism and Jungianism (psychology and anthropology), and Structuralism (linguistics and anthropology). The majority of literary critics did not clearly or unequivocally subscribe to any of these paradigms. Instead, most critics operated as eclectic free agents, spontaneously gleaning materials for interpretive models from the whole field of human discourse—from science, literature, philosophy, social science, history, current events, and common knowledge. This method can be designated "pluralistic humanism." The method is something like that of the Bower Bird, an artistic scavenger who carefully combs his territory, looking for shells, feathers, stones, or other bits of brightly colored material with which to decorate his bower, interrupted only by the necessities of eating, mating, and attacking and disrupting the artistic constructions of his competitors.

Old-fashioned literary Marxism, Freudianism, and structuralism sought to produce rhetorical "knowledge"—that is, interpretive commentary—in rough concord with a conceptual order supposed by its proponents to possess some solid grounding in scientific fact. Practitioners of pluralistic humanism, in contrast, typically conceived of their work as an alternative and autonomous order of knowledge—an order imaginative, subjective, and qualitative—and thus independent of scientific knowledge and incommensurate with it. In practice, it is not possible for any humanist to operate in a realm untouched by scientific information, but the claim for autonomy left the individual humanist free to pick and choose his rhetorical materials with no constraint other than that exercised by his or her own individual sense of what was plausible or rhetorically striking.

Over the past four decades or so, all these older forms of literary criticism have been partially assimilated to a new critical episteme and partially superseded by it. The new episteme is called by various names: "poststructuralism," "postmodernism," "cultural constructivism," "cultural critique," "critical theory," or most broadly and simply, "Theory." For convenience, we shall refer to the new episteme as "poststructuralism" but ask readers to understand that term in its broadest signification, including in it the whole array of attitudes and assumptions associated with the various alternative designations. Whatever one chooses to call it, the new episteme has incorporated Freudianism and Marxism (particularly in their Lacanian and Althusserian forms), but it has also overtly rejected the idea that empirical research can produce "objective" knowledge. Instead, it has envisioned science itself as a form of ideologically driven rhetoric, and it has thus subordinated scientific forms of knowledge to the kind of speculative theory that more typically characterizes the humanities. As Stanley Aronowitz puts it, science "is no more, but certainly no less, than any other discourse. It is one story among many stories." Within the poststructuralist frame of thinking, it is not permissible to say that a given scientific idea is "true" or that it "corresponds" closely to a "reality" that exists independently of the human mind. Consider, for instance, Gowan Dawson's commentary on efforts to integrate evolutionary psychology with studies in the humanities. As Dawson rightly observes, adopting a "realist" or "objectivist" approach to science "undermines the entire premise of recent literature and science studies." In his own work and that of his colleagues, Dawson explains, conceptions of science as an "intellectually authoritative mode of knowledge" have "long been proscribed."[3]

In literary studies, the key to subordinating science to rhetoric can be found in deconstructive philosophy. As practiced by Jacques Derrida, Paul de Man, J. Hillis Miller, Geoffrey Hartman, and their associates, deconstruction envisions all human cognition as operating within an all-encompassing realm of unstable and self-undermining semiotic activity. Deconstruction is no longer very prominent as a distinct school, but it remains a core element in poststructuralist thinking. The epistemological skepticism for which deconstruction provided a rationale was a theoretical prerequisite for the political criticism that has dominated literary studies since the 1980s. In the absence of progressive, empirical knowledge, all signs, even scientific signs, can be conceptualized as media for power politics. Current political criticism typically interprets discursive formations as symbolic enactments of a struggle between ruling social groups and subversive forms of group social identity, especially those of gender, race, and class.

One often now hears that "Theory," meaning poststructuralist theory, is a thing of the past.[4] In reality, most literary scholars have not left poststructuralist theory behind but have only internalized it. The categories they use derive chiefly from Foucauldian traditions: versions of Marxism and Freudianism filtered through deconstructive epistemology. Despite the many eulogies pronounced over the corpse of "Theory," in a survey of citations of books in the humanities in the year 2007, the most frequently cited authors were either the main luminaries in poststructuralist theory or thinkers who have been assimilated to the poststructuralist paradigm, especially Marxists, Freudians, and contributors to "the cultural construction of science."[5] The top three, in this order, were Foucault, Bourdieu, and Derrida. The top ten included Habermas, Judith Butler, and Bruno Latour. Freud and Deleuze ranked eleventh and twelfth. A group of 37 authors whose books had been cited 500 times or more included Marx, Nietzsche, Heidegger, Barthes, and Lacan. Perhaps needless to say, it did not include Darwin, Huxley, Edward O. Wilson, Sarah Hrdy, Robin Dunbar, Steven Pinker, or any other writer closely associated with evolutionary thinking in the human sciences.

Louis Menand, a distinguished senior literary scholar and an advocate of poststructuralist theory, recognizes that younger scholars in the humanities can declare themselves "post-theory" only because they have so completely internalized its axioms:

> There is a post-theory generation, bristling with an "it's all over" attitude, but when people of my generation look at the post-theory people, we recognize them immediately. They're the theory people. And their attitude is not "You've got it all wrong." It's "Stop repeating yourselves; we know this stuff better than you do."
>
> The profession is not reproducing itself so much as cloning itself. One sign that this is happening is that there appears to be little change in dissertation topics in the last ten years. Everyone seems to be writing the same dissertation, and with a tool kit that has not altered much since around 1990.[6]

Though Menand himself thinks "Theory" is profoundly right, he deplores the way in which younger scholars simply take it as a given. They seem unable to think critically about the fundamental ideas that guide their practice.

In short, for decades now nothing much has really changed in the way most humanists think. For close to two decades, though, the humanities have clearly been in crisis, demoralized by falling enrolments and funding, by eroding prestige within and beyond the academy, and by a sense of repetition and intellectual exhaustion. Monographs, edited volumes, and special journal issues have been devoted to "the crisis in the humanities," but few effective solutions have been proposed.[7] The most common response is to deplore the dismal conditions, blame public misperceptions or the degrading influence of late-capitalist consumerism, suggest a stepped-up campaign in public relations, and advise humanists to do precisely what they are already doing, only more vigorously. Menand offers a fairly typical instance. He cites all the usual statistics indicating institutional decline and registers the widespread contempt with which the educated public regard the academic humanities. Even so, he can envision no real alternative to the paradigm within which he himself works. While casting about desperately for almost any form of renewal in the humanities, he sternly admonishes his colleagues that the one course they must not on any account pursue is "consilience," that is, integrating literary study with the evolutionary human sciences. That option, he declares, would be "a bargain with the devil." Instead, what scholars in the humanities need to do is "hunt down the disciplines whose subject matter they covet and bring them into their own realm."[8] That strategy has not worked before, but perhaps if we keep trying…

As literary culture has been moving steadily further away from the epistemological standards that characterize scientific knowledge, science has been approaching ever closer to a commanding and detailed knowledge of the phenomena most germane to literary culture: to human motives, human feelings, and the operations of the human mind. Evolutionary biology, psychology, and anthropology—along with all contiguous disciplines such as behavioral ecology, affective and social neuroscience, developmental psychology, and behavioral genetics—have begun to penetrate the inner workings of the mind and make it accessible to precise empirical understanding. In Steven Pinker's provocative and stimulating title phrase, scientists are now in a position to give an ever more convincing account of *How the Mind Works.*

Over the past 15 years or so, a group of literary scholars has been assimilating findings from what Pinker calls "the new sciences of human nature."[9] Many "literary Darwinists" aim not just at creating another "approach" or "movement" in literary theory; they aim at fundamentally altering the paradigm within which literary study is now conducted. They want to establish a new alignment among the disciplines and ultimately to encompass all other possible approaches to literary study. They rally to Edward O. Wilson's cry for "consilience" among all the branches of learning.[10] Like Wilson, they envision nature as an integrated set of elements and forces extending in an unbroken chain of material causation from the lowest level of subatomic particles to the highest levels of cultural imagination. And like Wilson, they regard evolutionary biology as the pivotal discipline uniting the hard sciences with the social sciences and the humanities. They believe that humans have evolved in an adaptive relation to their environment. They argue that for humans, as for all other species, evolution has shaped the anatomical, physiological, and neurological characteristics of the species, and they think that human behavior, feeling, and thought are fundamentally constrained and informed by those characteristics. They make it their business to consult evolutionary biology and evolutionary social science in order to determine what those characteristics are, and they bring that information to bear on their understanding of the products of the human imagination. For the most part, the evolutionists in the humanities have been assiduous in incorporating new knowledge and scrupulous about speculating within the constraints of a biological understanding of human nature. So far, though, only a few have made use of empirical methods. As it seems to us, including empirical methods in the toolkit for literary scholarship is an important final step in bridging the gap between the two cultures.[11]

Not surprisingly, the ambitions of the literary Darwinists have often met with a skeptical response: "There have been previous efforts to establish a scientifically based criticism—Marxism, psychoanalysis, structuralism. All these efforts have failed. Why would yours be any different?" A fair question. Here is our answer: This effort is different because the historical conditions are different. We now have, for the first time, an empirically grounded psychology that is sufficiently robust to account for the products of the human imagination. Darwin's speculations about human nature in *The Descent of Man* were prescient, but evolutionary social science did not become a cumulative research program until the last quarter of the twentieth century.

Until the past few years, three theoretical deficiencies hampered efforts to form a paradigm in evolutionary social science. Early sociobiologists insisted that "selection" takes place only at the level of the gene and the individual organism. David Sloan Wilson has spearheaded the now largely successful effort to resuscitate the idea of "multi-level selection" and use it as the basis for a more adequate understanding of human sociality.[12] In the 1990s, "Evolutionary psychologists" distinguished themselves from sociobiologists by emphasizing "proximate mechanisms" that in ancestral environments fostered reproductive success, but in constructing their model of "the adapted mind," they left out the idea of flexible general intelligence. Books such as Kim Sterelny's *Thought in a Hostile World* (2003) and David Geary's *The Origin of Mind* (2005) demonstrate how that deficiency can be corrected.[13] The third major deficiency was an inadequate appreciation of "gene-culture co-evolution"—the idea that culture operates in reciprocally causal ways with the genetically transmitted features of human nature. That barrier, too, is now giving way. Theorists such E. O. Wilson, Ellen Dissanayake, John Tooby, Leda Cosmides, Brian Boyd, and Denis Dutton have made increasingly effective arguments that the arts are functionally significant features of human evolution.[14]

We believe these three gradual corrections have now produced a conceptual framework with the explanatory power of a true paradigm. Over the next few years, research in evolutionary literary study will provide a crucial test for the validity of this belief. The decisive evidence will be whether the literary Darwinists generate a cumulative body of explanatory principles that are in themselves simple and general but that nonetheless encompass the particularities and complexities of literature and the other arts. The research described in this book is offered as one contribution to that effort.

Agonistic Structure

The central concept in this study is "agonistic" structure: the organization of characters into protagonists, antagonists, and minor characters. We asked this question: does agonistic structure reflect evolved dispositions for forming cooperative social groups? Within the past decade or so, evolutionists in diverse disciplines have made cogent arguments that human social evolution has been driven partly by competition between human groups. That competition is the basis for the evolution of cooperative dispositions—dispositions in which impulses of personal domination are subordinated, however imperfectly, to the collective endeavor of the social group. Suppressing or muting competition within a social group enhances group solidarity and organizes the group psychologically for cooperative endeavor. Drawing on our own impressions about the features of temperament and moral character that typify characters in novels of the nineteenth century, we hypothesized that protagonists would form communities of cooperative endeavor and that antagonists would exemplify dominance behavior. And this is indeed what we found. In these novels, protagonists and their friends typically form communities of affiliative and cooperative behavior. Antagonists are typically envisioned as a force of social domination that threatens the very principle of community.[15]

Three Main Arguments

On the basis of the data collected through the questionnaire, we make three main arguments (1) that the novels in this study contain determinate structures of meaning that can be captured using the categories in our research design (chapter 3); (2) that differences between protagonists and antagonists are much more structurally prominent than differences between male and female characters (chapter 4); and (3) that agonistic structure in these novels fulfills an adaptive social function (chapter 5).

Under the influence of deconstructive skepticism, literary theorists have often affirmed that meanings are inherently indeterminate because they are inescapably caught up in semiotic slippages that produce irreconcilable implications. Writing two decades ago, D. A. Miller puts it thus: "Whenever a text makes confident claims to cognition, these will soon be rendered undecidable."[16] Adopting strong versions of Kuhn's theory of "paradigms," literary theorists have often also affirmed that every structure of meaning changes systemically in accordance with the interpretive framework being used. In the most extreme version of this idea, meaning is always preemptively determined—essentially created—by an "interpretive community."[17] Our findings lead us to conclusions different from both deconstructive indeterminacy and strong interpretive constructivism. We asked questions about the attributes of characters and the emotional responses of readers. The high degree of convergence in the answers to these questions suggests that authors determine which attributes readers see in characters and how they respond emotionally to those attributes.

For several decades now, no feature in personal and social identity has received more critical attention than sex and gender. Much of this criticism has taken as its central theme struggles for power based on sex. In chapter 2, in the section "Male and Female Characters by Male and Female Authors," we describe data on the way female authors depict female protagonists. In that data, we detect an undercurrent of feminist revolt. In chapter 4, though, we describe data indicating that struggles for power based on sex are less important than struggles for power based on the conflict between dominance and cooperation. Despite differences of sex, male and female protagonists are much more similar to each other than either are to male and female antagonists. Male and female antagonists, also, are much more similar to each other than either are to male or female protagonists. In the features that distinguish characters, being a protagonist or antagonist matters more than being male or female. This finding leads us to reconsider some of the basic assumptions that have guided feminist literary theory. We argue that feminist theory is troubled by a nagging, unresolvable conflict between "social constructivism" and "essentialism"—the contrasting ideas that sexual identity is an arbitrary social convention and that it is an irreducible, transcendent category. We identify the elements of truth in both constructivism and essentialism, reconcile them, and suggest a more consistent and comprehensive framework for analyzing gender in both life and fiction.

One of the most hotly debated issues in evolutionary studies in the humanities is whether the arts fulfill any adaptive function at all.[18] Various theorists have proposed possible adaptive functions, for instance, reinforcing the sense of a common social identity, fostering creativity and cognitive flexibility, enhancing pattern recognition, serving as a form of sexual display, providing information about the environment, offering game-plan scenarios to prepare for future problem-solving, focusing the mind on adaptively relevant problems, and making emotional sense of experience.[19]

One chief alternative to the idea that the arts provide *some* adaptive function is that literature and the other arts are like the color of blood or the gurgling noise of digestion—a functionless side-effect of adaptive processes. The data on agonistic structure point to a different conclusion. The ethos reflected in the agonistic structure of the novels replicates the egalitarian ethos of hunter-gatherers, who stigmatize and suppress status-seeking in potentially dominant individuals.[20] By supporting group solidarity, the egalitarian ethos fulfills an adaptive function for hunter-gatherers. If agonistic structure in the novels engages the same social dispositions that animate hunter-gatherers, our study would lend support to the hypothesis that literature can fulfill at least one adaptive social function. We argue that the novels enable readers to participate vicariously in an egalitarian social dynamic like that in hunter-gatherer societies. That vicarious participation presumably influences actual behavior.[21] If participating in an egalitarian social dynamic had adaptive value for ancestral populations, artistic media designed to foster egalitarian dispositions would presumably fulfill the same adaptive function.

Not all novels deploy morally polarized forms of agonistic structure in the clear-cut way exemplified by the average scores across the whole body of novels in this study. Agonistically problematic novels such as *Wuthering Heights* and *The Mayor of Casterbridge* suggest a still deeper, more general way in which novels fulfill evolved human needs. Theorists such as E. O. Wilson, Ellen Dissanayake, Terrence Deacon, and one of the present authors (Carroll) have argued that stories create imaginative virtual worlds through which we orient ourselves psychologically. Evolved and adaptive political impulses are deep and powerful—powerful enough to form the largest organizing feature in the ethos reflected in these novels of the nineteenth century. But human nature consists of more than evolved political dispositions. In the final section of chapter 5, after presenting the argument on the adaptive function of agonistic structure, we reflect on the agonistically problematic characters who display typically protagonistic intellectual traits but do not display typically protagonistic social traits.

The Scope of Our Claims

Assuming that we can make a convincing case for all three of the arguments described in the previous section, how far can we generalize from those conclusions to all literature, in every period and every culture? Logically, it is possible that no other literary texts anywhere in the world contain determinate meanings, display differences between protagonists and antagonists more prominent than differences between male and female characters, or fulfill any adaptive function at all. Hypothetically possible, but not very likely. If our arguments hold good for this body of texts, they demonstrate that determinate meaning is at least possible, that in at least one body of classic narratives, agonistic role assignment—being a protagonist or antagonist—looms larger than gender role assignment, and that the organization of characters in at least one important body of fictional narratives reflects evolved social dispositions that in ancestral populations fulfilled adaptive functions. It seems unlikely that in these three important respects this body of novels is wholly anomalous.

In proposing that agonistic structure in these novels fulfills an adaptive social function, we do not imagine that we have isolated the sole adaptive function of all literature. Quite the contrary. Along with other evolutionary theorists, we strongly suspect that literature fulfills other functions. Even if it is only one among other possible adaptive functions for narrative and drama, could we reasonably conclude that agonistic structure is a human universal—a formal structure that would appear in the narrative and dramatic productions in all cultures, at all periods, everywhere in the world? We argue that the social dynamics animating these novels derive from ancient, basic features of human nature. Such features would in all likelihood appear in some fictional narratives in most or all cultures. If morally polarized agonistic structure is in fact a human universal, we would be interested to know how it varies in form in different cultural ecologies. Marriage—the "publicly recognized right of sexual access to a woman deemed eligible for childbearing"—is a human universal but varies in form from culture to culture.[22] We might expect agonistic structure, like marriage, to vary in form.

These questions would make good topics of research for other studies. Until those studies are conducted, though, the topics are only a matter for theoretical speculation. For this current study, we can positively affirm only the conclusions we think that our data allow us to draw.

Audience

As a literary topic, British novels of the longer nineteenth century (Austen to Forster) is fairly broad, but our theoretical and methodological aims ultimately extend well beyond the specialist fields of British novels, the nineteenth century, British literature, narrative fiction, or even literary scholarship generally. We aim at engaging literary scholars in all fields and evolutionary scientists too. We hope to persuade literary scholars that empirical methods offer rich opportunities for the advancement of knowledge about literature, and we hope to persuade evolutionary human scientists that the quantitative study of literature can shed important light on fundamental questions of psychology. Our own research team combines these two prospective audiences. Two of us (Carroll and Gottschall) have been trained primarily as literary scholars, and two of us (Johnson and Kruger) primarily as psychologists.

While reaching out to these two academic audiences, we also hope to interest readers, inside and outside academe, who read classic novels and/or serious nonfiction for the sheer pleasure of it. Agonistic structure is deeply embedded in the human imagination. It influences most phases of our imaginative life—religion, philosophy, history, political ideology, workplace gossip, video games, sports, movies. An evolutionary understanding of agonistic structure can illuminate many dark corners of our cultural experience.

The Organization of the Book

In the first chapter, we describe the main features of our research design, explain methods for scoring characters, and offer guidance on assessing the reliability of the scores. In chapter 2, we lay out the results and give examples of scores in each set of categories. In chapters 3 through 5, we discuss the significance of our findings in three main areas: the determinacy of meaning, sexual politics, and the adaptive function of agonistic structure. Chapters 6 and 7 consist of case studies for authors and novels about which we have especially abundant data. In the conclusion, we come back to the largest themes in this introduction, comparing our approach with other approaches current in literary study, evaluating the charge that literary Darwinism is "reductive," and assessing our own results in relation to an ideal of a complete and comprehensive form of interpretive criticism.

Part I

Methods and Results

In the first chapter in part I, we explain the procedures that we used in collecting data, examine the pool of respondents, and weigh the validity of our methods. In the second chapter, after delineating the model of human nature that is the source of the categories on which we collected scores, we summarize all our main findings across the whole data set. In part II, we shall draw out the implications of those findings and then in part III look closely at results for particular novels

Chapter 1

A User's Manual

Procedures

Overview: Collecting Data and Sorting Characters into Sets

We created an online questionnaire, listed about 2,000 characters from 201 canonical British novels of the nineteenth and early twentieth centuries, and asked respondents to select individual characters and answer questions about them. Potential research participants were identified by scanning lists of faculty in hundreds of English departments worldwide and selecting specialists in nineteenth-century British literature, especially scholars specializing in the novel. Lists of English departments are available on the web, and most departments give a listing of faculty that contains information about their teaching and research interests. Invitations were also sent to multiple listservs dedicated to the discussion of Victorian literature or specific authors or groups of authors in our study. Approximately 519 respondents completed a total of 1,470 questionnaires on 435 characters from 134 novels. A copy of the questionnaire used in the study can be accessed at the following URL: *http://www-personal.umich.edu/~kruger/carroll-survey.html.* (The form is no longer active and will not be used to collect data.)

The questionnaire contains three sets of categories. One set consists of elements of the characters' personal identities: age, attractiveness, motives, the criteria of mate selection, and personality. (The sex of the characters was a given.) A second set of categories consists of readers' subjective responses to characters. Respondents rated characters on ten possible emotional responses and also signified whether they wished the character to succeed in achieving his or her goals.

The third set consists of four possible "agonistic" role assignments: (1) protagonists, (2) friends and associates of protagonists, (3) antagonists, and (4) friends and associates of antagonists. Respondents were free to fill out questionnaires on any character from the list.

Dividing the four agonistic character sets into male and female sets produces a total of eight character sets, with each set defined along three dimensions: a contrast between *major* and *minor* characters (Salience), a contrast between *good* and *bad* characters (Valence), and a contrast between *male* and *female* characters (Sex). We refer to protagonists and antagonists together as major characters and to their associates as "minor" characters. Following popular usage, we refer to protagonists and their associates as "good" characters and to antagonists and their associates as "bad" characters. In adopting the common terms "good" and "bad," we intend no preemptive moral judgments. As it happens, though, the data indicate that good and bad characters are heavily inflected with morally relevant traits. Popular usage evidently has its reasons.

Scoring the Characters

The questions on the attributes of characters are designed to produce summary impressions about characters. For instance, respondents are required to assess how much a given motive counts in the total set of all motives over that part of a character's life that is depicted in a novel. If motives change in changing circumstances, or if one motive conflicts with another, the respondents must weigh those differences and choose a score that reflects the relative importance of the motive in that character's life. The same principle applies to the emotional responses of readers. A reader might feel anger at a character but nonetheless feel sadness for his or her misfortunes. The scores that are registered for each emotion must be weighed in proportion to the total range of emotional effects produced by any given character.

Most of the categories in the questionnaire were coded on a five-point scale running from "unimportant" to "very important." ("I do not remember" was also included as an option but was seldom used by our respondents.) For instance, under the questions on motives, respondents were asked to rate a character on each of twelve motives by clicking a circle in a scale of one to five, with one being unimportant and five being very important. A respondent would thus have to decide whether, for instance, "gaining or keeping power" was, for a given character, unimportant, moderately unimportant, of average importance, moderately important, or very important. Multiple scores for individual characters were averaged, and that individual average was included in the average score for the character set to which that character was assigned.

The scores on motives, the criteria of mate selection, and emotional responses produced data that we condensed into smaller sets of categories through a statistical process known as "factor analysis." Factor analysis identifies items that tend to cluster together. (The details on each factor analysis can be found in appendix 6.) From 12 motives, factor analysis produced five motive factors; from seven mate-selection criteria, three mate-selection factors; and from ten emotional responses, three emotional response factors. For instance, under motives, factor analysis revealed that the desire for wealth, the desire for power, and the desire for prestige cluster together, forming a single factor that we call "Social Dominance." Under mate selection, the criteria of intelligence, kindness, and reliability cluster together, forming a single factor that we call "Intrinsic Qualities." Under emotional response, anger at a character correlates with disgust and contempt *for* the character and with fear *of* the character, and all these emotions together form a single factor that we call "Dislike." The personality terms that we used are from an already established set of factors, the "five-factor" or "Big Five" personality system. (The five factors are Extraversion, Agreeableness, Conscientiousness, Emotional Stability, and Openness to Experience.)

Motive factors, mate-selection factors, and emotional response factors are all composite categories. These composite categories are very useful in revealing large-scale patterns of relationship among the character sets. It is sometimes useful to look also at the scores on the constituent elements that go to make up each factor, especially when analyzing individual characters. For instance, the emotional response factor "Dislike" is a composite category in which the main components are anger, disgust, contempt, and fear. Count Dracula from Bram Stoker's *Dracula* and Mr. Collins from Jane Austen's *Pride and Prejudice* both score high on Dislike, but the largest constituent score for Count Dracula is fear, and for Mr. Collins contempt. At the level of character sets, such differences are merged into the large-scale patterns of relationship among factors. At the level of individual characters, the differences sometimes matter.

Averaging Scores and Using Majority Rule in Role Assignments

For characters who received multiple codings, the averaged scores for each such character are counted only once in the total set of scores. For instance, Elizabeth Bennet from Jane Austen's *Pride and Prejudice* was coded by 81 respondents. On each category, the scores of all respondents were averaged, and that average score is counted only once in the total data set. (We discuss the range of variation among multiple coders in a subsequent section: "Assessing Intercoder Reliability.") Elizabeth's averaged scores count precisely as much in the larger data set as the scores for any character who was coded only once. In each case, only one set of scores is averaged into the total of scores for all characters.

When multiple readers did not agree on role assignments, we assigned characters to the role designated by the majority of the respondents. Differences in designations of Salience usually involve only divided views as to whether a character should be designated a major character in his or her own right or, alternatively, as a friend or associate of a major character. Differences in designations of Valence usually involve judgments about whether a certain borderline blend of protagonistic and antagonistic features could more reasonably be located in a protagonistic or antagonistic category.

Big multiplot novels like *Bleak House*, *Vanity Fair*, and *Middlemarch* contain dozens of characters and more than one protagonist, but most of the characters are minor, and competent readers usually recognize the difference between the large group of characters who are distinctly minor and the small group of characters who form the chief focus of narrative attention and interest.[1] Differences in attributions of Salience do not usually reflect any difference of opinion as to whether some one main character should be designated a protagonist. Nor do such differences usually concern distinctly minor characters. Differences in designations of characters as major or minor occur chiefly with respect to characters within an inner protagonistic group of characters. The main source of uncertainty is just how narrowly to circumscribe the term "protagonist." Emma in Austen's *Emma*, for example, is clearly a protagonist. (So say 72 of 74 respondents.) But is her consort George Knightley also a protagonist, or only an associate of a protagonist? (One respondent designates him a protagonist, but 14 declare him only an associate of a protagonist.) The chief question that produces ambiguity in designating characters major or minor is whether to limit the application of the term "protagonist" to just one main character.

The process of creating a narrative focus and thus registering differences of Salience often begins with the title of a novel. Starting with the first fictional prose narratives that are generally recognized as "novels" in the English tradition—in the early eighteenth century—many of the titles of canonical novels consist of the name of some one main character or small group of characters, or with some close, descriptive proxy for such names, for instance: *Robinson Crusoe*, *Moll Flanders*, *Pamela*, *Clarissa*, *Joseph Andrews*, *Tom Jones*, *Humphrey Clinker*, *Ivanhoe*, *Rob Roy*, *Emma*, *Jane Eyre*, *Agnes Gray*, *Frankenstein*, *Oliver Twist*, *Barnaby Rudge*, *Dombey and Son*, *Nicholas Nickleby*, *Martin Chuzzlewit*, *David Copperfield*, *Little Dorrit*, *Barry Lyndon*, *Henry Esmond*, *Pendennis*, *The Virginians*, *The Newcomes*, *Mary Barton*, *Ruth*, *The Warden*, *Phineas Finn*, *Phineas Redux*, *The Prime Minister*, *The Duke's Children*, *Adam Bede*, *Silas Marner*, *Felix Holt*, *Romola*, *Daniel Deronda*, *A Little Princess*, *Little Lord Fauntleroy*, *The Return of the Native*, *Tess of the d'Urbervilles*, *The Mayor of Casterbridge*, *Jude the Obscure*, *Dr. Jekyll and Mr. Hyde*, *Alice's Adventures in Wonderland*, *Dracula*, *Kim*, *The Picture of Dorian Gray*, *Portrait of a Lady*, *The Princess Casamassima*, *The Ambassadors*, *The Secret Agent*, *Lord Jim*, and *Nostromo*. As this list should suggest, the idea of "Salience" is not an artificial theoretical construct fabricated by literary theorists. It is an idea that is implicit in the organization of narratives around the fortunes of some one main character or some small set of characters.

We could also take a set of titles from place names, for instance, *Mansfield Park*, *Wuthering Heights*, *Villette*, *The Old Curiosity Shop*, *A Tale of Two Cities*, *Bleak House*, *Barchester Towers*, *The Small House at Allington*, *The Mill on the Floss*, *Middlemarch*, *The Secret Garden*, and *Howard's End*. In virtually all such cases, the narrative is clearly organized around the fortunes of some one main character or small group of characters who happen to be associated with the place identified in the title. A similar observation applies to novels with titles that consist of thematic tags and symbolic images, as, for instance, *Sense and Sensibility*, *Pride and Prejudice*, *Persuasion*, *Vanity Fair*, *The Wings of the Dove*, *The Golden Bowl*, and *The Heart of Darkness*. The main characters in such novels typically exemplify the themes or symbols registered in the title. Without doing violence to the narrative focus, we could hypothetically retitle all these novels in the fashion of novels that take their names from the chief characters, for instance, *Catherine and Heathcliff* (*Wuthering Heights*), *Maggie Tulliver* (*The Mill on the Floss*), *The Dashwood Sisters* (*Sense and Sensibility*), *The Rise and Fall of Becky Sharp and the Fall and Rise of Amelia Sedley* (*Vanity Fair*), *The Death of Millie Theale and the Spiritual Trial of Merton Densher* (*The Wings of the Dove*), and *Marlow's Encounter with Kurtz* (*Heart of Darkness*). Novels are, above all else, stories about characters. They are fabricated biographies of imaginary people, sometimes whole life histories, sometimes just part a life.

Some of the most frequently coded characters occupy a border territory between the characteristics that typically define protagonists and antagonists. Becky Sharp in Thackeray's *Vanity Fair*, Catherine and Heathcliff in Brontë's *Wuthering Heights*, the Monster in Shelley's *Frankenstein*, Lucy Graham in Braddon's *Lady Audley's Secret*, and Dorian Gray in Wilde's *The Picture of Dorian Gray.* Agonistically ambiguous characters tend to be disagreeable or dangerous but adventurous and open-minded, and readers tend to respond to them with antipathy but also with pity or grudging admiration. For characters such as this, role assignments are often split. For instance, out of 17 codings for Frankenstein's Monster, eight respondents identified him as an antagonist; four as a protagonist; one as the friend or associate of a protagonist; and four as "other." Out of 26 respondents, 11 identified Heathcliff as a protagonist; 10 as an antagonist, and five said "other."

Agonistically ambiguous characters are extremely interesting—hence their disproportionate representation in the list of most frequently coded characters (appendix 3)—but their deviation from the norm does not subvert the larger pattern of agonistic structure. The larger pattern stands out clearly *despite* the blurring produced by the exceptions. An analogy might clarify this issue. When social scientists select a population of humans and score them on sexual orientation, a small percentage of their subjects have scores that are sexually ambiguous or that reverse heterosexual dispositions. The average scores for the total population nonetheless display clear patterns of heterosexual polarization—men preferring women, and women preferring men. Once one begins thinking statistically, one no longer gives undue prominence to special cases and exceptions. One thinks instead in terms of population averages. Within those population averages, one can make good analytic sense of the special cases and exceptions. If a protagonist or antagonist deviates from the average, that deviation enters deeply into the imaginative qualities that distinguish one novel from another. If a pattern of such deviations emerges across an author's whole body of work (as is the case, for example, with Jane Austen's protagonistic males), those deviations can help us to define the imaginative qualities that distinguish that author from other authors.

Borderline characters can be contrasted with characters who are clearly central or modal in their agonistic role assignments. For instance, the three most frequently coded characters are Elizabeth

Bennet of Austen's *Pride and Prejudice*, Emma Woodhouse of Austen's *Emma*, and Jane Eyre of Charlotte Brontë's *Jane Eyre*. Eighty of 81 respondents identified Elizabeth as a protagonist; 72 of 74 identified Emma as a protagonist; and 66 of 68 identified Jane as a protagonist. (Simple clicking mistakes might account for the absence of complete unanimity in these assignments.) So also for frequently coded antagonists: 11 of 12 respondents identified Count Dracula as an antagonist, and 6 of 7 identified Mrs. Norris as an antagonist. Mrs. Norris is Fanny Price's nemesis in Austen's *Mansfield Park*, and Fanny herself was identified as a protagonist by 17 of 18 respondents.

Standardizing the Scores

Since we are aiming at an audience that includes humanists and general readers who might not be familiar with the technical idiom of statistics, we summarize our results in largely discursive form. Most of the technical detail on the statistical analyses has been relegated to the appendices. To follow the results in the main text, a reader need understand only how to read the "standardized" scores used in the graphic displays. Standardized scores make comparison easier by reflecting the position of one character or character set relative to the average for all scores. The average score is set at zero, and one can tell instantly whether any standardized score is above or below average by whether it is a positive or negative number, respectively. Moreover, standardized scores derived from scales with different numbers of steps—say, from a three-point and a five-point scale—can be directly compared because both have the same new reference point: an average of zero.

The unit of measurement in standardized scores is the "standard deviation"—that is, the average distance from the average score. Each standard deviation is equal to one point. A score of .5 would thus equal one-half a standard deviation; a score of 1.5 would equal one-and-one-half standard deviations; and a score of 2 would equal two standard deviations. A score of –1 would equal a standard deviation *below* the average, and so on.

Units of standard deviation correlate with percentiles. For instance, on any given factor, for either a character set or an individual character, if a score is one standard deviation above the average, that score is higher than about 84 percent of all other scores on that factor. Half a standard deviation (.5) is higher than about 69 percent of all other scores. One-and-a-half standard deviations (1.5) is higher than about 93 percent of all other scores. For negative scores (below average rather than above average), the percentiles are the same, with the direction reversed. For instance, a score of one standard deviation below average is lower than about 84 percent of all other scores.

Displaying the Scores in Graphs

Looking at an example should quickly make readers comfortable with standardized scoring. Consider the scores on the three elements of "character success": Root For, Main Feature, and Achieves Goals. The scores for each of these categories were produced by responses to a single question. "On the whole, do you want this character to achieve his or her goals?" (= Root For). "In your opinion, is the success or failure of this character's hopes or efforts a main feature in the outcome of the novel?" (= Main Feature). "Does this character accomplish his or her main goals?" (= Achieves Goals). The graph in figure 1.1 displays the average scores on character success for four character sets—male and female protagonists and male and female antagonists:

The horizontal line at the zero point is the average score for all characters. All bars extending below that line signify scores below the average. All bars extending above the line signify scores above the average. Thus, the average male and female protagonists score above the average of all characters on all three categories: Root For, Main Feature, and Achieves Goals. Female protagonists score a higher than male protagonists on all three categories. Male and female

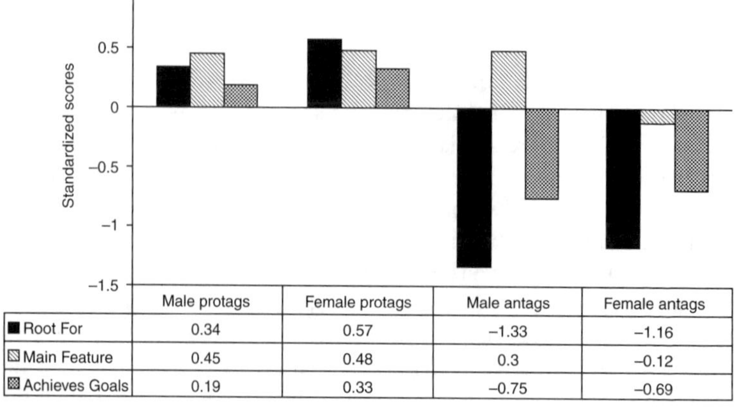

	Male protags	Female protags	Male antags	Female antags
Root For	0.34	0.57	−1.33	−1.16
Main Feature	0.45	0.48	0.3	−0.12
Achieves Goals	0.19	0.33	−0.75	−0.69

Figure 1.1 Character success for protagonists and antagonists.

antagonists score far below average (more than one standard deviation below average) on Root For, and they also score below average on Achieves Goals. Male antagonists score somewhat above average on Main Feature, and Female antagonists score a little below average on Main Feature. The scores are given in the data table below the bars. Negative scores indicate below-average scores, and positive scores indicate above-average scores.

The same principles of scoring hold good for individual characters. The graph in figure 1.2 includes both the average scores on character success for all female protagonists and also the scores for three specific female protagonists:

Lucy Snowe from Charlotte Brontë's *Villette* is a lonely young woman teaching in a Belgian school for girls. She watches other young people achieve the happiness denied to her. Our respondents wish her to succeed, but her successes are limited. Though she is a protagonist, she scores a little below the average female protagonist on Main Feature. For much of the action, she is merely an observer.

Isabel Archer is the protagonist of Henry James's novel *Portrait of a Lady*. She is unequivocally the center of attention in the story. She is an attractive person—beautiful, imaginative, adventurous, and generous. James himself is deeply sympathetic to her and expects the readers also to wish for her success. And they do. Isabel inherits a fortune, but she is young and inexperienced. Misled both by her own naive cultural idealism and by the intrigues of older, more cynical people, she makes a disastrous marriage choice. This choice is the

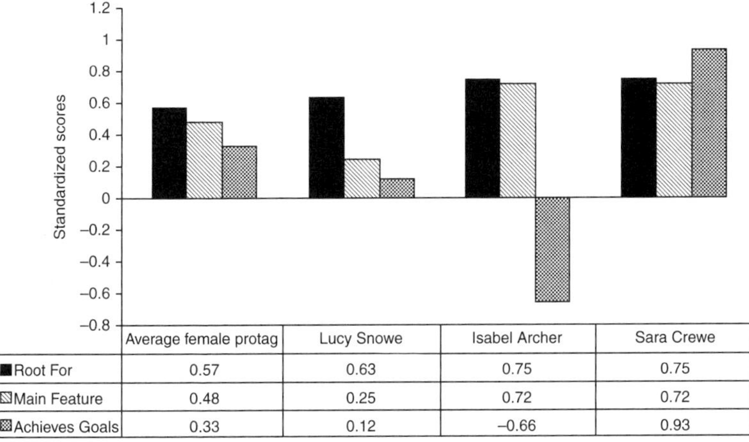

	Average female protag	Lucy Snowe	Isabel Archer	Sara Crewe
Root For	0.57	0.63	0.75	0.75
Main Feature	0.48	0.25	0.72	0.72
Achieves Goals	0.33	0.12	−0.66	0.93

Figure 1.2 Character success in three female protagonists.

culmination of her efforts to use her wealth for a noble purpose, and her score on Achieves Goals reflects this central failure in her career.

Sara Crewe is the child protagonist of Frances Hodgson Burnett's *A Little Princess*. She is the daughter of a wealthy man who leaves her at a boarding school but showers her with luxuries. When he dies, her funds are cut off and she is turned into a servant by the malevolent headmistress of the school. Despite the rigor of her lot, she befriends and teaches other children in the school, and eventually her wealth is restored to her. Though a child, she is in some respects a paradigmatic protagonist. She is a character of exceptional personal merits who is thrust into difficult circumstances, but retains her sense of honor and humanity. Readers very much wish her to succeed; her success or failure is unequivocally the main feature of the story; and she succeeds splendidly both in struggling against adversity and in attaining ultimate good fortune.

Evaluating the Reliability of the Scores

Demographics of the Respondents

The questionnaire included questions on the demographics of our respondents. We asked for their sex, age, and level of education, and we asked when they had read the novel they were coding and why they had read it. All participation was anonymous, but by using information about the age, sex, level of education, and how the respondents found out about the study, we produced identification strings that we can use to estimate the total number of individual respondents and segregate them into demographic categories.

Our data set contains a total of 519 unique identification strings. A few of these identification strings might contain multiple coders. For instance, a string might identify a coder as a 43-year-old female with a PhD who heard about the website through a listserv. That same string might apply to two or more respondents. Probably the number of such duplications is small. In any case, for our current purposes, we shall assume that each unique string identifies a distinct respondent. The figures that result from that assumption should provide a fairly accurate idea about the actual distribution of characteristics in our pool of respondents.

Out of 519 unique coders, 178 (34 percent) were male and 341 (66 percent) female. The youngest coder was 15; the oldest was 83, and the mean age was about 40. The standard deviation—the average distance from the mean—for the age of coders was about 15 years.

The majority of the respondents thus ranged between 25 and 55 years of age. Eighty-one percent of the respondents had a bachelor's degree or higher; 58 percent had advanced degrees; and 32 percent had doctorates. Fifty-two percent of the respondents had read the novel within the past year, and 85 percent within the past five years. Sixty percent read the novel for their own enjoyment, 20 percent for a class they were taking, and 19 percent for a class they were teaching.[2]

Experts and Amateurs

Most of our respondents are students or teachers of literature. Does this mean that our pool is biased, too narrow to give results that could be generalized beyond the habits of mind that distinguish this particular population? An analogy from personality rating studies can be used to illuminate our thinking on this issue. There are basically two kinds of people used in studies designed to rate personality. The first kind is what we call "knowledgeable acquaintances." These are people who know the targets to be rated very well because they have spent significant amounts of time with them, sometimes even living with them. They include family members, good friends, employers, and coworkers. The second kind of raters are those who have never met the targets before. These include just ordinary persons or professional psychologists who either interact with the person or observe them in a structured situation (an interview or task) for a limited period of time. If the raters simply observe the targets behind a one-way mirror or watch films of them without interacting with them, these are called "zero-acquaintance" raters.

There are advantages and disadvantages to using either type of rater. The knowledgeable acquaintances have the advantage of seeing the targets in a wide variety of situations, and therefore have an extensive experiential basis for rating the targets. However, because they are usually family members or friends, there are vested interests involved that can bias their ratings. For the other kind of raters, especially zero-acquaintance raters, biases that arise from personal relationships are avoided. But the amount of information on which their ratings are based is sparse and incomplete.

The analogy to our study is not perfect but still applies. We have chosen experts who are thoroughly familiar with the characters in the novels and probably Victorian literature in general. They therefore have a good familiarity with the characters and a rich context on which to base their codings. They have probably read the novels more than once, have studied and analyzed the characters, and even previously formulated their thoughts on the characters in writing. They are "knowledgeable acquaintances." But they are not necessarily biased. We could have gone the other route, asking naive persons with no particular expertise in literature and who had never read a Victorian novel to read novels that we select. It would have been a one-shot, zero-acquaintance type of study. Perhaps such coders would be more objective, but their level of motivation and background familiarity would be lower than the knowledgeable acquaintances. It is a trade-off. Whether one would find similar or different results is an empirical question.

Intercoder Reliability

In studies involving multiple raters or judges, psychologists often compute a statistic, *Cronbach's coefficient alpha estimate of reliability,* that quantifies the agreement among judges. Coefficient alpha amounts to the average correlation between two sets of judges' ratings, across all possible ways of dividing the judges into two groups. Coefficient alpha can vary from zero (no agreement) to one (perfect agreement). Psychologists generally agree that measurements need to show an alpha of at least .70 to be considered sufficiently reliable, although some argue that alphas as low as .40 are acceptable for a very small number of judges (four or less). When a set of measurements shows an acceptably high level of alpha, the standard procedure is to average all of the judges' ratings into a single aggregate measure.

We computed coefficient alpha estimates of intercoder reliability for a sampling of characters that were coded by two or more respondents. A fundamental axiom of psychometrics states that measurement reliability will increase as the number of judges increases. This is precisely what we found in our data. Consider the following sampling of characters with the number of coders and corresponding Cronbach alphas: Adam Bede (2, .73); Weena (3, .83); Augusta Elton (7, .94); Elizabeth Bennet (81, .99). Several observations can be drawn about these findings. First, the reliability coefficients are remarkably high, indicating that our respondents took the task seriously and provided high-quality data. Reliability coefficients from as few as two coders are above .70, clearly in a psychometrically acceptable range. Although we cannot compute reliabilities for characters based upon one coder, it is not unreasonable to assume that these coders also took their task seriously. Finally, these high-coefficient alpha coefficients justify averaging the responses for characters who were judged by two or more respondents (almost half of the characters in the study).

Levels of Consensus on Characters Who Received Multiple Codings

Respondents could choose either to assign a character to one of the four roles or check "I do not remember" or "other." To calculate the level of consensus in assigning characters to roles, we added up the total number of respondents who agreed with the majority in assigning a character to a role, and we divided that total number by the total number of respondents. If we retain the missing values ("other" and "I do not remember"), the average consensus rating for all 206 multiply coded characters is 81 percent (about eight out of ten agreeing). If we eliminate the missing values, the average consensus rating for all 206 multiply coded characters is about 87 percent (about nine out of ten agreeing).

Fifty-three characters are not included in character sets, either because respondents chose not to assign them to an agonistic role, or because of a "tie vote," that is, characters assigned to different agonistic roles by an equal number of respondents. The character sets contain a total of 382 characters (88 percent of the total of 435), but scores for all 435 characters are included in the average scores on all the substantive categories (motives, emotions, and the rest.).

Weighing the Reliability of Results for Characters with Only a Few Codings

For any singly judged character, we have no direct way of ascertaining if the judge's perceptions are normal and typical or idiosyncratic. But if we had too many idiosyncratic judges, the data would have been so noisy that no meaningful results would have emerged in subsequent statistical analyses. The fact that interpretable patterns did emerge argues against the idea that readers' perceptions of characters were unreliable.

Now, ideally, it is nice to have multiple raters so that when one computes average profiles across the raters, idiosyncratic biases can cancel each other out. In the examples of scores for individual characters given in chapter 2, we select characters from a group of characters who received at least seven codings. We understand that some readers might question whether seven readers is a sufficiently large sample, as seven seems intuitively like a very small number. Why do we feel fairly confident about results with as few as seven raters for a given character? There is a mathematical answer to this question, laid out by Jack Block in his book *The Q-Sort Method in Personality Assessment and Psychiatric Research.* With his 100-item California Q-set, he demonstrates that one can improve the reliability of the composite of multiple raters up to about seven raters. After that, adding additional raters does not make much of a difference. The type of items in the questionnaire that we used are not all that different from the kinds of items in the CQ-set; in fact, it would be easier to rate people with our questionnaire than the CQ-set. When we calculated alpha reliabilities for some of our characters, we found that we were getting perfectly acceptable reliabilities with as few as four judges. Indeed, we have no way of computing the reliability for singly judged characters, but the pattern of reliability analyses indicated that the judges were giving us good data.

There are two situations in which it is crucial to have multiple raters for a character: (1) a case study of a single character and (2) a comparison of the profiles of individual characters. When we focus on individual characters, it is essential that we have reliable profiles based on a sufficient number of judges because we are asserting that each of these profiles is precise and accurate. These kinds of analyses require more precision at the level of individuals than analyses that compare the averages of, say, protagonists versus antagonists, or correlations among variables. The latter kinds of analyses are employing the full sample size of 435, so it doesn't much matter if a character here or there has idiosyncratic ratings; limited noise from a few oddball ratings are not going to distort real patterns in the data. But if we want to claim that Michael Henchard, the title character in Hardy's *Mayor of Casterbridge*, has a high level of Social Dominance and low level of Constructive Effort, we need to have enough judges to give us a reliable, accurate assessment of those motives.

The Sex of Readers

Since the sex of characters is so clearly important in novels, one might reasonably anticipate that differences of sex would also be manifested in the responses of readers. If that were the case, the analysis of scores on characters would have to be divided into separate sets for male and female respondents. Accordingly, we conducted tests to compare scores by male and female respondents. What we actually found is that male and female respondents display negligible differences in scores on the same characters. (For details on the statistical analyses, see appendix 4.) That finding suggests that authors exercise a high degree of control in determining both the substantive attributes of characters and the emotional responses readers have to characters.

Competence in reading evidently requires that readers objectively register the meanings with which authors have invested their texts. With respect to the attributes of characters, that result is perhaps not very surprising. Writers signify that their characters possess certain definite qualities, and readers register the existence of those qualities in the characters. With respect to the emotional responses of readers, the convergence of male and female readers is more arresting. It suggests that the emotional responses of readers are tightly linked with the actual attributes of characters. It suggests also that emotional responses are strongly constrained by attributes that are created by authors. Rumors about "the death of the author," it would seem, have been greatly exaggerated.[3] Authors are people who mean to say certain definite things about their characters, and to evoke certain definite responses. Readers are people who understand what the authors mean to say and respond in ways that correspond to the authors' expectations of response.

Speaking as devil's advocates, we could propose an alternative explanation for the high level of agreement in male and female responses—an alternative concordant with Stanley Fish's concept of "interpretive communities."[4] According to that concept, readers converge not because they share objectively valid understandings of determinate meanings intended by an author; they converge because, at any given time, their responses are dominated by the norms and conventions of the community in which they live. Fashions and prejudices do of course enter into the responses of readers: that is the truistic part of Fish's theory. The element of radical innovation in the theory is to isolate and universalize the idea of fashion. From the Fishean perspective, no reader is capable of thinking outside the range of a monolithic set of shared assumptions. This Fishean view has had its own day of fashion, and it is still an active component in the organon of postmodern literary theory, but it will not stand serious inspection.[5] In reality, readers never operate under a single monolithic set of norms. They are not passive media for the transmission of transcendent interpretive conventions. They are critical agents capable of assessing evidence and evaluating degrees of probability in alternative, competing hypotheses.

We are confident that our readers will exercise their own critical judgment about the scores that characters receive in this study. Is it the case, or not, that Dorothea Brooke in *Middlemarch* is strongly motivated to seek education? Does sorrow form a relatively slight part of Jane Austen's tonal palette, or not? Does Henchard in *The Mayor of Casterbridge* have a volatile and aggressive personality, or not? Does the fate of Tess Durbeyfield produce sadness in readers, or not? Our respondents' scores on these and other such questions can be weighed against specific citations from the novels. In our own judgment, on the whole and on the average, bias in response seems to have had very narrow limits.

We can envision one alternative explanation for the homogeneity of subjective responses in male and female respondents. The characters and authors in our study are both from the longer nineteenth century (Austen to Forster), and the respondents are from the present. One might argue that the characters are sex-differentiated because social roles during the nineteenth century were more sex-differentiated than they are now. Respondents at the present time would recognize the sex differences attributed to characters, but would not themselves differ in their subjective responses to characters. Empirical support for that hypothetical argument would require evidence that males and females at the present time do not, in fact, differ in various ways related to subjective response—to motives and the criteria of mate selection, personality, behavioral patterns, cognitive styles, and styles of interpersonal behavior. As it happens, there is massive evidence that points in the other direction. Research in many fields—in developmental psychology, personality psychology, social psychology, cognitive neuroscience, sexual behavior, and quantitative literary analysis—consistently points toward pervasive differences of sex.[6] Male and female respondents do not differ substantially in subjective response to characters, but the absence of difference in subjective response cannot plausibly be attributed to a general absence of sexual differences between contemporary males and females. Unlike the Eloi in H. G. Wells's *The Time Machine*, men and women at the present time have not ceased to be significantly differentiated by sex.

Some Gentle Encouragement about the Statistics

Using just a few common concepts, readers with no statistical training should be able to grasp our findings and follow our arguments. The word "correlation" is part of the common idiom. We all intuitively grasp the idea that some traits tend to appear in company with other traits. In its technical, mathematical aspects, factor analysis can be demanding, but the basic concept—traits clustering into groups—is part of the way we all naturally think. We naturally sort related items into categories. Standardized scores are easy to read. In a bar graph with standardized scores, bars that rise above the horizontal centerline indicate scores that are above average, and bars that fall below the centerline indicate scores that are below average. To follow in detail the procedures involved in conducting *t*-tests and analysis of variance (ANOVA) would require technical training, but to understand the results of the significance tests we report, one need only register that a "statistically significant" difference between two character sets means a difference that is so large that it is unlikely to have resulted from chance. For readers who wish to follow the statistical analyses in more detail, we have included a guide to the basic procedures in appendix 4. We have also published two articles on this study for a professional social science audience with advanced training in statistics.[7]

Chapter 2

Agonistic Structure Differentiated by Sex

Does Agonistic Structure Exist?

The organization of characters into eight sets forms an implicit empirical hypothesis—the hypothesis that agonistic structure, differentiated by sex, is a fundamental shaping feature in the organization of characters in the novels. We predicted (1) that each of the eight character sets would be sharply defined by a distinct and integrated array of features, that these features would correlate in sharply defined ways with the emotional responses of readers, and that both the features of characters and the emotional responses of readers would correlate, on the average, with character role assignments; (2) that characters identified as protagonists and their friends and associates would have attributed to them, on average, the features to which readers are most attracted and that they most admire; (3) that characters identified as antagonists and their friends and associates would have attributed to them, on average, the characteristics for which readers feel an aversion and of which they disapprove; (4) that protagonists would most completely realize the approbatory tendencies in reader response; and (5) that antagonists would most completely realize the aversive tendencies. Taken individually, each of these propositions might seem obvious, but only if one presupposes the validity of the terms "protagonist" and "antagonist"—the very terms our study is designed to put to the test.

The very existence of agonistic structure is a topic about which speculative opinion could easily differ, and about which speculative arguments could go on endlessly and inconclusively. Are characters divided in authors' intentions and readers' responses into protagonists, antagonists, and minor characters? From one perspective, the categories that make up agonistic structure could be deprecated as so obvious, so self-evident, that they need no confirmation. The terms "protagonist" and "antagonist" are, after all, part of the common parlance. From this perspective, a research design oriented to substantiating the existence of agonistic structure could not fail to produce positive results, and would thus be trivial. From another perspective, suppositions about the self-evident nature of agonistic role assignments could be deprecated as naive and misconceived, moralistic and simple-minded. A theorist adopting this second perspective might argue that characters in novels, like real human beings, are complex, that they have both egocentric and cooperative dispositions, and that consequently they cannot be neatly categorized into good guys and bad guys. Some such idea is at work behind all contrasts between "serious" fiction, which depicts morally complex characters, and "melodramas," which depict morally polarized good and bad characters. (F. R. Leavis provides a canonical instance of this contrast.)[1] Or the theorist might argue that values are context-dependent, so that what counts as good and bad alters with circumstances, with varying cultural norms, and with differences in personal identity. Such contentions would be consistent with "reader-response" theories and with the forms of "cultural relativism" that have bulked so large in literary studies over the past few decades.

By themselves, the claims originating from either of these perspectives might seem plausible enough, but the contrast between them enables us to reject one of them out of hand. If it can plausibly be claimed that the idea of agonistic structure is naive and misguided, it cannot be the case that the idea of agonistic structure is so obvious as not to need support or argument.

The four categories on which we collected data—motives, mating, personality, and emotional responses—provide evidence for the reality and force of agonistic structure in these novels. Motives are the basis for action in human life. Selecting a sexual or marital partner drives reproductive success and evokes, accordingly, exceptionally strong feelings. Personality traits are dispositions to act on motives. Emotions are the proximal mechanisms that activate motives and guide our social judgments, including our judgments of imaginary people.[2]

These four categories take in a very broad swath of human experience, the depiction of characters in novels, and readers' responses to those depictions. If the agonistic patterns produced by the categories had been dim, feeble, and muddled, vague in outline and inconsistent in their relations to one another, that result would have strongly suggested that agonistic structure does not actually exist, or if it exists at all, does not account for much in the novels. As it turns out, though, the patterns are not vague and inconsistent. They are clear and robust.

In this chapter, we first outline the concept of human nature from which we derived the categories, then take up each of the four categories in turn, describing the dimensions in each, displaying scores for protagonists and antagonists, and giving examples of scores for particular characters in each category. The scores for protagonists and antagonists are more sharply polarized than the scores for all good versus all bad characters. Accordingly, we display graphic results only for the major character sets. Those results most clearly illuminate the forces at work in the system as a whole. Differences between major and minor characters are noted along the way.

A Model of Human Nature

The categories on which we measure attributes of character and responses of readers derive from an evolutionary concept of human nature—that is, the genetically transmitted dispositions that characterize the human species as a whole. One of our chief aims in this study was simply to demonstrate that categories from evolutionary psychology could be effectively used to capture major features in the organization of characters in these novels. In the degree to which the research design in *Graphing Jane Austen* proves successful, it gives evidence in support of the concept of human nature implicit in the questionnaire. Until fairly recently in literary history, most writers and literary theorists presupposed that human nature was their subject and their central point of reference. Dryden following Horace, who follows others, offers a representative formulation. In "Of Dramatic Poesy," Dryden's spokesman Lisideius defines a play as "a just and lively image of human nature, representing its passions and humours, and the changes of fortune to which it is subject; for the delight and instruction of mankind" (25).[3] The understanding of human nature in literature is the most articulate form of what evolutionists call "folk psychology."[4] When writers invoke human nature, or ordinary people say, "Oh, that's just human nature," what do they have in mind? They almost always have in mind the basic animal and social motives: self-preservation, sexual desire, jealousy, maternal love, favoring kin, belonging to a social group, desiring prestige. Usually, they also have in mind basic forms of social morality: resentment against wrongs, gratitude for kindness, honesty in fulfilling contracts, disgust at cheating, and the sense of justice in its simplest forms—reciprocation and revenge. All of these substantive motives are complicated by the ideas that enter into the folk understanding of ego psychology: the primacy of self-interest and the prevalence of self-serving delusion, manipulative deceit, vanity, and hypocrisy. Such notions of ego psychology have a cynical tinge, but they all imply failures in more positive aspects of human nature—honesty, fairness, and impulses of self-sacrifice for kin, friends, or the common good.

The most comprehensive scientific concepts for the systemic organization of the parts of human nature derive from "human life history theory." All species have a "life history," a species-typical pattern for birth, growth, reproduction, social relations (if the species is social), and death. For each species, the pattern of life history forms a reproductive cycle. In the case of humans, that cycle centers on parents, children, and the social group. Successful parental care produces children capable, when grown, of forming adult pair bonds, becoming functioning members of a community, and caring for children of their own. "Human nature" is the set of species-typical characteristics regulated by the human reproductive cycle.[5]

Human beings have a life history that is similar in some ways to that of their nearest relatives the chimpanzees (Boehm; A. Buss; de Waal; Stanford), but humans also have unique species characteristics deriving from their larger brains and more highly developed forms of social organization. Unlike chimpanzees and most other mammals, humans display pair-bonded male-female parenting; and unlike all other animals, they combine pair bonding with complex social organizations that include cooperative groups of males. Humans take longer to grow up, allowing time for their brains to mature and their social skills to develop.[6] And finally, for humans culture has an importance that it does not have in other species. Other species have adaptations for cooperation in social groups with specialized functions and status hierarchies. Other animals engage in play, produce technology, and share information. Humans alone produce imaginative artifacts designed to provide aesthetic pleasures, evoke subjective sensations, express emotions, depict nature or human experience, and delineate through symbols the salient features of their experience. Dispositions for the arts have evidently coevolved with the other genetically transmitted dispositions of human nature—survival, mating, kinship, friendship, dominance, cooperative group endeavor, and intergroup competition. If the arts are adaptively functional, that kind of causal interdependence would be part of the evolutionary process that evolutionists denote as "gene-culture co-evolution."[7]

In an earlier phase of thinking in the evolutionary human sciences, some theorists gave too little attention to intellect and imagination as motives and needs. More recent work has been correcting this deficiency. By including intellect and imagination in our model of human nature, we obtained higher resolution in our profiles of characters in the novels. Conversely, the correlation among all the elements in our design offers empirical support for the proposition that intellect and imagination need to be taken into account in building a model of human nature.[8]

Attributes of Characters and Emotional Responses of Readers

Motives

For the purposes of this study, we divided human life history into a set of 12 basic motives—that is, goal-oriented behaviors regulated by the reproductive cycle. For survival, we included two motives—survival itself (fending off immediate threats to life), and performing routine work to earn a living. We also asked about the importance of acquiring wealth, power, and prestige, and about the importance of acquiring a mate in both the short term and the long term. In the context of these novels, short-term mate selection would mean flirtation or illicit sexual activity; long-term mate selection would mean seeking a marital partner. Taking account of "reproduction" in its wider significance of replicating genes one shares with kin ("inclusive fitness"), we asked about the importance of helping offspring and other kin. For motives oriented to positive social relations beyond one's own kin, we included a question on "acquiring friends and making alliances" and another on "helping nonkin." And finally, to capture the uniquely human dispositions for acquiring complex forms of culture, we included "seeking education or culture" and "building, creating, or discovering something."

We predicted (1) that protagonists would be generally affiliative in their motives—concerned with helping kin and making friends; (2) that antagonists would be chiefly concerned with acquiring wealth, power, and prestige; and (3) that protagonists would on average be much more concerned than antagonists or minor characters with acquiring education and cultural knowledge.

When we submitted scores on the 12 separate motives to factor analysis, five main factors emerged: Social Dominance, Constructive Effort, Romance, Subsistence, and Nurture. Seeking wealth, power, and prestige all have strong positive loadings on Social Dominance, and helping nonkin has a moderate negative loading. That is, helping nonkin correlates negatively with seeking wealth, power, and prestige. Constructive Effort was defined most strongly by loadings from the two cultural motives, seeking education or culture, and creating, discovering, or building something, and also by loadings from two prosocial or affiliative motives: making friends and alliances and helping nonkin. Romance is a mating motive, chiefly loading on short-term and long-term mating. Subsistence combines two motives: survival and performing routine tasks to gain a livelihood. Nurture is defined most heavily by loadings from nurturing/fostering offspring or other kin, and that motive correlates negatively with short-term mating. Helping nonkin also contributes moderately to this factor, bringing affiliative kin-related behavior into association with generally affiliative social behavior.

Male and female antagonists both display a pronounced and exclusive emphasis on Social Dominance (figure 2.1).

Male protagonists score higher than any other character set on Constructive Effort and on Subsistence. Female protagonists score higher than any other character set on Romance, but their positive motives are fairly evenly balanced among Constructive Effort, Romance, and Nurture. In these novels, female protagonists are largely restricted to the nubile age range. That restriction corresponds with a pronounced emphasis on Romance as a motive.

The opposition between dominance and affiliation in the novels can clearly be linked to a robust and often-replicated finding

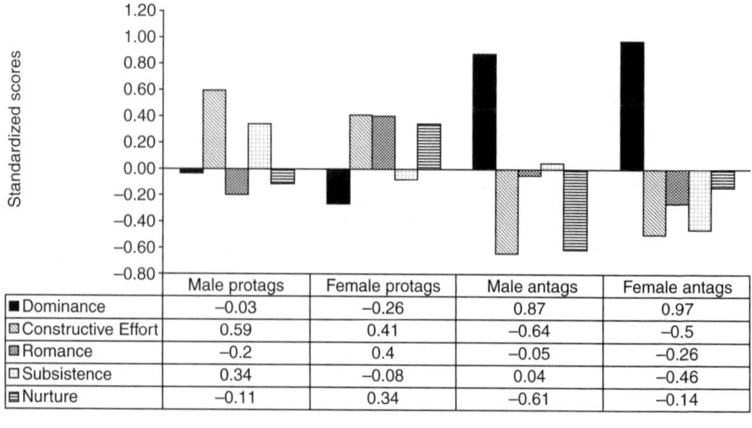

	Male protags	Female protags	Male antags	Female antags
Dominance	–0.03	–0.26	0.87	0.97
Constructive Effort	0.59	0.41	–0.64	–0.5
Romance	–0.2	0.4	–0.05	–0.26
Subsistence	0.34	–0.08	0.04	–0.46
Nurture	–0.11	0.34	–0.61	–0.14

Figure 2.1 Motive factors in protagonists and antagonists.

in psychological studies of motives and personality. Summarizing research into basic motives, David Buss observes that in cross-cultural studies the two most important dimensions of interpersonal behavior are "power and love." Surveying the same field and citing still other antecedents, Paulhus and John observe that in debates about "the number of important human values," there are two, above all, that are "never overlooked." They designate these values "agency and communion" and associate them with contrasting needs: the need for "power and status" on one side and for "approval" on the other.[9]

Examples

Dorothea Brooke in George Eliot's *Middlemarch* is an exemplary female protagonist. She scores low on Dominance (–.9), very high on Constructive Effort (1.39), somewhat above average on Romance (.19), and fairly high on Nurture (.52). In contrast, Mrs. Norris, an antagonist from Austen's *Mansfield Park*, scores very high on Dominance (1.46) and low on Constructive Effort (–.76). The narrator-protagonist in Dickens' *Great Expectations*, Pip (Philip Pirrip), is a more equivocal, borderline character. He scores unusually high on Dominance (.55), but he also scores high on Constructive Effort (.94) and on Romance (.75).

Criteria for Selecting Mates

Evolutionary psychologists have identified mating preferences that males and females share and also preferences that differ by sex. Males and females both value kindness, intelligence, and reliability in mates. Males preferentially value physical attractiveness, and females preferentially value wealth, prestige, and power. These sex-specific preferences are rooted in the logic of reproduction and have become part of human nature, because they had adaptive value in ancestral environments. Physical attractiveness in females correlates with youth and health—hence with reproductive potential. Wealth, power, and prestige enable a male to provide for a mate and her offspring.[10] We anticipated that scores for mate selection would correspond to the differences between males and females found in studies of mate selection in the real world. Since protagonists typically evoke admiration and liking in readers, we anticipated that protagonists would give stronger preference than antagonists to intelligence, kindness, and reliability. We reasoned that a preference for admirable qualities in a mate would evoke admiration in readers.

We asked questions about selecting mates in both the short term and the long term. In the results of the factor analyses for mate selection, the loadings for short-term and long-term mating are almost identical and divided with the sharpest possible clarity into three distinct factors: Extrinsic Attributes (a desire for wealth, power, and prestige in a mate), Intrinsic Qualities (a desire for kindness, reliability, and intelligence in a mate), and Physical Attractiveness (that one criterion by itself).

We anticipated differences in mate preferences in the short and long term, but our respondents evidently read the question on short-term mating to mean something different from what we had in mind. We had in mind illicit sexual activity. But respondents gave scores on short-term mating to many characters who do not engage in illicit sex. In many cases, the respondents evidently interpreted short-term mating to mean any romantic excitement in its early phases, even for relations that eventually culminate in marriage. The scores on selecting mates in the short and long term are essentially equivalent. We give the results here only for the long term (figure 2.2), but the examples will include a couple of instances of criteria for mating in the short term.

Female protagonists and antagonists both give a stronger preference to Extrinsic Attributes—wealth, power, and prestige—than male protagonists or antagonists, but female antagonists exaggerate the female tendency toward preferring Extrinsic Attributes. The emphasis female antagonists give to Extrinsic Attributes parallels their

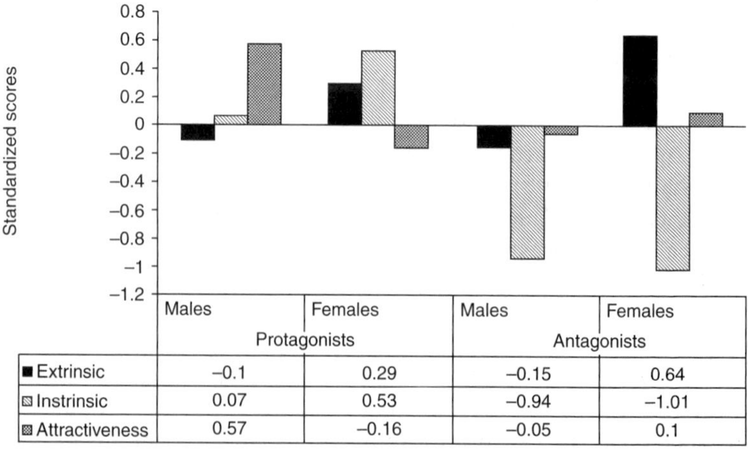

	Males	Females	Males	Females
	Protagonists		Antagonists	
■ Extrinsic	−0.1	0.29	−0.15	0.64
▨ Instrinsic	0.07	0.53	−0.94	−1.01
▩ Attractiveness	0.57	−0.16	−0.05	0.1

Figure 2.2 Criteria used by protagonists and antagonists in selecting marital partners.

single-minded pursuit of Social Dominance. Female protagonists give a more marked preference than male protagonists to Intrinsic Qualities—intelligence, kindness, and reliability.

We did not anticipate that male protagonists would be so strongly preoccupied with Physical Attractiveness relative to other qualities, nor did we anticipate that male antagonists would be so relatively indifferent to Physical Attractiveness. The inference we draw from these findings is that the male desire for physical beauty in mates is part of the ethos in the novels. It is part of the charm and romance of the novels, part of the glamor. Male antagonists' relative indifference to Physical Attractiveness seems part of their general indifference to affiliative relationships.

If one were to look only at the motive factors, one might speculate that male antagonists correspond more closely to their gender norms than female antagonists do. Male antagonists could be conceived as personified reductions to male dominance striving. The relative indifference male antagonists feel toward any differentiating features in mates might then look like an exaggeration of the male tendency toward interpersonal insensitivity. Conceived in this way, male antagonists would appear to be ultramale, and female antagonists, in contrast, would seem to cross a gender divide. Their reduction to dominance striving would be symptomatic of a certain masculinization of motive and temperament. They would be, in an important sense, desexed. Plausible as this line of interpretation might seem, it will not bear up under the weight of the evidence about male antagonists' relative indifference to Physical Attractiveness in a mate. Like female antagonistic dominance striving, that also is a form of desexing. Dominance striving devoid of all affiliative disposition constitutes a reduction to sex-neutral egoism. The essential character of male and female antagonists is thus not a sex or gender-specific tendency toward masculinization; it is a tendency toward sexual neutralization in the isolation of an ego disconnected from all social bonds.

Examples

Elizabeth Bennet from Austen's *Pride and Prejudice* offers an exemplary instance of criteria for selecting mates in female protagonists. She scores moderately high on seeking Extrinsic Attributes in a mate (.32), very high on seeking Intrinsic Qualities (1.15), and just about average on seeking Physical Attractiveness (–.03). In contrast to Elizabeth, Augusta Elton, an antagonist from Austen's *Emma*, scores very high on seeking Extrinsic Attributes (1.45) and very low on seeking Intrinsic Qualities (–1.15). Elizabeth's eventual marital choice, Fitzwilliam Darcy, deviates somewhat from the average male protagonist. He scores fairly high on seeking Physical Attractiveness (.59) but also high on seeking Extrinsic Attributes (.60) and exceptionally high, for a male, on seeking Intrinsic Qualities (.81). Oscar Wilde's Dorian Gray displays a hyper-male mating profile. He mates only in the short term, scores low on seeking Intrinsic Qualities (–.85) and—typically for a male—high on seeking Physical Attractiveness (.87).

Tess from Hardy's *Tess of the d'Urbervilles* offers clear instances of both short- and long-term mating. Her short-term relations are with Alec d'Urberville, a sexual predator. She does not so much select Alec as reluctantly accept capture by him. Our respondents rate him low on Intrinsic Qualities (–.69). In contrast, she selects her husband Angel Clare chiefly for his Intrinsic Qualities (.62). Becky Sharp, from Thackeray's *Vanity Fair*, is a more problematic character. She is agonistically borderline—amoral but spunky and bright. Her mate-selection preferences, though, are unequivocally those of a female antagonist, with high scores for Extrinsic Attributes in both the short (1.32) and long (1.64) term, and with very low scores for Intrinsic Qualities in both the short (–.85) and long (–1.46) term.

Personality Factors

The standard model for personality is the five-factor or "big five" model. *Extraversion* signals assertive, exuberant activity in the social world versus a tendency to be quiet, withdrawn, and disengaged. *Agreeableness* signals a pleasant, friendly disposition and a tendency to cooperate and compromise, versus a tendency to be self-centered and inconsiderate. *Conscientiousness* refers to an inclination toward purposeful planning, organization, persistence, and reliability, versus impulsivity, aimlessness, laziness, and undependability. *Emotional Stability* reflects a temperament that is calm and relatively free from negative feelings, versus a temperament marked by extreme emotional reactivity and persistent anxiety, anger, or depression. *Openness to Experience* describes a dimension of personality that distinguishes open (imaginative, intellectual, creative, complex) people from *closed* (down-to-earth, uncouth, conventional, simple) people.[11]

We predicted that (1) protagonists and their friends would on average score higher on the personality factor Agreeableness, a measure of warmth and affiliation; and (2) that protagonists would score higher than antagonists on Openness to Experience, a measure of intellectual vivacity.

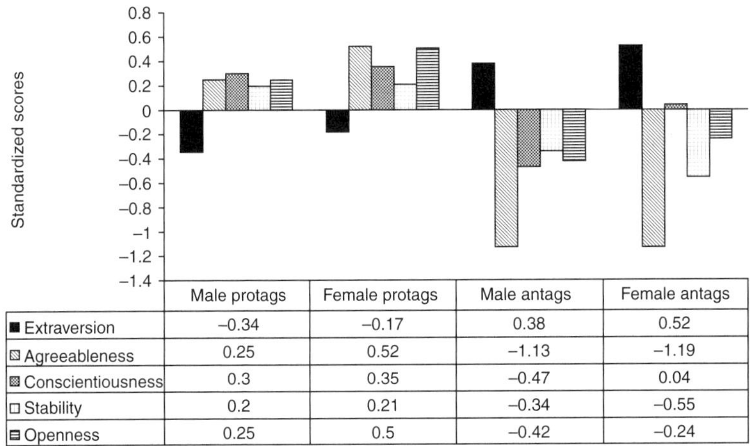

	Male protags	Female protags	Male antags	Female antags
Extraversion	−0.34	−0.17	0.38	0.52
Agreeableness	0.25	0.52	−1.13	−1.19
Conscientiousness	0.3	0.35	−0.47	0.04
Stability	0.2	0.21	−0.34	−0.55
Openness	0.25	0.5	−0.42	−0.24

Figure 2.3 Personality factors in protagonists and antagonists.

Male and female protagonists are both somewhat introverted, agreeable, conscientious, emotionally stable, and open to experience (figure 2.3).

Female protagonists score higher than any other set on Agreeableness, Conscientiousness, and Openness, and they score in the positive range on Stability. In personality, male protagonists look like slightly muted or moderated versions of female protagonists. Male and female antagonists are both relatively extraverted, highly disagreeable, and low in Stability and Openness. On each of the five factors, the protagonists and antagonists pair off and stand in contrast to one another.

The total profile for protagonists is that of quiet, steady people, curious and alert but not aggressive, friendly but not particularly outgoing. The antagonists, in contrast, are assertive, volatile, and unreliable, but also dull and conventional. Openness would be associated with the desire for education or culture and with the desire to build, discover, or create, and that whole complex of cognitive features is one of the two basic elements in Constructive Effort. As one would anticipate, then, Openness correlates with Constructive Effort (r =.41). The main antagonistic motive factor is Social Dominance, which correlates strongly and negatively with Agreeableness (r = −.54). Antagonists score in the extreme range both on Agreeableness (negatively) and on Social Dominance (positively).

We have to register one important limitation in the instrument that we used for obtaining scores on personality factors for our characters.

The larger the instrument, the higher the levels of resolution. We toyed with the idea of using a very large instrument but, with regret, rejected that idea. The larger the instrument, the higher the level of resolution, but also, the greater the drain on the limited patience of respondents to an online questionnaire. We chose then an instrument that is quite short, consisting of only ten items (two for each factor), the Ten Item Personality Inventory.[12] This instrument has proven empirical validity within its range, but in the nature of the case, some resolution is lost, and some adjustment has to be made. For our purposes, the most important adjustment concerns the personality factor Openness to Experience. For Openness, the two items on which characters received scores are "Open to new experiences, complex" and "Conventional, uncreative." Someone not already familiar with the broad construct Openness to Experience, as it is formulated, for instance, by Costa and McCrae, might think that the term "conventional" signifies conventional social attitudes and not consider the term in its cognitive aspect, as lack of imagination and intellect. The scores on Openness for a number of individual characters strongly suggest that in interpreting the term "conventional," our respondents did in fact tend to focus more on social attitudes than on cognitive interests. For instance, from among Jane Austen's protagonistic characters, the following characters all receive relatively low scores—average or below average—on Openness to Experience: Elinor Dashwood from *Sense and Sensibility*, Fanny Price from *Mansfield Park*, Fitzwilliam Darcy from *Pride and Prejudice*, and George Knightley from *Emma*. Even Anne Elliot from *Persuasion* scores only in the moderate range (.36). All of these characters are intelligent and cultivated, but also have relatively conservative attitudes toward social behavior. Darcy scores below average (–.15) on Openness, but he is described as "clever," and he devotes great care and attention to enhancing his library. The relatively heavy weighting of social attitudes in the scores on Openness can be illustrated by comparing Anne Elliot's score with that of Heathcliff from *Wuthering Heights*. Heathcliff's score on Openness (.37) is almost identical to Anne's, but Heathcliff has only a rudimentary education and displays no general cultural curiosity. He is merely indifferent to conventional standards of conduct. Anne is quiet and relatively conventional in social attitudes, but she is also highly educated, and she engages in serious, interesting conversations on literary subjects.

In compensation for having less resolution in the measurement of cultural curiosity, we gain more resolution in the measurement of cultural conservatism. The analytic utility of that feature of this particular instrument makes itself felt with particular force in our commentary of the relations between personality and ideology in the novels of Jane Austen.

Examples

Charlotte Brontë's Jane Eyre has a personality that is unequivocally protagonistic but that also has a distinctive cast common to Charlotte Brontë's protagonists and to those of her sister Anne: very low on Extraversion (–1.14), well above average on Agreeableness (.47) and Emotional Stability (.38), and high on Conscientiousness (.98) and Openness to Experience (.81). In contrast, Bertha Rochester, the madwoman in *Jane Eyre*, has a personality that is unequivocally antagonistic and that also reflects the character of her insanity: low on Agreeableness (–.80) and Openness to Experience (–.46), and ultralow on Conscientiousness (–1.46) and Emotional Stability (–1.61). Catherine Earnshaw, from Emily Brontë's *Wuthering Heights*, has a character profile that is fairly typical of agonistically problematic, borderline characters: high on Extraversion (1.14), low on Agreeableness (–.66), Conscientiousness (–1.06), and Emotional Stability (–1.01), but high on Openness to Experience (.94).

Emotional Responses

One of our chief working hypotheses is that when readers respond to characters in novels, they respond in much the same way, emotionally, as they respond to people in everyday life. They like or dislike them, admire them or despise them, fear them, feel sorry for them, or are amused by them. In writing fabricated accounts of human behavior, novelists select and organize their material for the purpose of generating such responses, and readers willingly cooperate with this purpose. They participate vicariously in the experiences depicted and form personal opinions about the qualities of the characters. Authors and readers thus collaborate in producing a simulated experience of emotionally responsive evaluative judgment.[13]

We sought to identify emotions that are universal and that are thus likely to be grounded in universal, evolved features of human psychology. The solution was to use Paul Ekman's influential set of seven basic or universal emotions: anger, fear, disgust, contempt, sadness, joy, and surprise.[14] These terms were adapted for the purpose of registering graded responses specifically to persons or characters. Four of the seven terms were used unaltered: anger, disgust, contempt, and sadness. Fear was divided into two distinct items: fear *of* a character, and fear *for* a character. "Joy" or "enjoyment" was adapted both to make it idiomatically appropriate as a response to a person and also to have it register some distinct qualitative differences. Two terms, "liking" and "admiration," served these purposes. "Surprise," like "joy," seems more appropriate as a descriptor for a response to a situation than as a descriptor for a response to a person or character. Consequently, in place of the word "surprise," we used the word "amusement," which combines the idea of surprise with an idea of positive emotion. One further term was included in the list of possible emotional responses: indifference. Indifference is the flip side of "interest," the otherwise undifferentiated sense that something matters, that it is important and worthy of attention.

We predicted (1) that protagonists would receive high scores on the positive emotional responses "liking" and "admiration"; (2) that antagonists would receive high scores on the negative emotions "anger," "disgust," "contempt," and "fear-of" the character; (3) that protagonists would score higher on "sadness" and "fear-for" the character than antagonists; and (4) that major characters (protagonists and antagonists) would score lower on "indifference" than minor characters.

Factor analysis produced three clearly defined emotional response factors: (1) Dislike, which includes anger, disgust, contempt, and fear *of* the character, and which also includes negative correlations with admiration and liking; (2) Sorrow, which includes sadness and fear *for* the character and a negative correlation with amusement; and (3) Interest, which consists chiefly in a negative correlation with indifference.

Male and female protagonists both score relatively low on Dislike and relatively high on Sorrow (figure 2.4).

Male and female antagonists score very high on Dislike—higher than any other set—low on Sorrow, and somewhat above average on Interest. Female protagonists score high on Interest, but male protagonists score below average on Interest. They score lower even than good minor males, though not lower than the other minor characters.

Once one has isolated the components of agonistic structure and deployed a model of reading that includes basic emotions as a register of evaluatively polarized response, most of the scores on emotional response factors are predictable. There is, however, one surprising and seemingly anomalous finding that emerges from the scores on emotional responses—the relatively low score received by male protagonists on Interest. This finding ran contrary to our expectation

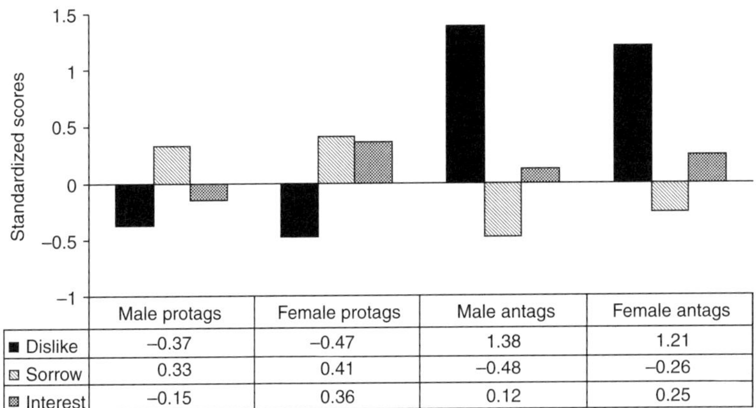

	Male protags	Female protags	Male antags	Female antags
■ Dislike	–0.37	–0.47	1.38	1.21
▧ Sorrow	0.33	0.41	–0.48	–0.26
▩ Interest	–0.15	0.36	0.12	0.25

Figure 2.4 Emotional response factors for protagonists and antagonists.

that protagonists, both male and female, would score lower on indifference than any other character set. We think this finding can be explained by the way agonistic polarization feeds into the psychology of cooperation. Male protagonists in our data set are relatively moderate, mild characters. They are introverted and agreeable, and they do not seek to dominate others socially. They are pleasant and conscientious, and they are also curious and alert. They are attractive, but they are not very assertive or aggressive. They excite very little Dislike at least in part because they do not excite much competitive antagonism. They are not intent on acquiring wealth and power, and they are thoroughly domesticated within the forms of conventional propriety. They serve admirably to exemplify normative values of cooperative behavior, but in serving this function they seem to be diminished in some vital component of fascination, some element of charisma. They lack power, and in lacking power, they seem also to lack some quality that excites intensity of interest in emotional response.

Examples

Count Dracula, from Stoker's *Dracula*, offers an unmistakably antagonistic profile: a very high score on Dislike (1.06), a respectable score on Interest (.33), and—despite having his head lopped off with a kukri knife—an only average score on Sorrow (–.06). In contrast, Jane Eyre scores low on Dislike (–.76), high on Sorrow (.81), and fairly high also on Interest (.48). These scores run closely parallel with those of Dorothea Brooke from *Middlemarch*: Dislike (–.74), Sorrow (.64), and Interest (.37). Jane Eyre's romantic counterpart,

Edward Rochester, scores just at average on Dislike, moderately high on Sorrow (.44), but—unusually for a male protagonist—high on Interest (.74). Rochester is evidently enough of the Dark Romantic Byronic type to spark higher than average interest for a male protagonist. Marlow from Conrad's *Heart of Darkness* tends in a different and more typical direction for a male protagonist: low on Dislike (–.44), average on Sorrow (.19), and low on Interest (–.50). Marlow's psychopathic counterpart, the renegade Kurtz, excites much more dislike (1.08) but rather more Interest (.19). Not surprisingly, the champions of Sorrow are characters from novels by Thomas Hardy, Tess (1.52) from *Tess of the d'Urbervilles* and Jude (1.48) from *Jude the Obscure* (1.48).

Male and Female Characters by Male and Female Authors

In the total set of 435 characters, characters by male authors outnumber characters by female authors by nearly two to one (281 versus 154). Nonetheless, because a greater percentage of characters by female authors are major females (protagonists or antagonists), 47 percent of the major females in the whole data set are from novels by female authors (45 percent of female protagonists and 52 percent of female antagonists). Female authors contribute close to half of all major females (47 percent), of all good females (protagonists and their associates, 47 percent), and of all minor females (associates of both protagonists and antagonists, 45 percent).

In order to determine whether the sex of the author significantly influenced the depiction of sex-specific features in the characters, we compared the depiction of male and female characters by male and female authors. Male and female authors converge in most of the ways that they depict male and female characters. (We found one statistically significant difference in criteria for selecting a partner for short-term mating.) For protagonists and antagonists, three features reach statistical significance. Male protagonists by female authors score significantly lower on valuing Extrinsic Attributes in a mate (wealth, power, and prestige). They also score significantly higher on Nurture. They are thus more domestic, more family oriented. Female protagonists by female authors score significantly higher on Constructive Effort. They are in this respect *less* domestic—more eager to occupy a place in the public sphere to which Constructive Effort gives access.

The constituent elements of Constructive Effort are seeking education or culture; creating, building, or discovering something;

making friends and forming alliances; and helping nonkin. Female protagonists by female authors score higher than female protagonists by male authors on making friends, seeking education, and helping nonkin. Out of all 12 motives that enter into the motive factors, the one motive with the largest difference for female protagonists by male and female authors is seeking "prestige." Across the whole set of 435 characters, prestige loads very strongly on the motive factor Social Dominance, where it clusters with seeking wealth and power. For female protagonists by female authors, in contrast, prestige separates out from the pursuit of wealth and power and clusters instead with the elements of Constructive Effort.

Characters with motivational profiles like those of female protagonists by female authors would scarcely be contented with purely domestic social roles. They want more education, a more active life in the public sphere, and greater public standing. In the advanced industrial nations, the social roles of women have of course changed dramatically in the past 100 years. The depictions of female protagonists by female authors give evidence of the undercurrents that ultimately helped to produce these changes. Male authors also contribute to this movement—female protagonists by male authors score moderately high on Constructive Effort—but female authors clearly take the lead.

Despite differences in cross-sexed depictions—male characters by female authors and female characters by male authors—male and female authors fundamentally concur on the motivational tendencies that distinguish male and female characters. In novels by both male and female authors, male characters score higher than female characters on Dominance, Constructive Effort, and Subsistence, and they score lower than female characters on Romance and Nurture. In novels by both male and female authors, male characters choosing long-term mates score higher than female characters on preferring Physical Attractiveness, and they score lower than female characters on preferring Intrinsic Qualities and Extrinsic Attributes. In all these factors, it is only the magnitude of the differences that vary in male and female characters by male and female authors, and the magnitude of that difference reaches statistical significance in none of the factors.

Correlation as a Test for the Validity of Role Assignments

We calculated the correlations on the scores among the various categories for all 435 characters in the larger data set. (For an explanation of what "correlation" means statistically, see appendix 4.) Since those correlations are derived independently of agonistic role assignments, they provide a cross-check on the validity of the structures revealed in the agonistic polarization between good and bad characters, and especially between protagonists and antagonists. The basic agonistic polarities produced by role assignments are replicated in the correlational analysis of scores for multiple categories. For instance, for all 435 characters, the emotional response factor Dislike (anger, disgust, contempt, and fear) and the personality factor Agreeableness have a large negative correlation ($r = -.63$), and Dislike also correlates positively with Social Dominance ($r = .44$). ("r" is the abbreviation for "correlation.") Social Dominance—the pursuit of wealth, power, and prestige—is the central antagonistic motive factor. The central protagonistic motive factor is Constructive Effort, which consists of affiliative social dispositions combined with a desire for education and creative endeavor. Constructive Effort correlates negatively with Dislike ($r = -.32$), positively with the personality factor Openness to Experience ($r = .41$), and positively with preferring Intrinsic Qualities (intelligence, kindness, and reliability) in a long-term mate ($r = .44$). The whole set of correlations produces clearly discernible patterns in the organization of characters, and those patterns correspond closely with the polarized emotional responses to the character sets.

A Circulatory System for a Social Ethos

Because the features attributed to characters correlate with role assignments and with the emotional responses of readers, we can infer relations between the attributes of characters and the outlook of authors and readers. On the average, the features that distinguish "good" and "bad" characters, and especially the features that distinguish protagonists and antagonists, reflect the positive and negative values that authors have invested in their characters and anticipate their readers will share. In general, good characters, and especially protagonists, reflect the normative values of the novels—values shared by authors and their readers. Bad characters reflect the inverse of normative values. Normative values provide a common frame of reference for authors and their readers.

The causal sequence in the diagram in figure 2.5 forms a feedback loop. The designs or intentions of the author, in the top left-hand corner of the diagram, serve as a starting point in the causal sequence, and the endpoint in the sequence, the ethos of a given culture, feeds back into the designs or intentions of the author. By drawing a line

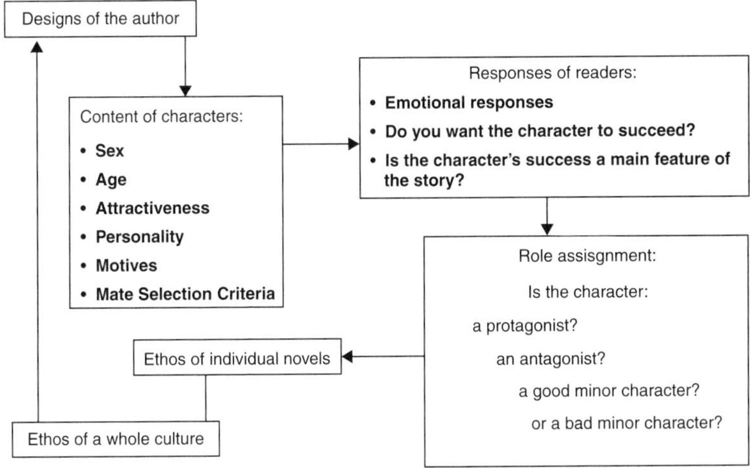

Figure 2.5 Circulatory system for a social ethos.

connecting "Ethos of individual novels" to "Ethos of a whole culture," we intend to signify that the whole body of novels in a given culture reflects the ethos of that culture. Individual novels are not of course the sole causal factors in producing the ethos of a culture; they are only contributing factors, both influencing and being influenced by other factors.

Authors and readers can and often do operate in tension with the normative values of their culture, but if authors are to communicate at all, their own idiosyncratic dispositions must define themselves in relation to the shared framework. By comparing the scores of individual novels with those of the larger data set, we can identify the features that distinguish one novel or novelist from another. In chapter 6, for instance, we examine the way scores for Austen's male protagonists deviate from the average for the whole set of novels. We also analyze the way that scores on emotional response differ between her novels and the other novels. By reflecting on the comparisons, we draw inferences about basic thematic and tonal features of her imagined world.

Novelists designate characters as persons intent on achieving goals. The success or failure of the character in achieving goals is the main action in the story—broadly, the "plot." Goals are the end-objects of motives—for instance, the desire to survive, to get married, to make friends, to obtain education, or to assist one's friends. Readers recognize characters as agents with goals and have emotional responses to the characters. In an obvious sense, an author is the first causal force in this sequence. The author creates characters and designates their features and fortunes. For a main character, the author fabricates a situation, identifies the hopes and fears of the character, invents a sequence of actions organized around those hopes and fears, and determines the outcome for that sequence of actions. In all of this, outside of recognizing what the author has stipulated, the reader has no part. The reader must take it as the author gives it. But in giving it, the author does not neglect to consult the reader, at least prospectively. The author anticipates the effects that his or her designs will have on the minds and emotions of readers.[15]

Despite the power exercised by authors, the causal force between an author and his or her readers does not move in only one direction, from author to readers. In anticipating the effects that their designations will have on readers, authors are themselves the cunning servants of their readers. They are themselves constrained in constructing meaning by their own sense of what readers expect and demand. Dickens' revision of the end of *Great Expectations* offers a case in point. Having done a little judicious prepublication market testing by consulting a savvy friend, Dickens decided that the original, unhappy conclusion he had written for his novel would not sell nearly so well as a hopefully upbeat ending, and he changed the ending accordingly. The author's ability to manipulate the responses of readers depends on keeping his or her depictions within the range of the readers' expectations or desires. Authors rule, but only because they provide their subjects with what the subjects want. Authors dominate the feelings and thoughts of the audience, but only because they allow the feelings and thoughts of the audience at least partially to determine the parameters within which the authors work. After the public outcry against *Jude the Obscure*, Hardy felt that he could no longer satisfy his own artistic impulses while also giving readers what they wanted. Accordingly, he quit writing novels and devoted himself to poetry.

Authors of a canonical standing on a level with that of the authors sampled in this study do not just passively reflect the established and conventional values and beliefs of their culture. That conception of the inert passivity of the authorial mind is, in our view, an important limitation in one form of Foucauldian cultural theory and the New Historical literary criticism that flows from it. Great writers tap into the deepest levels of the human psyche, connect their contemporary cultural forms with basic human passions, and give their own idiosyncratic and distinctive stamp to the world they envision.

Despite his willingness to play to his audience, Dickens is still "the inimitable Dickens." Great and original authors create new possibilities of understanding, but no matter how original and independent they might be, all authors feed off of the meanings that are available within their culture: the literary forms and traditions with which they work, and the forms of cultural imagination—ideological, religious, and philosophical—in which they participate. Authors, readers, and the larger culture are all locked into a reciprocal and interdependent relationship. The arrows in the diagram leading back from a cultural ethos to the designs of an author, and thus closing the feedback loop, are intended to reflect that reciprocal relationship.

Conclusion: The Global Evaluation Factor

Agonistic structure in these novels clearly serves as a central organizing principle. It is a center of gravity for the whole solar system constituted by motives, personality traits, mate selection, and emotional responses. The characters display an integrated array of agonistically polarized attributes, and readers respond to those attributes in emotionally polarized ways. The antagonists display a single-minded preoccupation with wealth, prestige, and power—egoistic striving wholly segregated from social affiliations. That motive profile extends itself into their criteria for choosing mates. Male antagonists have no particular preferences in mates, and female antagonists seek only to marry for wealth and status. The sociopathic dispositions revealed in motives and mating correspond to low scores on the personality factor Agreeableness. Antagonists are both emotionally isolated and also incurious. They are interested in nothing except enhancing their power and prestige. The protagonists, in contrast, care about friends and family, respond to romantic attractions, and become readily absorbed in cultural pursuits. They are affectionate, reliable, and open to experience. They are also on average younger and more physically attractive than antagonists. Agonistic structure thus presents a sharply etched picture—youth, beauty, and positive emotional energy meeting resistance and opposition from malevolent forces seeking only personal domination for its own sake. The polarized emotional responses of readers correlate strongly with this integrated array of attributes. Readers respond with aversion and disapproval to antagonists and with admiration and sympathy to protagonists.

Humans share with amoebas a fundamentally dichotomized orientation to the world. "Approach" and "avoidance" are the two mechanisms that govern an amoeba's activity. Chemical signals direct it to approach nutrients and to retreat from toxins. People do the same thing. They approach those things—food, sex, warmth, friends, status—that make them feel good, and they turn away with aversion from those things that make them feel bad. Egoistic displays of dominance evidently have a toxic impact on the nervous system of our respondents.[16]

Amoebas react. Humans react and judge. As the scores on emotional responses indicate, judgments can be complex, nuanced, ambivalent. Even so, those complications are only that, complications. They work variations on a basic theme, and that theme is polarized evaluative response. As a team of personality psychologists led by Gerard Saucier explains, in many contexts, across a diverse array of concerns, psychologists identify "a global evaluation factor (good versus bad)" (857). When personality psychologists use statistical techniques to reduce multiple personality attributions to superordinate factors, they can choose the number of factors to extract. If only one factor is extracted, that factor constitutes a "contrast between desirable and undesirable qualities" (Saucier and Goldberg 854). Scores on motives, mating, and personality reveal in detail what counts as desirable and undesirable qualities in characters. Scores on emotional responses lock down these evaluative judgments by placing them in the court of first and last appeal—the court of actual feeling.

Most of the novels included in this study are "classics." Classics gain access to the deepest levels of human nature. They evoke universal passions and fulfill deep psychological needs, but they do not always produce mimetically accurate representations of human nature. They hold a mirror up to nature, but this mirror, unlike that in *Snow White*, is under no obligation to tell the simple, unvarnished truth. The images produced are filtered through an imaginative lens that adds its own twist to the images that it reflects. In the novels in this study, agonistic structure creates a virtual imaginative world designed to give concentrated emotional force to the clash between dominance and affiliation. That imaginative virtual world provides a medium in which readers participate in a shared social ethos. The social ethos shapes agonistic structure, and agonistic structure in turn feeds back into the social ethos, affirming it, reinforcing it, integrating it with the changing circumstances of material and social life, and illuminating it with the aesthetic, intellectual, and moral powers of individual artists.

Part II

Implications

The standard format of scientific papers consists of four parts: an introduction, an explanation of the methods used in the study, an exposition of the results, and a discussion of the results. The first chapter in this book was our methods chapter; the second gave the main results of collecting and analyzing the data. The next three chapters are "discussion." In these chapters, we draw out the implications of the data for three issues of broad general interest: the determinacy of meaning, the relations between sex and agonistic role assignments, and the adaptive function of agonistic structure.

Chapter 3

Determinate Meanings

Understanding What Writers Mean to Say

Literary theorists have reached no consensus about whether literary "meaning" can be objectively determined. Most critics have an at least half-conscious conviction that in reading a novel they are deciphering a determinate structure of significations in the sequence of words and sentences. That kind of intuitive conviction is grounded in the evolved social psychology that makes communication possible. But critics who adopt this stance in a merely intuitive way also often assume, as a more conscious theoretical belief, that no determinate structure of significations is ultimately possible. Every structure of meaning, so the reasoning goes, is fundamentally dependent on some "community of discourse." All particular statements assume meaning only within such communities, and the discourses of those communities are both arbitrary and incommensurate.[1] From this perspective, "meaning" is always up for grabs, dependent entirely on the interpretive framework that critics might choose to deploy. Many critics caught somewhere in between intuitive determinacy and theoretical relativism compromise by adopting one or another version of "pluralism"—the idea that many possible interpretive frameworks are valid; that they can be grounded in heterogeneous theoretical systems and nonetheless get at different aspects of a text.[2] Critics adopting this stance become practitioners of principled "bricolage." Despite their cheerful resignation to deep theoretical incoherence, within the range of ideas currently active in literary theory, pluralists represent a relatively "rational" stance toward the determinacy of meaning. Relatively rational, because pluralism stands as an alternative to deconstruction, a much more aggressively irrationalist theory.

As an independent theoretical school, deconstruction did not last long, but its epistemology remains a core element in the poststructuralist episteme that still dominates current literary theory. In the late seventies and early eighties, deconstruction swept through departments of literature like a form of contagious delirium, infecting almost everyone, and then just as suddenly departed, supplanted by the political criticism of Foucault and the Althusserian Marxists, various forms of identity politics, and Lacanian psychoanalytic criticism. As an element unto itself, Derridean wordplay offered too thin an atmosphere in which to breathe. Literary study has to deal with human realities, with psychological impulses and social forces. Althusserian Marxism, Lacanian psychoanalytic theory, and the brooding Foucauldian preoccupation with social "power" provided the chemical elements necessary to make the atmosphere in "Theory" breathable. But to this gaseous mix deconstruction contributed three vital bonding agents: a spirit of subversion, a mystified belief in the transcendent reality of "discourse," and a conviction that all meaning is unstable, indeterminate, ambiguous—caught in an endless flux of semiotic slippages and interdependent but contradictory significations.

How do our results speak to this deconstructive vision? Psychologists presuppose that when multiple respondents agree about features of people, those features actually exist. The subjects in this study are imagined people rather than actual people, but the principle is the same. We found high levels of agreement on the attributes of characters and thus assume that those attributes actually exist in the characters. Moreover, we found a high degree of correlation between attributed features and the emotional responses of readers. Now, if the features that readers identify in characters actually exist, those features are determined by authors. Authors stipulate a character's sex, age, personality, motives, and criteria for selecting mates. They also stipulate the character's actions, which are based on motives and the personality dispositions that orient characters to motives. Our data indicate that readers largely agree in recognizing and identifying all these features. If readers' emotional responses to characters correlate strongly with attributed features, and if readers tend to respond in emotionally similar ways to those features, we can reasonably infer that authors have a high degree of control in determining readers' emotional responses.

Constructing the World

Poststructuralists like to say, in various ways, that words construct the world. Social and sexual identity, especially, are "constructed," or so we are told. There is of course a half truth in this declaration. Like so much of poststructuralist theory, the declaration consists of two parts, the truistic part, and the false part.[3] The truistic part is the idea that social and sexual identity are heavily influenced by the norms that prevail in any given culture. The false part has two elements. One element is the idea that cultural norms are not themselves heavily constrained by genetically transmitted dispositions—"human universals." The other element is the idea that individual identity consists exclusively of cultural norms. This idea implies that individuals are not powerfully driven by biological forces: their own particular genetic designs, the hormones that flood them *in utero*, the peculiarities of their individual brains, and the characteristics of their individual bodies. In reality, individual human identity grows in culture in the way that plants grow in soil and air, but a tree is not dirt and cannot be reduced to atmospheric gas.

Is it too much to say that authors construct readers? Yes. Readers have minds of their own. They can resist, reflect, like and dislike, laugh at a book, throw it across the room, or write critical essays likening it to infectious effluvia. In all of this, the author and reader stand on a footing like two people meeting person to person. We "read" the people that we meet just as we read authors. That is, we look at them curiously, inquiringly. We compare them to other people. We catalog them using various criteria—family relation, social function, personality factors, sex, ethnic identity, or profession. We assess them in relation to our own needs and purposes—friend, enemy, business associate, sexual partner, customer, predator or prey. And ultimately, even if only subliminally, we locate them within our total imaginative universe. Readers are active observers and judges, not passive vessels. Is it then too much to say that readers construct authors? Yes. However much we might observe and judge the person before us, there is a person there, and that person can be well and truly observed, or not. This is in fact the plot situation for many a classic novel—*Pride and Prejudice*, for example—with a protagonist making a false early judgment of some other character, and gradually coming to see more clearly and accurately.

If authors do not construct readers, and readers do not construct authors, where does meaning come from? The structure of meaning in any given novel—the kind of meaning that can be empirically defined and quantified—comes from the author. It is the author who stipulates the features of characters and situations, describes a setting, delineates a sequence of actions, and orchestrates the whole to produce a continuous sequence of recognitions and emotional responses that vary little from reader to reader. If the reader is competent, the reader registers precisely what is in the text, just as an observer; if he or she is alert, registers precisely the physical features and expressive character of some actual person. There is a novel there, just as there is a body and mind there, and we can either read it well and truly, or not. We can also judge it, evaluate it, analyze it, describe how all the parts fit together to form an effective whole, assess the forces that influence it, whether the author is conscious of those forces or not, detect undercurrents of feeling or bias of which the author might not be aware, translate its particular idiom into other idioms, compare and contrast it with other novels, explain its origins, trace its effects, draw out its implications, and locate it, ultimately, within a total explanatory system of our own.

Can any one set of descriptive and analytic terms (or their close synonyms) be used to define meaning in a given text, assigned priority over other, competing terms, and presented in such a way that the weight of empirical evidence overwhelmingly confirms its validity? The suppositions in most current literary theories tend to run strongly in the other direction. Problems start of course with identifying the very meaning of the word "meaning." One common usage appears in declarations such as this: "This book *means* so much to me. It was an inspiration during a difficult period in my life." In that usage, "meaning" denotes the relative personal value a text has for some individual person. It suggests that the text helps define the identity themes that matter most to that person, providing moral guidance or emotional solace. The idea that texts can have this kind of value is implicit in the argument we make, in chapter 5, for the adaptive function of agonistic structure: that literature influences beliefs and values. In the context of this current discussion, though, the word "meaning" does not denote the relative significance that a given text might have in the personal life of individual readers.

In this current context, when we use the word "meaning," what we have in mind is this: the attributes of characters, the emotional responses of readers to characters, character role assignment, and the implications for thematic and tonal organization that arise out of relations among these elements. Although we have not included "style"—the formal organization of verbal elements such as word choice and syntax—among the topics in this study, we feel confident that stylistic analysis can also be conducted in quantitative ways and can be coordinated with thematic and tonal analysis.[4] So far as thematic and tonal organization go, we have aimed at demonstrating the concurrence between meanings intended by authors and recognized by readers. We have tested and confirmed the proposition that authors assign definite attributes to characters and organize characters in such a way as to produce definite, determinate forms of conceptual and emotional order in the minds of readers. We also tested the proposition that readers accurately recognize these structures and very largely agree among themselves about them. We have assessed the degree to which authors control the recognitions and even the emotional responses of readers, and we have found that authors exercise a very high degree of control.

The film theorist David Bordwell offers an illuminating three-level scheme for the interpretive responses of people viewing films: perception, comprehension, and appropriation, or (in our terms), observation, analytic summary, and theoretical explanation.[5] At the perceptual level, most viewers with normal hearing and sight hear and see more or less the same thing. The level of consensus—as could be measured, for example, by a simple quiz—is extremely high. Did Charlie Chaplin get caught in that great gear, or not? Yes, he did. No statistically significant level of disagreement among viewers. At the next higher level in the organization of meaning, readers or viewers put together the discrete moments of perception into larger patterns like those of plot, agonistic structure, and thematic and tonal organization—all combining into the composite categories of genre (romantic comedy, tragedy, satire, and the like.). One recognizes connected sequences of events, patterns of emotions, and moral and psychological themes linking events and characters. At this level, too, agreement is often remarkably high. Most people recognize and agree on the basic patterns in the relations of characters and the basic sequence of emotional responses that the author implicitly assumes that the readers will feel at the sequence of events. Readers of *Pride and Prejudice* are angry at Darcy when he is rude to Elizabeth at the ball—they recognize that his behavior is rude, and they are angry at it. When he proposes marriage, they recognize that the proposal is presented in an arrogant, presumptuous way, and they are thrilled at the eloquence of contained rage with which Elizabeth not only rejects his proposal but also denounces and condemns his entire character. And they are pleased and happy when Darcy and Elizabeth, both humbled and chastened, overcome their misunderstandings and become engaged. They recognize that this sequence of events constitutes the main plot of the novel. They are aware, that is, that the motives and concerns are those of a marriage plot with a happy conclusion. They also recognize that other characters in the novel, Darcy's conceited aunt Lady Catherine de Bourgh and the fatuous clergyman Mr. Collins, for instance, are objects of amused contempt and that their qualities stand in sharp contrast, morally and psychologically, to the admirable qualities in the main characters. That is, readers recognize that the novel is not just a romantic comedy but also a social satire. Our respondents provide statistically compelling evidence for a rational consensus on these and other thematic and tonal features in the novels of Jane Austen and other novelists.

As a rough impression, based on reading thousands of essays in literary criticism, well more than half of all commentary on novels, plays, and films consists of analytic summary, virtually interchangeable from essay to essay on any particular work. In each essay, the summary is usually presented not as an end in itself but as supporting evidence for some thesis at the third level. It is at this third, theoretical level that critics can normally generate enough difference of opinion to provide a rationale for the proliferation of critical essays. This is the level at which critics offer explanations by invoking some overarching set of interpretive analytic terms—Marxist, deconstructive, feminist, archetypal, phenomenological, psychoanalytic, Christian, Aristotelian, structuralist, and so on—as many interpretive terms as there are theoretical schools. And no way to decide among them? For theorists who reject the idea of determinate meanings, the usual answer would be "no." The terms of the theoretical schools are matters of choice, the argument would go, no more susceptible to empirical adjudication than matters of religious faith. Each theoretical school would elicit somewhat different theoretical implications from the same analytic summary, translating the characters and events of the story into allegorical embodiments of the chief terms of the theory. Each theory would be able to make some kind of interpretive sense of the materials available at the level of analytic summary, and there could be no way to determine the relative validity of these competing interpretations. Moreover, each theoretical slant would have an imaginative quality peculiar to itself, like the flavors characterizing different national cuisines. Those flavors have intrinsic aesthetic value. Not only is it not possible to identify the one "true" cuisine; any effort at limiting the variety would merely impoverish the range of our gustatory experience. Theoretical schools could hypothetically proliferate without limit, not just through their own spontaneous generation, each individually, but through a kind of quasi-sexual reproduction, feeding off each other, producing hybrids and blends, and stimulating alternative and opposing structures in a Hegelian, dialectical way. Given the current variety of theories and the conditions ensuring endless theoretical proliferation, we can look forward with confidence to an endless succession of rereadings of the same finite body of canonical literary texts. What's not to like about that? Graduate students need fear no exhaustion of the fields to which they will be called to labor. And in any case, there is no alternative to the efflorescence of theoretically modulated interpretive variation.

We think there is a good deal not to like about this situation, and we think there is an alternative. The generation of theoretical variety has a frivolous air. Within the larger intellectual community, it has brought literary study into general and merited disesteem.[6] The various theoretical schools are not in fact quasi-theological constructs beyond discourse of reason. Each consists of propositions about matters susceptible to empirical confirmation or falsification—the nature of the human mind, the laws of social organization, language, sex, and gender. Some of these propositions are true, some partly true, and some false. The evolutionary human sciences now provide us with an encompassing framework through which we can make reasoned assessments of what is true and false in the claims of the speculative theoretical schools. The evolutionary human sciences are grounded in evolutionary biology, itself firmly established as a scientific paradigm concordant with knowledge in the other sciences. Evolutionary biology has a prima facie epistemic validity that can be claimed by none of the competing theoretical schools in literary study. Whatever is empirically sound and conceptually rich in the speculations of other theoretical schools can be assimilated to the evolutionary paradigm. The evolutionary human sciences thus now, for the first time in our history, form the basis for a rational interpretive consensus at the highest level. With that consensus in place, meaning becomes determinate all the way to the top, from the perceptual level, to the level of analytic summary, to the level at which the largest implications of the lower levels are explained and linked with concepts across the whole field of the human sciences.

Again, when we speak of determinate meaning, we do not intend to signify the relative personal value that any given text has for its readers. We intend to signify the recognition of what authors mean to say and the forms of explanation that most adequately account for authorial motives, depicted behavior, and reader response. Unlike intended meaning and objective explanations of that intended meaning, relative personal value necessarily varies with the needs and interests of individual readers. Many readers respond passionately to the stories of Guy de Maupassant, thinking that "these richly sensual, earthy stories accord very closely with the forms of feeling that matter most to me." Other readers, responding to Jane Austen, think that "the elegance and propriety of her ethos is precisely the atmosphere in which I would like to conduct my own life." Different temperaments, different tastes. And yet our data indicate that both sets of readers would probably agree very closely on what Maupassant and Austen mean to say; they would probably respond in just the way Maupassant and Austen intend their readers to respond—rooting for some characters and hoping others will fail. And if the readers were all evolutionists, they would also probably agree that the same basic set of causal principles could account both for determinate meanings in different writers and for their own personal preferences.

When we propose that an evolutionary framework can make meaning determinate all the way to the top, we are not of course suggesting that all authors are themselves proponents of an evolutionary perspective. Historically, that is not even possible. Many authors are Christians. Some are Marxists. Some few have been taken with Freudian ideas, and a small set of recent writers might even account themselves among the deconstructionists. Most writers could hardly be categorized in any simple way as adherents of any theoretical school. Like the public at large, they are eclectic. They trust more to their own genius, along with the accumulated stores of insight in the common idiom, than to the reductions of any one theoretical school. The claim we are making, then, is not that all writers are evolutionists. It is, rather, that writers write in the common idiom, that the common idiom contains determinate meanings, that all determinate meanings can ultimately be explained within the framework of evolutionary biology, and that evolutionary biology is a scientifically valid framework that encompasses and either subsumes or supplants all these other competing theoretical systems.

Among readers who find such claims disturbing, perhaps the most common word that will come to mind, to express their uneasiness, is "reductive." Yes, we aim at reduction. We aim to reduce the phenomenal particularity of a diverse body of literary texts to underlying patterns of meaning. In this respect, we join company with most literary scholars, from all schools. Efforts at explanation necessarily identify underlying patterns of meaning. Hence titles such as *Culture and Anarchy*, *The Great Chain of Being*, *The Mirror and the Lamp*, *Anatomy of Criticism*, *The Realistic Imagination*, *Blindness and Insight*, *The Female Imagination*, *Fiction and Repetition*, *The Political Unconscious*, *Desire and Domestic Fiction*, *Gender Trouble*, and *Culture and Imperialism*. Even the most rudimentary form of literary commentary—paraphrase and summary—constitutes an exercise in analytic reduction. In seeking to reduce texts to a specific set of terms, evolutionists do not differ from critics in other theoretical schools. They differ only in the terms to which they seek to reduce texts.

The differences among encompassing theoretical terms do not render different theoretical schools incommensurate with one another. All the schools have to bring their larger concepts into congruence with common observation. We all agree that Charlie Chaplain did get caught in that giant gear, whether we interpret that event as a symbol of capitalist oppression, a symptom of castration anxiety, a self-reflexive image of semiotic entanglement, or a tragicomic image of common humanity trapped in technological and social mechanisms operating in destructively autonomous ways. Even at this highest level of interpretation, large-scale theories share a great deal in the way of common understanding, overlapping on such conceptual features as folk physics, folk biology, and folk psychology. Such concepts are fundamental to the organization of our thoughts but are often held so instinctively that they are not even consciously recognized.[7] They function like Kantian a prioris, as preconditions for the possibility of thinking. The shared and overlapping elements in large-scale theories do much to limit the range of interpretive disagreement at the middle level, the level at which we analyze thematic and tonal structure in novels.

Bordwell persuasively argues that large-scale interpretive concepts exercise more influence on interpretation at the middle level—thematic and tonal summary—than at the level of simple observation. But just how much influence? That would be an excellent question for empirical research. As soon as the theoretical and methodological blockage in the established and allowed ways of conducting literary study breaks up, we hope to see graduate students, no longer shunted away from training their minds empirically, take up such topics, submit them to empirical inquiry, and advance our understanding on them. Meanwhile, our own experience is that the degree of influence varies from case to case. Some novels (and plays, films, and poems) generate a broad critical consensus, not just at the level of rudimentary analytic summary but also at the level of thematic and tonal structure. Everybody recognizes the conceptual and emotional organization of the story. There is very little disagreement. Jane Austen is a signal instance. Upping the bid, *Middlemarch* is brilliant and complex, arguably the most "intelligent" of all English novels, but it presents few real challenges at the level of thematic and tonal summary. It is unambiguous, self-conscious, and highly explicit. Readers generally agree about how it is put together to produce meaning. Other novels are more challenging, more difficult, harder to "read," just as we say of certain actual people. Walter Pater's novel *Marius the Epicurean*, for instance, is a singularly enigmatic, opaque work. In this respect, the novel is like the man.[8] *Tess of the d'Urbervilles* and *Jude the Obscure* are "modern" and unconventional in various ways, but they are thematically and tonally unambiguous. *The Mayor of Casterbridge*, in contrast, is a genuine "problem" novel, hard to read, easy to get confused about, so difficult to get a fix on that it has generated relatively little activity at the third, highest level of interpretation, that of "appropriation." Critics have had to struggle too hard, and with too little success, simply to make sense of the novel at the second level, that of "comprehension." Jane Austen, in contrast, is so easy to understand that critics have been almost forced to generate metatheoretical accounts—allegorical reductions of characters and events to governing terms in arcane theoretical systems—simply to have something to say that is not obvious to every common reader.

The interpretive history of *The Mayor of Casterbridge* demonstrates that "meaning" is not always simply given, transparently available, sitting there on the page to be picked up and deposited in a sack, like bolls of cotton or bunches of grapes. We think that the methods we use in analyzing both *Mayor* and its critical history demonstrate a complementary truth. Objectively determinate meaning—the actual thematic and tonal structure of a novel—is not always immediately apparent, but it does exist and can be discovered. Discovering determinate meaning does not require that the critic share the beliefs of the author. Nor does it require that the critic share with the author some privileged category in contemporary identity politics—sex or sexual orientation, race or ethnicity, social class, or any other form of social identity. What it does require is access to a set of analytic categories that are sufficiently basic, simple, and comprehensive so that they can account for all things human. It requires an understanding of human nature and an understanding of literature as a mimetic and communicative medium. It requires, at a minimum, a sufficient number of analytic dimensions to register differences in motives, including criteria for selecting mates, differences in personality, and differences in emotional response. With a sufficient number of such analytic components, one can break down thematic and tonal structures into their component parts, building interpretive models from the bottom-up, rather than taking them off the rack of ready-made critical concepts and using them to construct observations from the top-down.

When any critic, however deconstructive he or she might feel, declares that some observation is wrong or misleading, or even just trivial, that critic is implicitly appealing to the intuitive realism that has made it possible for humans to survive as a species. One cannot safely deconstruct hungry lions. Like the three paleolithic protagonists in the film *Quest for Fire*, it is necessary sometimes just to sit in a tree, waiting for the lions to go away. While sitting there, one can eat leaves, or in a literate culture, carry on a philosophical discussion about the meaning of meaning. Deconstructionists and their poststructuralist progeny freely acknowledge their own "naive" but irrepressible realism. They hold that realism *sous rature* and regard this equivocation—erased and not erased, there and not there—as a particularly exquisite form of epistemological sophistication. From our perspective, that sort of equivocation is idle. There are other, more interesting things to do with one's mind. Discovering determinate meanings in particular texts and locating them in relation to human nature, its characteristic passions and modes of thought, is one of those more interesting things.

Chapter 4

Sexual Politics

The Predominance of Valence in the Organization of Characters

By obtaining quantitative results on readers' responses to male and female characters, and by comparing those results with readers' responses to good and bad characters and to major and minor characters, we can give decisive evidence as to whether responses to Sex vary independently of responses to Valence (good versus bad) and Salience (major versus minor). The results are unequivocal. Sex has no correlation with either Valence or Salience. (In appendix 4, see the section "The Independence of Sex from Valence and Salience.") Sex does not explain any of the variance in Valence (whether a character is good or bad) or Salience (whether a character is major or minor). On the categories of emotional response and character success, there are no statistically significant differences between the sets of all male and all female characters (appendix 6). Our respondents do not like males or females more; they do not wish one sex to succeed more than the other; and they do not regard the success of either sex as more frequently a main feature in the outcome of the narratives. What this means is that "agonistic structure" does not divide along lines of male and female. Characters are not good or bad, major or minor, *because* they are male or female. Sex is a separate, independent category.

Valence bulks much larger than either Sex or Salience in the organization of characters in the novels. The features that distinguish good from bad characters, and especially the features that distinguish protagonists from antagonists, display divergences in scores much wider than the divergences that distinguish male from female characters or major from minor characters. These divergences are manifested in the constitution of the characters—in motives, mate selection, and personality—and in the emotional responses of readers. That fact suggests basic corrections for critical theories that attribute a predominating significance to conflicts of gender in the novels.

The predominance of Valence can be demonstrated by comparing the differences in scores between each paired set in the three character set pairs—the differences between male and female, good and bad, and major and minor characters. For example, on the category Root For, good characters score .41 (nearly half a standard deviation above average), and bad characters score –1.13 (more than a standard deviation below average). When we subtract .41 from –1.13, we get 1.54. So, the difference in the scores between good and bad characters on Root For is 1.54—more than one-and-a-half standard deviations, a huge difference. In contrast, the difference in scores on Root For between male characters (.01) and female characters (.16) is only .15—a negligible difference. For major characters (–.13) and minor characters (.29), the difference in scores on Root For is .42, not negligible, but not nearly so large as the difference between good and bad characters.

The difference between the scores for two character sets is designated a "difference score." The difference between the scores of all good and all bad characters on Root For is 1.54. So the difference score for good and bad characters on Root For is 1.54.

A difference score of .5 or above can be taken as a rough measure of medium to large differences in the scores between the paired character sets on any given category. Twelve categories display scores in which the difference between character sets in one of the three pairs is .5 or greater. In 10 of the 12 categories with these relatively large difference scores, the differences are between good and bad characters. Differences between major and minor characters are most prominent in only one category—Main Feature (difference score of .73). The difference between male and female characters is most prominent only in preferring Extrinsic Attributes in long-term mates (difference score of .69; females score higher). The differences between good and bad characters are most prominent in the other ten categories and are often very large: Root For (1.54), Dislike (1.42), Agreeableness (1.31), preferring Intrinsic Qualities in long-term mates (1.27), preferring Intrinsic Qualities in short-term mates (1.08), Achieves Goals (.95), Social Dominance (.88), Constructive Effort (.88), Emotional Stability (.62), and Nurture (.55). It should be clear, then, that in agonistic structure differentiated by Sex, Valence overwhelmingly provides the predominating structural principle.

Sex, Valence, and Community

In the world of these novels, males hold positions of political, institutional, and sometimes of economic power denied to females, but females hold a kind of psychological and moral power that is exemplified in their status as paradigmatic protagonists. The most important distinguishing features of antagonists, male and female, are high scores on the motive factor Social Dominance (the desire for wealth, power, and prestige), low scores on the personality factor Agreeableness, and low scores on a preference for Intrinsic Qualities (intelligence, kindness, and reliability) in a mate. Female protagonists score lowest of any character set on Social Dominance and highest on Agreeableness and on preferring Intrinsic Qualities in mates. They also score highest in the typically protagonistic personality factors Conscientiousness, Emotional Stability, and Openness to Experience. In these important ways, female protagonists hold a central position within the normative value structure of the novels. The ethos of the novels is in this sense feminized or gynocentric.[1]

In the past few decades, more criticism on the novel has been devoted to the issue of gender identity than to any other topic. The data in our study indicate that gender can be invested with a significance out of proportion to its true place in the structure of interpersonal relations in the novels and that it can be conceived in agonistically polarized ways out of keeping with the forms of social affiliation depicted in the novels. In this data set, differences between males and females are far less prominent than differences between protagonists and antagonists. If polarized emotional responses were absent from the novels, or if those polarized responses covaried with differences between males and females, the differences between male and female characters could be conceived agonistically, as a conflict (as it is, for instance, in Gilbert's and Gubar's *Madwoman in the Attic*). The differences between male and female characters in motives and personality could be conceived as competing value structures. From a Marxist perspective, that competition would be interpreted as essentially political and economic in character (as it is, for instance, in Nancy Armstrong's *Desire and Domestic Fiction*). From the deeper Darwinian perspective, it would ultimately be attributed to competing reproductive interests. The predominance of Valence in the organization of characters suggests, in contrast, that in these novels conflict between the sexes is subordinated to their shared and complementary interests. In the agonistic structure of plot and theme, male and female protagonists are allies. They cooperate in resisting the predatory threats of antagonists, and they join together to exemplify the values that elicit readers' admiration and sympathy. Both male and female antagonists are massively preoccupied with material gain and social rank. That preoccupation stands in stark contrast to the more balanced and developed world of the protagonists—a world that includes sexual interest, romance, the care of family and friends, and the life of the mind. By isolating and stigmatizing dominance behavior, the novels affirm the shared values that bind its members into a community.

Feminist Sexual Agonistics

Commentary on gender in fiction has been dominated by feminist theory. Feminist critics vary a good deal in their conceptual alignments, but the term "feminist" nonetheless denotes a distinct school—a shared set of beliefs, attitudes, and values. That shared set can be synoptically characterized as a specific imaginative structure: an agonistically polarized vision of human sexual identity. Within this agonistically polarized vision, "patriarchy," the system of male domination, embodies the desire for Social Dominance as an end in itself. Patriarchy is thus a paradigmatically antagonistic force. The counterposing protagonistic force consists of a specifically female ethos of affiliative social interaction.

The imaginative structure that most broadly characterizes feminist cultural critique incorporates two distinct concepts of human sexual identity. These two concepts are not logically consistent with one another, but they serve complementary imaginative functions. One concept is that "gender" consists exclusively of roles arbitrarily imposed by society and culture. The other concept is that males and females are radically separate forms of life characterized by independent and incompatible systems of affect, cognition, and value. The first concept is "constructivist," and the second "essentialist." In the constructivist concept of sexual identity, the anatomical, physiological, and neurological differences between males and females, if they are not actually produced by culture, consist of merely physical features that have no significant impact on motives, emotions, or behavior. In the essentialist concept, male and female dispositions are themselves primary and irreducible constituents of the moral universe. The constructivist concept of sexual identity dislodges sexual identity from the causal constraints of human life history, and the essentialist concept identifies human sex differences as autonomous moral forces within an agonistically polarized field of action.

The idea that sexual identity is the product of arbitrary social role assignments is congruent with the cultural constructivist ideas that dominated mainstream social science until the Darwinian revolution three decades ago, and it is congruent also with the Foucauldian cultural critique that still holds sway in academic literary study. The constructivist concept has often been explicitly formulated.[2] The essentialist concept, in contrast, makes a tacit appeal to biologically based, genetically encoded dispositions in males and females. That appeal conflicts with the idea that culture exercises autonomous causal force, and the essentialist concept is consequently seldom formulated in a clear and straightforward way. Across the spectrum of feminist theoretical writing, the essentialist concept is equivocally evoked—implied, repudiated, suggested, evaded, intimated, and dodged. It is often explicitly disavowed, but it does not go away. It leads a subliminal but potent imaginative life. The imaginative force of the essentialist concept makes itself felt in repudiations of "phallocentric discourse," "the phallocentric tradition," and "Phallic Criticism."[3] It makes itself felt also in countervailing appeals to "the female imagination," "the specificity of the female," and the "female counter-tradition."[4] Most strikingly, it makes itself felt in the frequency with which feminist theorists have themselves charged one another with inadvertently violating the ideological taboo against essentialism.[5]

In feminist discourse, as Naomi Schor explains, the charge of essentialism is "the prime idiom of intellectual terrorism and the privileged instrument of political orthodoxy." For feminists, the term "essentialism" has "the power to reduce to silence, to excommunicate, to consign to oblivion." Writing in the mid-nineties, Jane Martin notes that "at meetings, workshops, and conferences in the 1990s one is told that the debate about essentialism is dead." She expresses concern that the debate ended not because it was resolved, but because tactics of intellectual intimidation had suppressed any deviation from the constructivist orthodoxy. As it happens, proclamations about the death of essentialism, like those about the death of the author and the death of Theory, have been greatly exaggerated. Surveying the field of feminist theory a decade after Martin, Mary Dietz observes that "no philosophical matter is more tenacious within feminist theory's subjectivity problem than essentialism, 'the issue which simply refuses to die,' partly because its status within feminism cannot be readily resolved." No matter how vigorously an intellectual orthodoxy punishes dissent, and no matter how sincerely theorists might wish to conform to an established creed, they can never wholly suppress basic contradictions in their own thinking. Feminism as a theoretical program depends fundamentally on the idea that women are in some important way different from men, but any feminist theorist who seeks "to articulate an identity for women" makes herself vulnerable to "charges of (latent) essentialism." When they simultaneously invoke and repudiate the idea of essential sexual differences, feminist theorists make it impossible to speak coherently about the nature of men and women. As a result, "intense debates about 'risking essence' proliferate within feminist theory." Writing in this current year (2011), Greta Gaard surveys the history of ecofeminism and identifies "essentialism" as the pivotal issue shaping its development. "After the charges of gender essentialism—accurately leveled at cultural feminism, a branch of thought in both feminist and ecofeminist theory—most feminists working on the intersections of feminism and the environment thought it better to rename their approach to distinguish it from essentialist feminisms and thereby gain a wider audience." Names that have been tried on for size include "ecological feminism," "feminist environmentalism," "social ecofeminism," "critical feminist eco-socialism," and "gender and the environment." The proliferation of alternative names has not of course solved the underlying conceptual problem. Changing the names only gives evidence of the chronic anxiety produced by the problem.[6]

Pure cultural constructivism must blind itself to the overwhelming body of empirical evidence confirming that biological factors influence differences of gender. Both in embryonic development and throughout the life span, the hormones that are produced by sexual organs, which are themselves produced by sex chromosomes, massively influence motives, emotions, behavior, and even cognitive style.[7]

The only way to give pure cultural constructivism a spurious color of plausibility is to presuppose a false dichotomy and fabricate a straw man. One must presuppose, wrongly, that gender identity can be produced only by culture, alone, or by biology, alone. One can then demonstrate easily enough that culture influences gender identity, draw a correct inference that pure biological determinism cannot be correct, and conclude, wrongly, that the only alternative to biological determinism is cultural determinism. In reality, no serious researcher claims that biology alone, independently of culture, creates gender identity. All empirically oriented researchers understand that biology and culture are reciprocally causal. There are thus only two actual positions in this debate—positions held by actual people, rather than by straw men: pure cultural determinism, and biocultural interactionism. Only one of these positions is internally coherent, and only one accords with the evidence from empirical research.

Both the cultural constructivist and the essentialist conceptions of human sexual identity make contact with important aspects of human sexual reality. Sociosexual roles vary greatly from culture to culture, but each sex also has genetically transmitted dispositions that transcend cultural differences and constrain cultural formations. The longer, Darwinian perspective on human life history captures the elements of truth in both these observations and integrates those elements into a comprehensive and consistent understanding of human sexual identity. The complex functional structures that distinguish males and females at the present time are features that on the average most effectively contributed to the reproductive success of their ancestors. The sexes are not separate and autonomous systems of motivation and affect. Males and females have coevolved, in reciprocally causal ways, under the constraining force of partially shared and partially conflicting reproductive interests. Human males and females are reproductively interdependent. Human sexual relations require humans to negotiate conflicts between reciprocal benefits and competing interests, and in that respect, human sexual relations are like all other affiliative human social relations, including those of parents and children.

Understanding the evolutionary basis for the conflicted interdependence of males and females does not eliminate the need for sexual politics. Quite the contrary. It suggests that all sexual relations necessarily involve a process of perpetual political negotiation. An evolutionary understanding of human sexual relations can contribute to this process in a constructive way. In its very nature as an empirical explanatory system, the evolutionary approach is politically, emotionally, and ethically neutral. By providing a causal explanation of the forces that enter into sexual politics, evolutionary theory can provide a perspective that, compared to current forms of explanation in the humanities, is more objective, more empirically sound, and more conceptually coherent.[8]

How Much Does Sex Matter?

In virtually all cases, the amount of time people actually spend copulating is miniscule in comparison to the time they spend eating, working, or talking to friends and family. The organization of reproductive relations is nonetheless a fundamental shaping force in most lives and in most novels. The emotional quality of a life depends crucially, in most cases, on the quality of its romantic relations. Plots are often organized around love stories because human passions are densely concentrated on making and sustaining sexual bonds. To evoke the proportion of imaginative life occupied by love and sex, we can compare it with those pictures of the human body that have been drawn not according to the scale of the physical parts of the body but according to the proportion of the cortex devoted to sensing them. In such pictures, the trunk—the bulkiest physical part—is small because it is not a concentrated center of sensation. The eyes, tongue, ears, nose, lips, and hands, in contrast, are monstrously large.[9] In the proportion of imaginative attention invested in love and sex, love and sex are like those enlarged body parts. They loom large in imaginative space.

From an evolutionary perspective, the disproportionate force of sex and romantic love is hardly surprising. An individual human being is merely an elaborate mechanism designed by natural selection for the purposes of replication.[10] Human organisms are adaptively designed to be emotionally preoccupied by the social relations that cluster around reproduction. Those relations involve family and parenting as well as sex, but without the sex, nothing else follows.

Because humans are social animals, survival and reproduction necessarily involve social relations, but in both phylogenetic and causal sequence, social relations follow reproduction. That is, the genetically transmitted dispositions that enable humans to construct society and culture have been shaped through natural selection by the requirements of reproduction. Within a biological context, these observations are almost truistic, but if one takes them seriously, they have the broadest possible bearings on the assumptions that govern literary study at the present time. The broadest assumptions are those of cultural constructivism, most often from a Marxist angle. Constructivists suppose that in seeking ultimate causal terms we should always look to social relations, especially relations of class. From an evolutionary perspective, social class is indeed important, but not ultimate. It is important because it correlates with acquired resources and potential to acquire resources, which, in turn, affects one's ability to attract desirable mates and provide for offspring. By abstracting themes from the depiction of social relations, and by intermingling those themes with the core elements of sex and family, critics can go a long way in analyzing character and point of view. By gaining a better sense of the phylogenetic sequence, they should be able to go still further. They should be able to incorporate all that we now know about social identity with what we also now know about "nature" and "human nature." That kind of analysis would provide a more complete and adequate form of knowledge, and it would also bring criticism much more closely into touch with the intuitive vision of writers such as Shakespeare, Dickens, Hardy, and Lawrence. Hardy, for instance, was acutely aware of how much social class relations, with all their attendant material conditions, affect individual lives. *Tess of the d'Urbervilles* offers a striking example. But Hardy also characteristically saw human life within the broader context of nature—in relation to the land and weather, to plants and animals, and to elemental needs and passions. He understood that much of the confusion of our lives derives from focusing too narrowly on social conventions and in mistaking those conventions for the ultimate forces of nature.

Reproduction matters, and the division of sexes into male and female reproductive units also matters. The partially shared and partially conflicting reproductive interests of males and females have anatomical, physiological, and psychological consequences. The social organization of biological sex differences varies enormously, but all forms of social organization are constrained by biological sex differences. Those differences have a direct impact on the moral and emotional qualities available within any culturally specific organization of reproductive relations.

Human life history entails species-typical differences in mating preferences for males and females. Those differences are manifested in the polarized preferences in the males and females in our data set. Plots are based on motives and desires; sex bulks large among the motives that drive plots, and biologically based mating preferences infuse passion and interest into motives. These observations have important implications for the interpretation of sex and gender in the novels. A critic who registers the way evolved sex differences shape stories and infuse them with passion and interest is unlikely to speak of the novels in quite the same way as a critic who believes that sex roles are determined solely by social convention. So also, in discussing the sexual politics in novels, a basic difference opens up between critics who see sex as a powerful, primary force and critics who see it chiefly as a medium for the circulation of sociopolitical energy. In an obvious way, all sex is political. That is, all sex is bound up with social power relations. But sex is not merely a product of social power relations. No cultural or literary theory that overlooks the deep adaptive history of human mating preferences is likely to capture the real force of sexual passion in novels, and without getting the sexual passion right, one cannot get the politics right, either.

Sex is interesting in itself, but we find a still deeper interest in the interaction between Sex and Valence. Female characters prefer Extrinsic Attributes in their mates, and male characters prefer Physical

Attractiveness. Well and good—just what, from an evolutionary perspective, one would expect.[11] But that is not the whole story, or even the main story. The main story concerns the opposition between good and bad characters, both male and female. Among the good characters, esteem and gratitude count for something, and romantic love is possible. The bad characters are interested in neither love nor sex. They are interested only in power, wealth, and prestige. In discussing sex and sexual politics in the novels, we need to be sure that we are talking about the whole emotional world of the novels, not just about the preoccupations with power that distinguish the antagonists. In our own preoccupations with sociosexual power relations, we should not lose sight of love. The novelists themselves generally do not.

Chapter 5

Adaptive Function

The Controversy over the Adaptive Function of the Arts: Three Hypotheses

Arguments on the adaptive function of literature and the other arts have occupied more of the shared attention of evolutionary psychologists and evolutionary literary scholars than any other topic. The amount of attention theorists have devoted to this issue signals that it is both crucially important and heavily disputed. By providing empirical evidence that bears on this issue, we hope to advance the argument in ways that can reduce the range of reasonable disputation. Before turning to our specific arguments on the adaptive function of agonistic structure in these particular novels, we summarize the current state of the discussion on this larger issue.

In *How the Mind Works*, Steven Pinker makes a provocative argument that the aesthetic aspects of the arts might not be adaptive at all; they might, he contends, merely be parasitic side effects of cognitive aptitudes that evolved for other functions.[1] To illustrate this idea, he draws parallels between art on the one hand and on the other pornography, psychoactive drugs, and rich foods like cheesecake. Pinker acknowledges that fictional narratives might have informational content of some utility in providing game-plan scenarios for practical problems that might arise at some point in the future.[2] All the other features of the arts, he suggests, reflect only the human capacity to exploit its evolved dispositions for the purposes of generating pleasure. This sort of pleasure, detached from all practical value for the purposes of survival and reproduction, would be equivalent to the pleasure derived from masturbation.

A second provocative hypothesis from the side of evolutionary psychology has been proposed by Geoffrey Miller. Miller argues that all displays of mental power, including those of the arts, might have had no adaptive value but might have served, like the peacock's tail, as costly signals indicating the general fitness of the person sending the signal. Miller's hypothesis identifies virtuosity in overcoming technical difficulty as the central defining characteristic of art.[3] Since Miller grants that the arts and other forms of mental activity, once they got started, might have been co-opted or "exapted" for adaptively functional purposes, his argument reduces itself to an argument about the original function of the arts. Miller's wider argument about the origin of all higher cognitive powers has an obvious weakness: it requires us to suppose that the enlarged human brain—so costly, so complex and functionally structured, and so obviously useful for so many practical purposes in life—evolved primarily as a useless ornament for the purposes of sexual display. Virtually all commentators would acknowledge that human mental abilities can be used for sexual display, as can almost any other characteristic. We use bodily powers, clothing, and housing for sexual display, but we do not suppose that physical strength, clothing, and shelter have no primary functions subserving the needs of survival and the forms of reproduction not associated with display. Acknowledging that adaptively useful capacities can be deployed in a secondary way for the purposes of sexual display tells us nothing about any specific adaptive function those capacities might have.[4]

Even if we overlook the weakness in Miller's broader hypothesis about the adaptive utility of the higher cognitive powers, his hypothesis about the arts says so little about the qualities and features that are specific to art that it has little explanatory value. Pinker's hypothesis is more challenging. He might be right that humanists object to his arguments at least in part because those arguments seem to diminish the dignity of the arts,[5] but we think many of these objections come from a deeper and more serious level—from a feeling that Pinker's hypothesis, like Miller's, fails to give an adequate account of his subject.

In contrast to Pinker and Miller, E. O. Wilson and others have proposed a hypothesis that attributes a basic adaptive function to the arts, a function that includes but is not limited to providing game-plan scenarios. Wilson directly poses the same question posed by Pinker:

> If the arts are steered by inborn rules of mental development, they are end products not just of conventional history but also of genetic evolution. The question remains: Were the genetic guides mere

> byproducts—epiphenomena—of that evolution, or were they adaptations that directly improved survival and reproduction? And if adaptations, what exactly were the advantages conferred?

Wilson's answer to this question draws a decisive cognitive line between the mental powers of humans and other animals. Other animals are "instinct-driven." Human behavior is much more open and flexible than the behavior of other animals. "The most distinctive qualities of the human species are extremely high intelligence, language, culture, and reliance on long-term contracts."[6] The adaptive value of high intelligence is that it provides the means for behavioral flexibility—for generating plans based on mental representations of complex relationships, engaging in collective enterprises requiring shared mental representations, and thus producing novel solutions to adaptive problems. To the human mind, the world does not present itself as a series of rigidly defined stimuli releasing a narrow repertory of stereotyped behaviors. What, then, determines human behavioral choice? Emotions activate motives.[7] But what prompts humans to feel in specific ways about the vast array of alternatives opened by their flexible general intelligence? In humans, Wilson argues, the arts partially take the place of instinct. Along with religion, ideology, and other emotionally charged belief systems, the arts form an imaginative interface between rational cognition and genetically transmitted behavioral dispositions.

It seems clear that humans do not operate automatically; but neither do they operate on the basis of purely rational deliberations about means and ends. They are prompted to action by emotions, but they also regulate their behavior in accordance with beliefs and values. Wilson and others argue that beliefs and values—and thus ultimately also behavior—are influenced by the depictions of art, including fictional narratives.[8]

Aesthetic and Imaginative Fulfillment

A predilection for abstract pattern is an essential component of what we describe as "aesthetic" experience. Pinker gives an incisive technical analysis of musical form, but he regards musical form as a nonfunctional elaboration of adaptively functional cognitive aptitudes. Brian Boyd, in contrast, makes the predilection for "pattern" the core of his hypothesis about the adaptive function of the arts. He defines art as cognitive play with pattern and argues that cognitive play develops and reinforces neural circuitry. This hypothesis overlaps with an idea formulated by John Tooby and Leda Cosmides: that the arts have organizing effects on "neurocognitive adaptations." Like Ellen Dissanayake, Tooby and Cosmides suggest that the arts concentrate emotional attention on the chief themes in human life history. Boyd would not disagree, but he regards cognitive flexibility as in itself an adaptive target of artistic activity. In his view, art not only displays "creativity" but also fosters it.[9]

The kind of "meaning" provided by art can operate entirely without words and virtually without concepts, through images, sounds, and aesthetic patterns alone. For literature or its oral antecedents, though, meaning typically does involve concepts, and it usually also involves the positioning of human subjects within some imagined world. As Terrence Deacon puts it, "We tell stories about our real experiences and invent stories about imagined ones, and we even make use of these stories to organize our lives. In a real sense, we live our lives in this shared virtual world."[10]

Theories attributing an adaptive function to the arts emphasize different aspects of art, but they all work variations on a common theme. They all concentrate on the way the arts develop the mind, enrich its powers, and make it more capable of dealing effectively with its physical and social environment. Such claims might seem little more than common sense. We have all experienced moments in which some song, story, or play, some film, piece of music, or painting, has transfigured our vision of the world, broadened our minds, deepened our emotional understanding, or given us new insight into human experience. Working out from this common observation to a hypothesis about the adaptive function of literature requires no great speculative leap. Literature and the other arts help us live our lives. That is why the arts are human universals. In all known cultures, the arts enter profoundly into normal childhood development, connect individuals to their culture, and help people get oriented to the world, emotionally, morally, and conceptually.[11]

If it is true that the arts are adaptively functional, they would be motivated as emotionally driven needs. The need to produce and consume imaginative artifacts would be as real and distinct a need as hunger, sex, or social interaction. Like all such needs, it would bear within itself, as its motivating mechanism, the impetus of desire and the pleasure and satisfaction that attend upon the fulfilling of desire. That kind of fulfillment would not be a parasitic by-product of some other form of pleasure, nor merely a means toward the end of fulfilling some other kind of need—sexual, social, or practical. Like all forms of human fulfillment, the need for art could be integrated with other needs in any number of ways. It could be used for sexual display or the gratifications of sexual hunger or social vanity, and it could be used as a medium for social bonding. Nonetheless, in itself it would be a primary and irreducible human need.

Agonistic Structure and Adaptive Function

The various hypotheses we have described about the adaptive functions of the arts involve the whole imaginative universe humans inhabit. Some theorists, most notably Dissanayake and Boyd, have also made more particular arguments that literature functions adaptively as a medium for social cohesion. Dissanayake describes many forms of collective artistic activity that help to create group cohesion—dance, song, collective sculpture, and physical adornments signifying tribal identity.[12] Boyd delineates a theory of art as a form of "shared attention."[13] On the basis of the data in this study, we are not arguing that the arts in general subserve the need for social cohesion. We are considering only one particular kind of art (literature and its oral antecedents); within that kind, we are isolating just one mode (narrative) in the literature of a single period; and within that mode, we are isolating a single formal feature (agonistic structure). Though thus tightly circumscribed, agonistic structure in these novels reflects social dispositions that are a basic part of human nature. Consequently, we would predict that literatures from other eras and cultures would portray similar patterns of agonistic structure. Further empirical study could confirm or falsify this prediction.

In *Hierarchy in the Forest: The Evolution of Egalitarian Behavior*, Christopher Boehm offers a cogent explanation for the way interacting impulses of dominance and affiliation have shaped the evolution of human political behavior. In an earlier phase of the evolutionary human sciences, sociobiological theorists had repudiated the idea of "altruistic" behavior and had restricted prosocial dispositions to nepotism and to the exchange of reciprocal benefits. In contrast, Boehm argues that at some point in their evolutionary history—at the latest 100,000 years ago—humans developed a special capacity, dependent on their symbolic and cultural capabilities, for enforcing altruistic or group-oriented norms. By enforcing these norms, humans succeed in controlling "free riders" or "cheaters," and they thus make it possible for genuinely altruistic genes to survive within a social group. Such altruistic dispositions, enforced by punishing defectors, would enable social groups to compete more successfully against other groups and would thus make "group selection" an effective force in subsequent human evolution. The selection for altruistic dispositions—and dispositions for enforcing altruistic cultural norms—would involve a process of gene-culture coevolution that would snowball in its effect of altering human nature itself.

Is it feasible to reason backwards from our findings on agonistic structure to formulate hypotheses about functions fictional narratives might have fulfilled in ancestral environments? By identifying one of the ways novels actually work for us now, can we produce evidence relevant to hypotheses about the evolutionary origin and adaptive function of the arts? We think so. Agonistic structure is a central principle in the organization of characters in the novels. Taking into account not just the representation of characters but the emotional responses of readers, we can identify agonistic structure as a simulated experience of emotionally responsive social interaction. That experience has a clearly defined moral dimension. Agonistic structure precisely mirrors the kind of egalitarian social dynamic documented by Boehm in hunter-gatherers—our closest contemporary proxy to ancestral humans. As Boehm and others have argued, the dispositions that produce an egalitarian social dynamic are deeply embedded in the evolved and adapted character of human nature. Humans have an innate desire for power and an innate dislike of being dominated. Egalitarianism as a political strategy arises as a compromise between the desire to dominate and the dislike of being dominated. By pooling their power so as to exercise collective social coercion, individuals in groups can repress dominance behavior in other individuals. The result is autonomy for individuals. No one gets all the power he or she would like, but then, no one has to accept submission to other dominant individuals. Boehm describes in detail the pervasive collective tactics for repressing dominance within social groups organized at the levels of bands and tribes.[14]

An egalitarian social dynamic is the most important basic structural feature that distinguishes human social organization from the social organization of chimpanzees. In chimpanzee society, social organization is regulated exclusively by dominance, that is, power. In human society, social organization is regulated by interactions between impulses of dominance and impulses for suppressing dominance. State societies with elaborate systems of hierarchy emerged only very recently in the evolutionary past, about six thousand years ago, after the agricultural revolution made possible concentrations of resources and therefore power. Before the advent of despotism, the egalitarian disposition for suppressing dominance had, at a minimum, a hundred thousand years in which to become entrenched in human nature—more than sufficient time for significant adaptive change to take place.[15]

In highly stratified societies, dominance assumes a new ascendancy, but no human society dispenses with the need for communitarian association. It seems likely, then, that morally polarized forms of agonistic structure in fictional narratives emerged in tandem with specifically human adaptations for cooperation and specifically human adaptations for creating imaginative constructs that embody the ethos of the tribe.

Agonistic structure in these novels seems to serve as a medium for readers to participate vicariously in an egalitarian social ethos. If that is the case, the novels can be described as prosthetic extensions of social interactions that in nonliterate cultures require face-to-face interaction. If suppressing dominance in face-to-face interaction fulfils an adaptive function, and if agonistic structure in narrative is a cultural technology that extends that interaction by imaginative means, one could reasonably conclude that agonistic structure fulfils an adaptive function. We hope to see further empirical research that opens up new ways of probing this important issue.

Our largest argument is that agonistic structure provides a medium of shared imaginative experience through which authors and readers affirm and reinforce egalitarian dispositions on a large cultural scale. At least one possible challenge to this conclusion could readily be anticipated. Could it not plausibly be argued that the novels merely depict social dynamics as they actually occur in the real world? If that were the case, one would have no reason to suppose that the novels serve as a medium for social dynamics in the community of readers. To assess the cogency of this challenge, consider the large-scale patterns revealed in our data and ask whether those patterns plausibly reflect social reality.

The world is in reality divided into two main kinds of people. One kind is motivated exclusively by the desire for wealth, power, and prestige. These people have no affiliative dispositions whatsoever. Moreover, they are emotionally unstable, undisciplined, and narrow minded. The second kind, in contrast, has almost no desire for wealth, power, and prestige. They are animated by the purest and most self-forgetful dispositions for nurturing kin and helping nonkin. Moreover, they are young, attractive, emotionally stable, conscientious, and open-minded. Life consists in a series of clear-cut confrontations between these two kinds of people. Fortunately, the second set almost always wins, and lives happily ever after. This is reality, and novels do nothing except depict this reality in a true and faithful way.

In our view, this alternative hypothesis fails of conviction. The novels contain a vast fund of realistic social depiction and profound psychological analysis. In their larger imaginative structures, though, the novels evidently do not just represent human nature; they embody the impulses of human nature. Those impulses include a need to derogate dominance in others and to affirm one's identity as a member of a social group. Our evidence strongly suggests that those needs provide the emotional and imaginative force that shapes agonistic structure in the novels.

The Politics of the Novels

For the past several decades, political criticism has typically adopted a subversive stance toward existing distributions of social power. To position themselves ideologically in relation to the novels, contemporary critics must almost necessarily adopt one of two positions: they must affirm either that the ethos of the novels supports the dominant ideology, or they must affirm that the ethos of the novels enacts resistance against the dominant ideology. (D. A. Miller's *The Novel and the Police* offers an instance of the former position, Nancy Armstrong's *Desire and Domestic Fiction* an instance of the latter.) The more common tendency among poststructuralist political critics is to affirm that the novels, like the critics, seek to undermine the values supporting the prevailing structures of power. In the next chapter, on Jane Austen, we offer some representative examples.[16]

The norms governing most current political criticism are egalitarian. Critics most commonly attack political systems because they contain unequal distributions of power and privilege with respect, especially, to class, gender, race, ethnicity, and imperial/subaltern status. Now, our data indicate that the novels, like the poststructuralist political critics, embrace egalitarianism. Should we then conclude that the ethos of the novels is fundamentally in accord with that in contemporary political criticism? We think not. In contrast to the ethos that characterizes most contemporary cultural critique, the ethos of the novels is neither revolutionary nor utopian. It is reformist. The novelists typically express hostility toward individual assertions of dominance based on wealth, power, and prestige, but they do not typically repudiate all existing structures of social power.

Dickens and Eliot are among the most aggressively political novelists in this study. Dickens is deeply suspicious of public institutions, passionately sympathetic to the sufferings of the poor, and uncompromisingly hostile to aristocratic arrogance. Nonetheless, most of his protagonists are solidly middle-class, well-educated and professionally trained. They display no anarchic impulses, and they have no tolerance for revolutionary violence. Madame Defarge, the virulent revolutionist in *A Tale of Two Cities*, is an antagonist. She is defeated and killed by an ideologically conservative servant of the English bourgeoisie, an elderly woman. Eliot's political sympathies are liberal, not revolutionary. Felix Holt, one of her protagonists, becomes involved in a political riot, but only in order to contain its violence. He pretends to assume leadership of a mob in order to divert it from its most destructive aims. After he is released from prison, he settles comfortably into the domestic life of a proletarian intellectual. His "Address to Working Men," an essay Eliot appended to the novel, concentrates on reform within the working class. He urges working men to gain more education so as to deploy more responsibly the political power he hopes them someday to gain. Real political "radicals" have always sniffed dismissively at the description Eliot gives to her hero in the title of the book—*Felix Holt, the Radical.*

Taking Dickens and Eliot as characteristic of the more radical novelists in this study, we can conclude that there is nothing very seriously subversive about the political ethos of the novels. The "industrial" novels of Disraeli (*Sybil, or the Two Nations*) and Gaskell (*Mary Barton*, *North and South*) adopt political stances very similar to those of Eliot—compassionate about the sufferings of the poor, implicitly advocating institutional reform, but offering no encouragement to impulses of revolt. Gissing's novels about the urban underclass (for instance, *The Nether World*) could scarcely be said to have a political dimension. They are naturalistic horror stories oriented to the tragedy of fine-grained people trapped in coarse and brutal environments. Similar sympathies animate Henry James's only political novel, *The Princess Casamassima.* James's characters include irresponsible aristocrats, but the most sinister characters are the proletarian subversives who sacrifice James's delicate interclass protagonist, Hyacinth Robinson, to gratify their own class animosities. In *The Secret Agent*, Conrad explores the underworld of political subversives from an unequivocally hostile perspective. His anarchists are uniformly a seedy, shady lot, distinguished chiefly by weaknesses of mind or character.

As we shall argue in chapter 6, Austen's politics are essentially conservative. She tacitly affirms the legitimacy of the larger social order. The same can be said of Trollope. The Palliser series, Trollope's novels about political life, do not deal with politics in the broader social sense. They deal only with the politics internal to a career in public office, just as his novels about religious life, the Chronicles of Barsetshire, deal only with the politics of ecclesiastical ambition, not with religion itself. Like Austen's characters, Trollope's characters are mostly from the upper classes. In both Trollope and Austen, agonistic conflict plays out from within those classes. Other authors register conflict among social classes, but few or none adopt a purely class-based system for the distribution of protagonists and antagonists. Some characters from the upper classes are depicted as arrogant and domineering, thus antagonistic, and some are depicted as kind and generous, thus protagonistic. In Dickens, some members of the proletariat, for instance Stephen Blackpool in *Hard Times*, are almost allegorical embodiments of kindness and decency in working class guise. Others, though, such as Orlick in *Great Expectations*, are vicious and brutal. Across the whole field of the novels, dominance and affiliation correlate with class identity in no systematic way.

Taken collectively, the novels in this study affirm egalitarian values. They thus nurture impulses that tend toward social reform—toward diminishing differences of wealth and rank, recognizing our common humanity, and thus improving conditions of life for the most vulnerable members of society. Even at their most political, though, the novels work at a level of motive and emotion deeper and more universal than any specific form of social organization. They affirm the qualities that make community possible.

The Division between Cultural and Prosocial Dispositions in the Ethos of the Novels

Ellen Dissanayake, E. O. Wilson, and others have proposed that literature and the other arts help to organize attitudes and beliefs in a basic, general way—a way that includes politics but is not limited to politics.[17] We have focused so far on the sociopolitical aspects of agonistic structure, but the values implicit in agonistic structure are not limited to issues of social power. If in its political aspects, agonistic structure conditions readers in adaptively functional ways, it might also be the case that other aspects of agonistic structure have adaptively functional effects.

In the ethos implicit in the agonistic structure of these novels, communitarian social dispositions are closely linked with an active mental and imaginative life—with curiosity, intelligence, imagination, and aesthetic responsiveness. The most distinctively protagonistic motive factor, Constructive Effort, consists in both prosocial and culturally acquisitive motives. Constructive Effort correlates positively both with the personality factor Agreeableness (a socially oriented factor) and the personality factor Openness to Experience (a culturally oriented factor).

These two sets of dispositions, the cultural and the prosocial, are both parts of human nature, but the ethos integrating them is only an ideal of civilization. Neither set is functionally dependent on the other. Either can function perfectly well in the absence of the other. In the minds of most of the protagonists in this study, communitarian and culturally acquisitive dispositions interact harmoniously—hence the average scores that distinguish protagonists as a group. In characters such as Sara Crewe, Dorothea Brooke, Isabel Archer, and Jane Eyre, the culturally acquisitive and prosocial motives converge. Such characters occupy the center of the cultural ethos embodied in agonistic structure across the whole data set. In a small minority of cases, the two sets of dispositions diverge. When that happens, as in *Great Expectations*, *Vanity Fair* and *The Picture of Dorian Gray*, the total ethos of the novel is likely to be sharply divided against itself.

A division in the ethos of a novel has distinct effects in a novel's tone and in the emotional responses of readers. Emotional disturbance in tone makes itself felt, for instance, in the self-alienation in Pip's first-person narrative persona, in the ironic reverberations in Thackeray's narrative voice, and in the psychodramatic horror in which Wilde's narrative culminates. In our research design, disturbances in readers' responses can be directly measured. Protagonists who display a fully integrated suite of normative dispositions typically elicit strongly positive, sympathetic emotional responses. Conversely, antagonists who conform to agonistic type—Count Dracula, for instance, or Austen's Aunt Norris—typically elicit emphatically negative responses. Agonistically ambiguous characters such as Becky Sharp and Catherine Earnshaw elicit emotionally ambivalent responses. Such characters satisfy impulses of rebellion, evoke compassion, or prompt the reader to identify with Machiavellian dispositions. They thus expose the fault line in a cultural ethos compounded of two ingredients—the prosocial and the cultural—that are both intrinsically attractive but that are not functionally interdependent. In charming but sociopathic protagonists like Becky Sharp, and in good-natured but dim-witted minor characters like those who typically gather around Dickens' protagonists, the ethos divides into its separate parts.

Machiavellian characters are sometimes attractive—charismatic, erotically fascinating, refreshingly free of social constraints. From the safe distance of their libraries, readers often find such characters highly diverting. In their actual social lives, few readers would wish to have much to do with people motivated chiefly by predatory impulses of social dominance. One might as soon wish to have a wolf or tiger for a house mate. Most protagonists can be counted among the beautiful people, but their personal charm is not the main reason that the novels form a viable virtual community. A "community" of egoists, however charming, would be a contradiction in terms. Community requires cooperation: subordinating individual interests, at least in part, to the common good. Agonistic structure produces a viable virtual community because it promotes that common good.

Part III

Case Studies

In the final two chapters, we shift back to looking at detailed results from the questionnaires. While collecting data across the whole body of novels in this period, we also set up a separate website for Hardy's *The Mayor of Casterbridge*, and we made a concentrated effort at enlisting participants with a special interest in Hardy. We wished to make sure we had enough data for a statistical analysis of one particular novel. The idea was that the results for the whole body of novels would provide a framework for considering one specific novel in detail. We could compare that one novel with the patterns produced by the data from all the novels in the study. Fortunately, the respondents who filled in questionnaires for the novels in the larger data set gave us a great deal of data on characters in the novels of Jane Austen. Consequently, we are able to offer two case studies, one on the whole body of Austen's novels, and one on *The Mayor of Casterbridge*.

Chapter 6

Jane Austen, by the Numbers

The Janeites among Our Respondents

Jane Austen bulks larger than any other single author in the data set. Out of the total of 435 characters in the data set, 56, or about 13 percent, are from Austen novels. All of her characters together received 423 codings, or about 29 percent of the 1,470 codings for the whole data set. Since we have averaged the ratings for characters who receive more than one coding, each Austen character, no matter how many codings he or she receives, counts only once in the total set of scores for all 435 characters.

The large number of characters coded from Austen's novels offers an opportunity to examine scoring patterns across the whole body of her novels. On many categories, scores for her characters converge with those of characters by other novelists seemingly very different—the Brontës, Dickens, George Eliot, Thomas Hardy, Joseph Conrad, Oscar Wilde. In other ways, though, in the characterization of male consorts of female protagonists and in the tonal quality captured in the emotional responses of readers, Austen stands apart from these other novelists. Quantifying those differences gives us a new angle of access in interpreting her work, enabling us to confirm the validity of some common views, refine insights from her most perceptive critics, offer new evidence on disputed issues, and locate all particular observations within a systematic organization of categories lodged in an evolutionary understanding of human nature.

Is Austen Too Sensible To Be Explained?

In order to claim legitimate standing as "explanation," interpretive criticism must reduce phenomenal surfaces to underlying causal patterns. The alternative is merely to describe, analyze, summarize, and appreciate. Most of the criticism that has been written on Austen's novels has departed relatively little from the phenomenal surface. Before the poststructuralist revolution in the 1970s, most interpretive criticism operated within the range of analytic summary and appreciative evaluation. More recent critics have sought to subordinate analytic summary to theoretical terms such as Class Struggle, the Phallus, the Mirror Stage, Compulsory Heterosexism, the Other, Desire, Patriarchy, Dialogism, Textuality, Semiosis, Discourse, and Power.[1] In criticism of Austen, though, these interpretive gestures often seem perfunctory or half-hearted. Austen's own commitment to "sense" at the common level seems to have chastened the more rhetorically flamboyant impulses of the theoretical schools. The bulk of more recent critical commentary on Austen overlaps heavily with traditional analytic summary couched in the common idiom.

By breaking down Austen's thematic and tonal structures to their component parts, we can discover patterns of meaning not readily apparent to the common understanding and can give an empirically grounded analysis of the total imaginative effect produced by her work. Our data indicate that Austen mutes male sexuality, feminizes male motives, and uses an emotional palette largely devoid of Sorrow. Her novels thus embody a female domestic ethos with a positive emotional tone. In the social vision implicit in her fiction, the primary function of the larger social order is to protect and nurture this female domestic ethos. The muting of Sorrow and the correlation between Root For and Achieves Goals give evidence that in her imagined world society largely succeeds in fulfilling this function.

In Austen's novels, the desexualized resolutions of domestic romance converge with the depoliticized resolutions of an agonistically isolated social order. By reducing her imagined world to a single social class, she eliminates any serious consideration of class conflict. Within that one class, though, she makes a strong appeal to evolved dispositions for suppressing dominance in individuals. By inviting readers to participate vicariously in an elite social class, she satisfies their impulse toward Social Dominance; by stigmatizing individual assertions of dominance within the elite class, she also fulfills readers' needs for communitarian cooperation.

For Austen's own protagonists, at least, romantic and social conflicts culminate in a near-perfect resolution. That dual resolution is an essential part of the total imaginative effect produced by her work. Our respondents' scores indicate that they recognize and resonate to this effect. They clearly distinguish major from minor characters and good from bad, recognize success in outcomes, and respond emotionally in predictable ways. Character role assignments and scores on Root For and Achieves Goals indicate that the outcomes of the novels give solid satisfaction to the respondents.

The research described here offers an advance on the critical consensus about Austen's work. Many of our particular findings, though, converge closely with that critical consensus. That convergence has complementary implications: it offers empirical evidence for the correctness of the critical consensus and also for the explanatory power of the model of human nature used to obtain the data. The empirical character of the model of human nature lends epistemological credibility to the critical tradition. The convergence between our results and the critical tradition gives evidence that this model, simple as it is, is nonetheless complex enough to replicate insights from generations of the most capable readers of a master novelist—replicate them, and also advance on them.

Integrating Empirical Methods with Traditional Literary Criticism

Many theorists and critics feel that theoretical explanation should be counterintuitive and produce imaginative impressions radically at variance with the common understanding. We think this feeling is misguided. Literary works are meant to be understood. They use the common language, depict common motives and features of personality, and elicit common emotional responses. The questions in the questionnaire are derived from an evolutionary model of human nature but couched in the common language. They are thus situated at the point at which the evolutionary model converges with the common understanding. The questions register the common understanding, quantify it, and locate it within the context of empirical social science. Quantification enables us to give an objective, formal analysis of the common understanding, assess statistically the relations among its elements, and draw new inferences from those relations.

While drawing large interpretive inferences from the scores on the attributes of characters and the emotional responses of readers, we also use our general knowledge of Austen and the critical tradition to help interpret the scores. To get the full benefit of the data, it is necessary to bring the data to bear on issues of authorial stance, reader response, and aesthetic quality. Consequently, we have drawn no hard and fast line between data-driven analysis and interpretive literary criticism. Even so, in the exposition that follows, we take care to identify claims that are primarily inferences from data and to distinguish them from interpretive propositions that depend heavily on literary judgment.

The Figure in Austen's Carpet

One of our findings—a finding we perhaps should have anticipated but did not—is that in motives and in the criteria for selecting long-term mates, Austen's female protagonists and their male consorts display few individual differences. They are all much the same. In personality, though, and in the emotional responses of readers, the individuals stand out sharply from one another. Evidently, the differences in the emotional responses of readers are produced chiefly through differences in personality among the characters. This finding has a practical bearing on the exposition that follows. For motives and the criteria for selecting mates, we present graphic displays only for the character sets as groups, not singling out individual characters. For personality and emotional responses, in contrast, we include graphic displays for both the groups and the individual characters.

Since we did not ourselves anticipate this difference between motives and mating, on the one side, and personality and emotional responses on the other, and since we are aware of no critical commentaries on Austen that clearly register the contrast between these two sets of categories, we regard this finding as a noteworthy result of having conducted an empirical, quantitative analysis of Austen's novels: *motives and mating are constants; personality is the key that opens up the possibility of meaningful variation in Austen's imaginative world.*

Analyzing relations among scores across all Austen's novels, we argue that the novels form a unified thematic and tonal field. The variations in personality and in emotional response for individual characters are contained within an overarching set of values—domestic and social—that we designate Austen's "ethos." In each novel, the female protagonist must use the resources of her own personality, different for each character, to solve the problem presented in the plot: achieving a satisfactory marital union. Our chief interpretive hypothesis is that in each novel solving this problem also fulfills the main thematic motive in the novel: depicting the female protagonist's successful effort at achieving emotional maturity. By "thematic motive," we mean what is really at stake with respect to the attitudes and beliefs of the protagonist. By "emotional maturity," we mean fulfilling the emotional potential available in human nature.[2] For Austen, that potential consists in achieving what she calls "rational happiness."[3] This, we think, is the main design, the figure in Jane Austen's carpet. In the course of each novel, the female protagonist must meet a moral and intellectual challenge: to achieve emotional and intellectual maturity in the sense defined by Austen's ethos.

The figure in this particular carpet is not startlingly unfamiliar. But it is decisively clear. It is based on the responses of knowledgeable readers giving quantitative evidence on simple, basic categories derived from an evolutionary model of human nature. It constitutes the first empirically grounded interpretive proposition about the chief constants and variables that produce meaningful order on a large scale in Austen's novels. Accordingly, we think that the results reported here could serve a useful function in future criticism of Austen's works. They could constrain interpretive commentaries, both limiting the range of plausible hypotheses and also stimulating scholars to develop, qualify, or correct the conclusions we draw.

Generalizing from our findings about the significance of personality in Austen's work, we draw one large theoretical inference that extends well beyond Austen's particular case: the factors of personality are themselves primary thematic terms, on a par, as terms of "meaning," with the allegorical reductions of the theoretical schools: the Mirror Stage, Class Struggle, Compulsory Heterosexuality, and all the rest. Personality is an ultimate interpretive term at the level of "appropriation" or "theoretical explanation."[4]

Sorting the 56 Austen Characters into Character Sets

All but five of the 56 characters from Austen's novels were assigned to a role either on the basis of a single respondent's decision or on the basis of a majority vote among multiple respondents. Four characters received tie votes, and one (Sir Walter Elliot of *Persuasion*) received only one coding and no role assignment ("other"). Table 6.1 displays the distribution of characters into character sets.

Table 6.1 Number of Austen characters in the eight agonistic character sets (and the unassigned characters)

Character Sex	Unassigned	Protagonists	Good minors	Antagonists	Bad minors	Total
Males	4	1	13	5	1	24
Females	1	7	16	8	0	32
Total	5	8	29	13	1	56

Good minor characters bulk largest, and bad minors smallest, as is also the case in the larger data set of the 382 characters assigned to agonistic roles. Female protagonists are in good supply, and the supply of antagonists, both male and females, constitutes a percentage of the Austen characters (23 percent) substantially larger than that in the larger data set. In contrast with the larger data set, characters from Austen contain a somewhat larger proportion of females, also. The proportion of male protagonists is miniscule compared to that in the larger data set.

Only one of the 20 male characters from Austen—Fitzwilliam Darcy of *Pride and Prejudice*—is officially identified as a protagonist, and even Darcy's assignment is marginal. Only 12 of 30 respondents identify him as a protagonist, 11 as a good minor character, 5 as an antagonist, and 2 as "other." (The five designations of Darcy as an antagonist can be attributed to the shift in his relation to Elizabeth and her family midway through the novel.) Five of Austen's six novels focus clearly on a single main character as a protagonist, and in every novel that character is female. (*Sense and Sensibility* has two female protagonists, sisters, Elinor and Marianne.) In each of her novels, Austen aligns her own perspective closely with that of a female protagonist, and we infer that it is for this reason that our respondents usually designate the leading male figures in the novels as "associates of a protagonist."

The paucity of official male protagonists in table 6.1 is misleading. Each of Austen's female protagonists has a male consort, and in each case for which we have scores, the male consorts score within the protagonistic range on the key features that distinguish characters as male protagonists. On the substantive attributes of characters and on Dislike, Root For, and Main Feature, the six consorts are typical male protagonists. The six consorts for the six novels are Darcy in *Pride and Prejudice*, George Knightley in *Emma*, Captain Wentworth in *Persuasion*, Edmund Bertram in *Mansfield Park*, Henry Tilney in *Northanger Abbey*, and Colonel Brandon in *Sense and Sensibility*. (We have no scores for Elinor Dashwood's consort Edward Ferrars, but in profession and temperament he is similar to Edmund Bertram in *Mansfield Park*. Both are quiet, conservative clergymen.)

Despite their official role assignments as good minor characters, the six male consorts of Austen's female protagonists stand out very distinctly from the profiles of good minor male characters who are not consorts of female protagonists. On Main Feature, Constructive Effort, Conscientiousness, Stability, Openness, and Interest, the consort males as a group score at least half a standard deviation higher than the other nine good minor males. Taking account of these signal differences, within this chapter we separate the six male consorts into a distinct group that we designate "male consorts." In the study as a whole, the scores for five of these six characters are designated good minor males. Such designations have much to do with the degree to which good minor males approximate, in scores on Constructive Effort, to male protagonists.

Motives

One of the two most important things to register about motives in Austen's novels is that she uses motives to diminish differences between the sexes. The unisex character of her imagined world enters fundamentally into the ethos and emotional tenor of the novels, shifting the balance of interest away from sexual romance and toward companionship. Unisexuality reduces conflicts of reproductive interest between males and females, thereby reducing also the struggle for power between them. It brings males and females into closer convergence than they are in the actual world or in the world depicted in the novels of the period as a whole. All these effects contribute to the completeness of the tonal resolutions in the novels—hence to the unusually high level of positive emotionality in readers' experience of Austen. A few critics have intuitively recognized some aspects of unisexuality in Austen's novels—particularly the diminution of specifically sexual romance.[5] No critic, to our knowledge, has combined all the aspects of Austen's unisexuality to form part of a comprehensive interpretive argument.

In contrast to male protagonists in the larger data set, Austen's male consorts score unusually high on Romance (figure 6.1).

Even more importantly, they stand far apart from the average male protagonist on Nurture. They score higher on Nurture than both major female sets. They are kinder, gentler males, not so sexually exciting as males in "romance novels"—the pulp fiction genre—but good for the long haul in domestic life. The erotic moment is never a culminating moment for Austen. She glosses over the passionate kiss that seals the deal, and dwells on the terms of the deal. Those terms are the terms of "domestic" romance. The males suitable for this sort of romance are socially decorous, responsible, steady, and companionable. Above all, they are good family men.[6]

The other most important thing to register about motives in Austen's novels is the peculiar way in which she reconciles rank

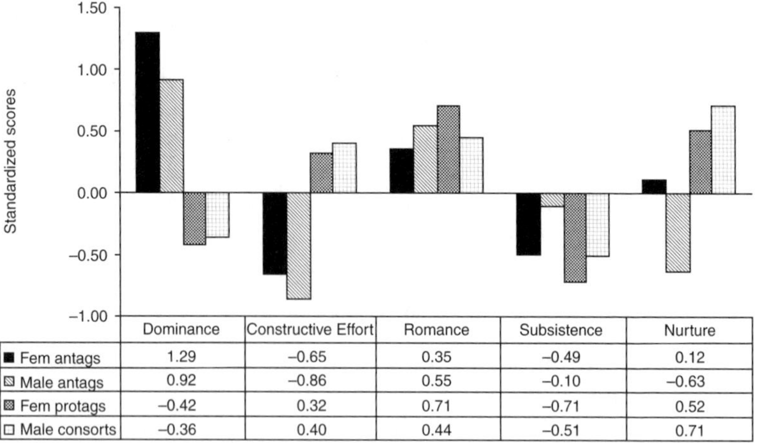

	Dominance	Constructive Effort	Romance	Subsistence	Nurture
■ Fem antags	1.29	−0.65	0.35	−0.49	0.12
▧ Male antags	0.92	−0.86	0.55	−0.10	−0.63
▩ Fem protags	−0.42	0.32	0.71	−0.71	0.52
□ Male consorts	−0.36	0.40	0.44	−0.51	0.71

Figure 6.1 Motive factors in Austen's antagonists, female protagonists, and male consorts.

and privilege with the evolved dispositions for an egalitarian ethos. Virtually all the characters in Austen's novels, good and bad alike, are overtly committed to seeking or sustaining high social rank and material prosperity. Now, high social rank and material prosperity are of course the chief constituents of Social Dominance. The difference is that the good characters, and especially the protagonists and their consorts, make fine discriminations of personal and moral value. Antagonists, in contrast, place rank and wealth above all other considerations, or leave other considerations out altogether. Antagonists either recognize better things but sacrifice them to social and material advantage, or they simply fail, out of stupidity or bad nature, to recognize any forms of value except rank and fortune. Instances of antagonistic characters who see the better and follow the worse include Wickham in *Pride and Prejudice*, Willoughby in *Sense and Sensibility*, Henry Crawford in *Mansfield Park*, and William Elliot in *Persuasion*. Instances of antagonistic characters who follow the worse because that is all they see include Isabella Thorpe and Captain Frederick Tilney in *Northanger Abbey*, Mr. Collins and Lady Catherine de Bourgh in *Pride and Prejudice*, the Reverend Philip Elton and his wife in *Emma*, John Dashwood and Robert Ferrars in *Sense and Sensibility*, Anne Elliot's father and sister in *Persuasion*, and Mrs. Norris in *Mansfield Park*.

Since Austen restricts all her major characters to the members of the leisure class, they receive uniformly low scores on Subsistence as a motive. Jane Fairfax's anguish at the prospect of becoming a governess, in *Emma*, suggests the intensity of the selective pressure for remaining within the leisure class. By restricting her major characters to a single social class, Austen restricts the conflict between communitarian motives and Social Dominance to interpersonal relations within that class. She thus derogates Social Dominance as an individual motive but also tacitly affirms the social legitimacy of the dominant class. Each of her protagonists wins a secure position within that class.

Long-Term Mate Selection

The feminizing of Austen's male consorts extends into their criteria for selecting mates (figure 6.2).

In this category, the male consorts are much more like Austen's female protagonists than they are like male protagonists in the whole set of novels in this study. With a minor qualification for Catherine Morland of *Northanger Abbey*, Austen's female protagonists are all attractive; there are no plain Jane Eyres. But physical attractiveness is not the main thing that attracts the males to them. Austen's male consorts select marital partners not on the basis of sexual passion, but on the basis of their admiration and respect for qualities of character and mind.

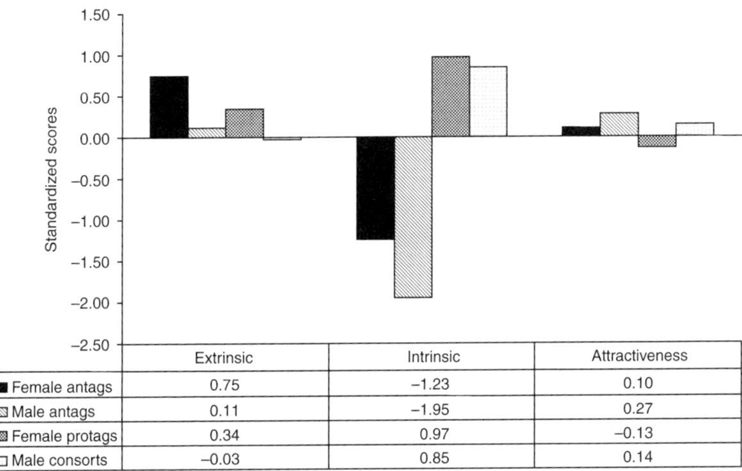

	Extrinsic	Intrinsic	Attractiveness
■ Female antags	0.75	−1.23	0.10
▧ Male antags	0.11	−1.95	0.27
▩ Female protags	0.34	0.97	−0.13
□ Male consorts	−0.03	0.85	0.14

Figure 6.2 Criteria for selecting marital partners in Austen's antagonists, female protagonists, and male consorts.

Austen is evidently aware that her sexual ethos differs from that in the world at large. She has Emma Woodhouse dramatize this issue and bring the reader's attention forcibly to it. Emma is a clever young woman, but she is inexperienced, and her inventive wit often leads her to false conclusions that correspond with her wishes or preconceptions. One of her chief projects is to find a husband for her protégée Harriet Smith. Harriet is physically attractive and has a pleasant temperament, but she is not well educated and not at all clever. Emma and her friend George Knightley engage in a warm debate over Harriet's value on the marriage market. Emma contends that men in general favor physical attractiveness over qualities of mind. "'Till it appears that men are much more philosophic on the subject of beauty than they are generally supposed; till they do fall in love with well-informed minds instead of handsome faces, a girl, with such loveliness as Harriet, has a certainty of being admired and sought after.'"[7]

Emma's generalization corresponds well with the data on mate selection in the whole set of novels in this study, and it corresponds also with findings on current male mating preferences.[8] But with respect to the male consorts in Austen's novels, Emma's judgment is mistaken. That kind of mistake indicates one way in which Emma must still be educated in the sexual norms that are specific to Austen's own imaginative universe. Emma's mistake about sexual norms in Austen's world manifests itself particularly in her judgment about Knightley's sexual preferences. She tells him, "'Oh! Harriet may pick and chuse. Were you, yourself, ever to marry, she is the very woman for you'" (1.8). As it happens, Emma is herself the very woman for Knightley. The resolution of the marriage plot—Emma's betrothal to Knightley—is thus also an embodiment of Emma's successful education in Austen's domestic ethos.

The scores on criteria for selecting mates indicate that Austen places a primary emphasis on intelligent companionship. Though Emma has not herself recognized her own proclivity for this kind of romantic bond, she has already begun, unconsciously, to school herself in it. Her judgment is often poor, and she has never submitted herself to disciplined study, but her mind is sharp and subtle. The dialogue that she has with Knightley over the criteria of male mate selection produces vexation for both of them, but it also displays the acuity and intellectual vigor, on both sides, that forms a chief basis for their companionship. This particular dialogue has a function very similar to that of the dialogue between Elizabeth and Darcy, early in their relations, on the limits of satiric laughter (1:11). Both couples argue, but the quality of their conversation, even as they disagree, tacitly forms the basis for a companionable bond between them.

The capacity to engage in intelligent and civilized dialogue is an essential criterion for the selection of marital partners among all of Austen's protagonists and consorts. It also serves a larger social function in the interactions among the author, the characters, and the readers. In conversations like those between Emma and Knightley and between Elizabeth and Darcy, the focal characters display qualities of perception, inferential acuity, and stylistic force commensurate with those in the narrator's own exposition. The dialogue tacitly brings the focal couple within the privileged circle of the narrator's own perspective. By responding with intelligent sympathy to the qualities of mind displayed by both the focal characters and the author, the reader also enters into this privileged circle. Author, characters, and readers all form a community of civilized and intelligent intercourse.[9] Our respondents evidently delight in joining this particular community.

Drawing more on general knowledge about Austen than on the scores in this particular study, we can affirm that the resolutions of the mating game in Austen also typically resolve, by proxy, conflicts in the larger structure of family life, kin relations, and the community. Elizabeth Bennet's parents are a model of conjugal frustration. Emma Woodhouse's and Anne Elliot's parents, like Elizabeth's, are ill-matched. The Dashwood sisters in *Sense and Sensibility* have an emotionally extravagant mother and a father who does not provide properly for them. Fanny Price's parents live in squalid disorder. In all of these novels, the concluding marital arrangement between the female protagonist and her consort offers a model of domestic propriety, coupled with warm affection, that replaces the defective parental model. The married couple is the nucleus of the family, and all Austen's protagonistic couples give good promise that they will be affectionate and responsible parents. Within the socioeconomic polity of the landed gentry, the family is also a nucleus for a harmonious social order organized around the estate. All these forms of resolution depend on the successfully completed quest of the female protagonist: to achieve emotional maturity within Austen's domestic ethos.

Male antagonists in Austen, like male antagonists in the larger data set, have no definite mating preferences. Mr. Collins in *Pride and Prejudice* is exemplary in this respect. (Because of his dual affiliations with the Bennett household and Lady Catherine de Bourgh, respondents sometimes assign him to the role of good minor or bad minor character, but his general profile is unambiguously that of an antagonist.) He shows up at the Bennet household intending to offer marriage to one of the five daughters, none of whom he has ever before met. He first chooses the oldest, Jane, is told she is spoken for, and within a couple of days proposes to Elizabeth; she turns him down; and within a few more days, he proposes to her much older and plainer friend, Charlotte Lucas, who accepts him. On all three criteria of long-term mate selection, Mr. Collins scores below average, and on the preference for Physical Attractiveness, he scores far below average (–.62). For him, one woman is as good as another. His lack of discrimination in choosing a wife is symptomatic of his general insensitivity to all finer qualities of individual identity.

Mr. Collins' lack of discrimination illustrates a chief function of antagonists: they provide a foil for the ethos embodied in the protagonists and their consorts. The ethos set off by the foil includes the communitarian social ethos and also goes beyond that ethos to include all the attractive features embodied in the protagonistic community: some social, some intimately personal, and some intellectual. As we argue in the final section of chapter 5, mental dullness has no necessary, intrinsic association with an egoistic craving for Social Dominance. In the ethos of the novels, though, the two are typically found in association with one another. In this respect, Austen's ethos conforms entirely with the ethos evident in the average scores for the novels in the period as a whole. Hence it is that Mr. Collins, like his patroness Lady Catherine, is not only a snob but a fool. Hence it is, too, that he has no real power of discrimination in evaluating the attractions of women. The attraction men and women feel for each other as individuals is an important part of the protagonistic ethos.

Personality in the Major Character Sets

The Explanatory Power of Personality

The terms Austen uses to distinguish shades of difference in personality are closely concordant with the five factor model that now dominates the field of personality psychology. This claim might at first seem far-fetched. Austen's observations on human psychology are those of a woman with very little formal education who lived for the most part in retired rural settings some two centuries ago. The five factor model has been produced only within the past few decades, not by an isolated artistic genius operating in a world in which systematic psychological research did not even exist, but by a collective, multigenerational scientific effort involving the statistical analysis of thousands of personality descriptors and tens of thousands of live human subjects.

The seeming oddity of this conjunction is superficial. Modern personality psychology is based on the "lexical" concept: the idea that if concepts are important enough to ordinary human social interaction, they eventually become embedded in the common lexicon—the idiom of ordinary speech. For good evolutionary reasons, humans are tireless and skilled social evaluators. The statistical analysis of personality descriptors identifies the underlying commonalities among multifarious lexical variants. Austen intuitively recognizes the same commonalities. Moreover, Austen did not in fact work in isolation. Though she had little formal education, she had access to the collected works of English literature—to Shakespeare and Chaucer, to Richardson and Fielding—and they too are psychologists of the first order. Austen's implicit psychological model is in some ways more reductive, schematic, and repetitive than that of these other writers. That simplicity is a crucial element in her artistic economy.

In deciding how to interpret Austen's imagined world, it would be a mistake to overlook the obvious. Personality is so much a part of our everyday lives, so thoroughly built into our intuitive folk psychology, that we can fail to register that it is a fundamental, biologically grounded feature of human nature. It is not just a counter or proxy for some other explanatory dimension—political, ideological, metaphysical, psychological, or aesthetic. It is a real and primary fact, a central organizing principle in our lives. Moreover, it is not amorphous, mysterious, infinitely complex, consisting only of nuances and shades of differences. It consists of a few basic features of temperament deriving from the realities of our lives as social animals.

If we strip away the now standard triad of race, class, and sex, what is left? More than has been taken away. Beneath ethnic and class identity, beneath even the two basic human morphs of male and female, personality forms a bedrock of personal identity. The composition of that bedrock can be assessed with the five factors of personality: the organism's drive outward toward rewarding stimulus in the environment (Extraversion); the capacity of all higher organisms to feel pain and react against it (Emotional Stability); the disposition of all mammals for affiliative bonding (Agreeableness); and the specifically human capacities for organizing behavior over time (Conscientiousness) and generating imaginative culture (Openness to Experience).

The depiction of personality in Austen's characters provides an explanation for a paradoxical sensation that many of her readers have felt: it is such a small world she depicts, with such a limited range of settings and plot situations; how can it be that Austen gives the impression of classic grandeur? A large part of the answer is personality. When Austen depicts her female protagonists making their way in the world by using the resources of their own personalities and learning to discriminate the pitfalls and hidden strengths in the personalities of others, she is moving with the precision of genius over ancient, evolved features of human nature.

Personality, Ideology, and Gender

Some of Austen's critics, most of them traditional humanists, have argued that Austen affirms the legitimacy of the social power structure depicted in her novels.[10] Others, especially among the more recent critics, have argued that through devices of style or characterization Austen casts doubt, if only surreptitiously, on the legitimacy of existing power structures.[11] Evaluating scores on personality offers a new angle of approach on this issue.

Personality has an ideological dimension that includes a contrast between conservative and unconventional personality types.[12] Knightley's scores on Extraversion (–.41), Conscientiousness (.78), Emotional Stability (.92), and Openness to Experience (–.05) offer one example of the conservative temperament—self-sufficient, reliable, stable, and conventional. Darcy's scores offer a still more extreme example: Extraversion (–1.61), Conscientiousness (1.05), Emotional Stability (.92), and Openness to Experience (–.15).

Across the whole body of her novels, Austen pairs off unconventional and conservative protagonists or consorts—Elizabeth with Darcy, Emma with Knightley, Catherine with Henry Tilney, and Marianne with Elinor and then finally also with Colonel Brandon. *Mansfield Park* varies the pattern by having two potential candidates for protagonistic status, Henry and Mary Crawford, paired off against two conservatives, Fanny Price and her consort Edmund Bertram. The one main exception is *Persuasion,* in which both Anne and Captain Wentworth are conservative. Maria Musgrove and William Elliott provide the foils in that case. Austen's pairing of unconventional and conservative personalities produces a struggle for moral authority, and in each case the unconventional personality types accept the moral authority exercised by their more conservative counterparts. In our judgment, this pairing gives decisive evidence of Austen's conservative ideological orientation.

Austen gives a distinctive ideological turn to the personalities of female protagonists and male consorts (figure 6.3).

The male consorts are much more introverted, on average, than the female protagonists, and they are also more conscientious and more stable. The females are more open to experience. In this gendered division of psychological labor, female protagonists are typically agents of cultural curiosity. They thus tend to put pressure on conventional social standards. The male consorts, in contrast, typically serve to anchor the conventional system of values. They are, in a word, conservative. Patriarchy is of course part of the conventional system of values, but within Austen's ideological dynamics, preserving differences of male and female power seem less important than preserving the privilege of the leisure class. Since so many of Austen's critics have taken gendered power relations as the central organizing theme in her work, this contention clearly cannot be taken as self-evident. What evidence can we adduce to support the idea that Austen subordinates gendered power relations to the desire, shared by female protagonists and their male consorts, to preserve genteel privilege?

Austen shows us little or nothing of the male sphere of activity—the world of work and war. Virtually all the action of the novels takes place within the domestic sphere, at social gatherings or intimate family encounters. None of Austen's female characters evinces any desire

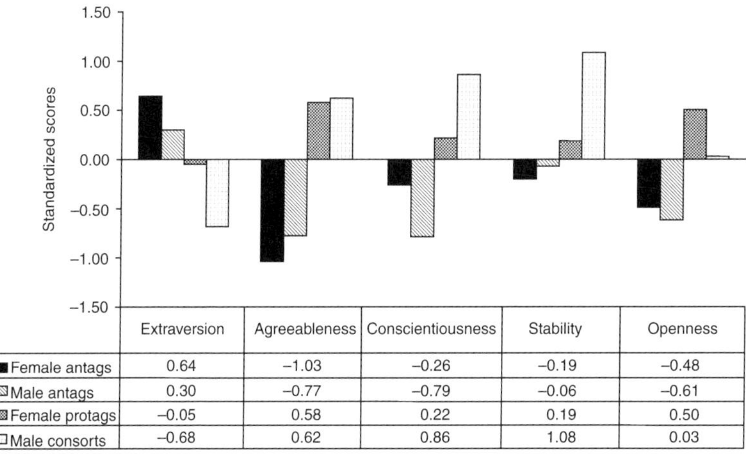

	Extraversion	Agreeableness	Conscientiousness	Stability	Openness
■ Female antags	0.64	−1.03	−0.26	−0.19	−0.48
▧ Male antags	0.30	−0.77	−0.79	−0.06	−0.61
▩ Female protags	−0.05	0.58	0.22	0.19	0.50
□ Male consorts	−0.68	0.62	0.86	1.08	0.03

Figure 6.3 Personality in Austen's antagonists, female protagonists, and male consorts.

to move outside this sphere, and many males clearly wish to remain wholly within this sphere. Frank Churchill in *Emma* yearns for an inheritance that will free him from any necessity of ever quitting the domestic sphere, and Bingley in *Pride and Prejudice* is delighted to have inherited enough money so that he will never have to enter the world of "trade" that is the source of his money. Barring an entail like that which disadvantages the Bennet sisters, males and females both can inherit wealth and exercise the power that derives from it, as is the case, for instance, with Lady Catherine de Bourgh in *Pride and Prejudice*, Willoughby's aunt in *Sense and Sensibility*, and Frank Churchill's aunt in *Emma*. Within the domestic sphere of the leisure class, males exercise no preemptive authority on the basis of their sex. Males and females fulfill complementary functions in sustaining a civil order.

The relationship between Elizabeth and Darcy in *Pride and Prejudice* is paradigmatic for the whole array of gendered personality relations within the protagonistic field of Austen's work. Elizabeth is lively and playful, outgoing, sociable, and flexible in wit. Darcy is taciturn, withdrawn, aloof, and rather stodgily conservative in his social views. He is "clever," but he is also grave and sober. He takes himself very seriously, and in the later phases of their relationship Elizabeth comes to depend fundamentally on his steadiness and reliability. Her own lively wit can play freely around the sobriety of his character, but it never leaves the gravitational field formed by his sober moral convictions. Elizabeth has the livelier mind, but Darcy has the greater power, and Elizabeth does not ultimately challenge the legitimacy of that power. Indeed, it would be strange if she did. Darcy's power is the basis for her security and much of her social prestige. As Claudia Johnson observes, *Pride and Prejudice* "is almost shamelessly wish fulfilling," and "it is Darcy himself who secures the happiness the novel celebrates."[13] The power does not run just one way, though. Austen's female protagonists exercise considerable force in dictating the tone of social relations. On more than one occasion, Darcy asserts his dominance in inappropriate ways—as on the occasion of the ball in which he first appears and offends everyone with his arrogance, and in his first proposal of marriage to Elizabeth. In rejecting this proposal, Elizabeth upbraids Darcy for his transgressions in manners, and he ultimately acknowledges the force of her criticisms. Mistakes of this sort are no small matter. In Austen's universe, a sustained pattern of such transgressions would make the decisive difference between being associated with antagonists rather than protagonists. In gradually altering her judgment of Darcy, Elizabeth must segregate him in her own mind from his antagonistic aunt Lady Catherine de Bourgh.

In order to secure the happiness of the main characters in *Pride and Prejudice*, Darcy must act on the basis of principles concordant with those implicit in the perspective of the narrator—Austen herself. Not all the conservative characters in Austen are male. Fanny, Elinor, and Anne, for instance, are not. And of course, Austen herself is not. Nonetheless, the pattern of gendered psychological relationships has an important function in the emotional organization of Austen's narratives. The diminution of sexual and social conflict in her novels suggests that she aims at an ultimate "felicity," to use her own word. To achieve this felicity, she must dissolve as much as possible any sense of injustice, oppression, and resentment in her imagined world. Patriarchy and class privilege are both background features in the political constitution of Austen's world. They are not foregrounded and made into explicit issues, subjects of controversy, as they are, for instance, in the novels of George Eliot. Nonetheless, they are latent in the conditions of the world that Austen depicts. It is important, then, that the aristocratic males in Austen's world display qualities of judgment that vindicate their positions of privilege and authority. Within Austen's imagined world, male consorts are conservative not because they are repressing the righteous self-assertion of oppressed minorities; they are conservative because they are conserving the principles of justice and order that make happiness possible for all, male and female alike, within the social world depicted in the novels. That social world consists exclusively of the gentry and their satellites: Anglican clergymen and officers in the army and navy. In Austen's imaginative universe, the boundaries of interest and sympathy are coterminous with the circle of privilege.

The fact that male consorts in Austen tend to be more conservative than female protagonists subliminally confirms the legitimacy of patriarchal power. Even so, specific male consorts have moral authority not because they are male but because they are conservative. The authority exercised by males like Darcy and Knightley is moral power based on personality, not on sex. In exercising moral force—as when Knightley rebukes Emma for humiliating the decayed gentlewoman Miss Bates—they appeal to social values that encompass both sexes. Female protagonists can also exercise this kind of moral power. Fanny Price and Elinor Dashwood are exemplary instances. Conversely, female antagonists such as Lady Catherine de Bourgh in *Pride and Prejudice* and Mrs. Ferrars in *Sense and Sensibility*, both beneficiaries of inherited wealth, assert their power in ways that violate the norms implicit in agonistic structure. In this respect, Lady Catherine and Mrs. Ferrars are like General Tilney in *Northanger Abbey*.

In chapter 4, discussing all the novels in this study, we argue that being male or female matters less than being good or bad. In Austen's case, we can make a further stipulation: being male or female matters less than having a conservative or unconventional personality. Subordinating sex to personality is all the easier for Austen in that the differences between her male and female characters, in motives and in the criteria for selecting mates, are much smaller than they are in other novelists or in the world at large. She reduces the distance between males and females not by reducing the differences from both sides of the gender divide but by feminizing her male consorts. Consequently, while indirectly affirming the legitimacy of patriarchy, Austen is also, paradoxically, affirming the gynocentric ethos that prevails in the novels of the period as a whole. To exercise moral authority in an Austen novel, a man must be more like a woman. Henry Higgins, perhaps, would not approve.

Personality in Individual Female Protagonists

The personality profiles of Austen's female protagonists display a rich variety, but all the variations are ultimately contained within a single ethos—a consistent vision of domestic happiness and social stability. This is the ethos that can be teased out of the scores on motives and mating. In each novel, the protagonists ultimately bring the particular features of their own individual personalities into concord with Austen's ethos. All the novels end happily. That observation accords with the experience of most readers, and it is confirmed by the convergence of the scores on Root For and Achieves Goals. The happy ending in each novel consists of the protagonists achieving what Austen calls "rational happiness"—"rational" meaning the very specific blend of prudence, intelligent companionship, and civil intercourse that constitutes Austen's ethos. Variations in personality place different kinds of stress on the ethos of the novels; and each specific personality offers different resources for meeting challenges to that ethos. Austen's novels thus form something like a psychological thought-experiment: a fictive exploration of the weaknesses and strengths inherent in a wide range of personalities. The constant in this experiment is the problem situation: young people seeking happy and stable marriages.

In the graphic array (figures 6.4 and 6.5), we have divided Austen's female protagonists into extraverts and introverts.

There are seven female protagonists in Austen's six novels (the Dashwood sisters double up in *Sense and Sensibility*). Four of the seven score above average in Extraversion, and three score below average. Marianne Dashwood received only four codings, and her sister Elinor only five, but we think most readers will consider the scores

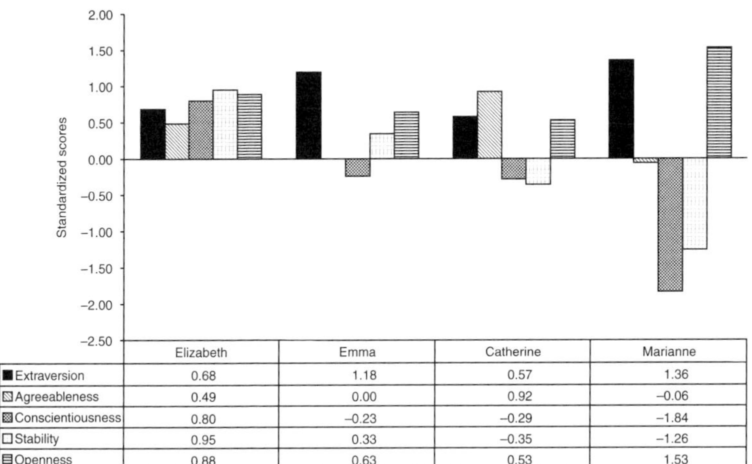

	Elizabeth	Emma	Catherine	Marianne
Extraversion	0.68	1.18	0.57	1.36
Agreeableness	0.49	0.00	0.92	−0.06
Conscientiousness	0.80	−0.23	−0.29	−1.84
Stability	0.95	0.33	−0.35	−1.26
Openness	0.88	0.63	0.53	1.53

Figure 6.4 Personality in Austen's female protagonists—the extraverts.

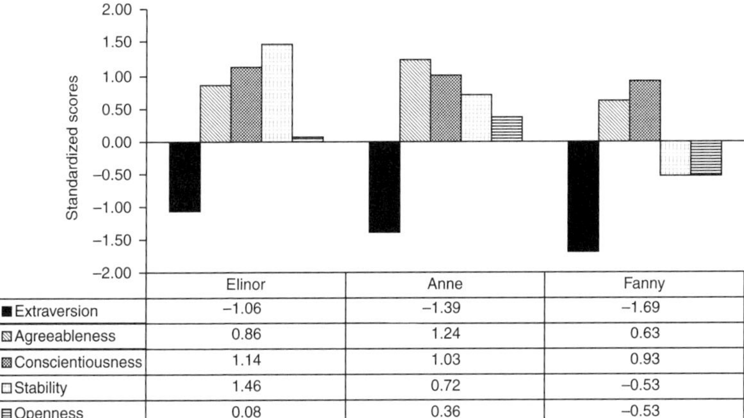

	Elinor	Anne	Fanny
Extraversion	−1.06	−1.39	−1.69
Agreeableness	0.86	1.24	0.63
Conscientiousness	1.14	1.03	0.93
Stability	1.46	0.72	−0.53
Openness	0.08	0.36	−0.53

Figure 6.5 Personality in Austen's female protagonists—the introverts.

reasonable. The alpha reliability estimates—a measure of consensus among respondents—are quite high for these two characters (.93 for Elinor, and .88 for Marianne).

The scores on personality gives us a clue to the reason that *Pride and Prejudice* holds a modal position in the body of Austen's novels. It is the most often read, most often filmed, most often critiqued, and most often taught. Elizabeth Bennet's personality almost certainly constitutes a chief reason for this preeminence. In comparison with Austen's other female protagonists, Elizabeth appears to have an ideal personality. She displays a balance in all five features of personality. She is lively and outgoing but also moderately agreeable, and she is conscientious, stable, and open to experience. None of the other female protagonists displays this full an array of desirable qualities set into balance. Emma, Catherine, and Marianne are all weak in conscientiousness, especially Marianne. Emma and Marianne are weak in Agreeableness. Catherine, Fanny, and Marianne all are weak in Emotional Stability, especially Marianne. The introverted protagonists are all highly conscientious, but they are also less open to experience than the extraverts. Like all of Austen's female protagonists, Elizabeth is young and inexperienced. (Anne Elliot in *Persuasion* is the exception; but her story line actually began several years before the novel opens, when she was young and inexperienced.) Like the other Austen protagonists, Elizabeth has some learning to do. But the distance she has to travel between her own natural disposition and that of the implied author is smaller than that of any other Austen protagonist.

This last claim is of course an interpretive judgment; it is based partly on the convergence of verbal style in Elizabeth and Austen, and we have no data on verbal style. The features of Elizabeth's personality, though, and the comparison with the features of the other characters, are matters of data.

In contrast to the patterns across all the novels in this study, Austen pairs Extraversion with Openness to Experience. All her extraverted protagonists score at or above average on Openness, and her most extraverted protagonist, Marianne, is also her most open. Her three introverted female protagonists score in the bottom three positions on Openness, and Fanny, the most introverted female protagonist, is also the least open to experience.[14] Fanny is timid and sensitive, but she holds a key position within the ultimately conservative ethos in Austen's fictive world. The conservative family in which Fanny lives comes apart under the anarchic influence of two characters, the Crawford siblings. Mary Crawford is in important ways very similar to Elizabeth Bennet—lively, clever, vivacious—but she and her brother are both deficient in the moral seriousness with which Elizabeth tempers her own vivacity. Mary's liveliness leads her into an indulgent tolerance of libertine amorality—that is, of a sexual license that threatens the monogamous marital norm. Fanny's temperament would not be ideal for every occasion, clearly, but it turns out to be exactly the right temperament to deal with the charming solicitations of anarchic self-release in *Mansfield Park*.[15]

The pairing of Extraversion and Openness is a main element in the charm exercised by Austen's extraverted female protagonists, but that pairing depends in each case on the female protagonist being set off in complementary relationship to a more conservative counterpart. Marianne provides the most obvious instance of why the conservative temperament holds a central place in Austen's ethos. Marianne comes close to disaster. She is ultimately saved by two conservatives, her sister Elinor and Colonel Brandon. Though she cannot change her own temperament, she expresses contrition for her self-indulgent emotional extravagance. She is thus allowed to participate in the happy comedy resolution of *Sense and Sensibility*. In contrast to Marianne, neither of the Crawford siblings succeeds in forming a permanent bond with a more stable, conservative counterpart—Mary with Edmund or Henry with Fanny. Consequently, they are ultimately expelled from the inner protagonistic circle. So also with Wickham, Willoughby, and William Elliot.

In situation, setting, verbal style, and the ethos of the implied author, Austen's novels are all of a piece. And yet, each of the six novels has its own distinct artistic character. Austen's critics savor the fine shades of difference among the novels, often articulating formal or ideological reasons to vindicate their personal preferences. Our data suggest that the deeper source for these evaluative differences are variations in emotional response corresponding to variations in the personalities of the characters. It is variation in personality, more than anything else, that invests each novel with its own distinct identity as a work of art. Nonetheless, Austen's pervasive pairing of conservative and unconventional characters forms a larger pattern that points toward the dominant ethos, domestic and social, that governs her fictive universe.

Emotional Responses to the Major Character Sets

Our data indicate that the emotional tone of Austen's novels is considerably more positive than the emotional tone in the average novel of the period. Across the whole body of novels, antagonists score below average in eliciting sorrow, and protagonists score above average. In Austen's novels, in contrast, protagonists and their consorts, along with antagonists, score below average in eliciting Sorrow (figure 6.6).

This too is a distinctive feature of Austen's imagined world. It no doubt accounts for a good deal of her extraordinary popularity. Everybody likes to be cheerful. But good cheer alone is not enough; we readily detect false cheer and find it jarring. Feminizing her male consorts makes it easier for Austen to maintain a positive emotional tone. Achieving a companionable marital bond is as much a need for the males as it is for the females. We have already observed that feminizing males reduces the tension of conflicting male/female reproductive interests. Male characters are also exceptionally well-integrated into the emotional fulfillment that the readers derive from the resolutions of the plot. In contrast to the pattern in the larger data set, Austen's male consorts score higher on Interest than either antagonistic set, though still not so high as female protagonists.

To maintain the cheerfulness of her imagined world, Austen must carefully control readers' emotional investment in the characters. Consider, for instance, the plot crisis in *Mansfield Park*. Fanny's married cousin Maria engages in sexual misconduct that brings ruin to herself and disgrace to her family. Austen gives the crisis its due

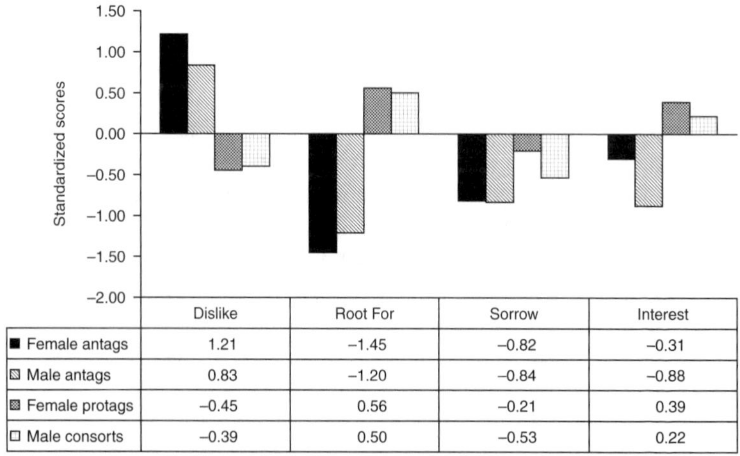

	Dislike	Root For	Sorrow	Interest
■ Female antags	1.21	−1.45	−0.82	−0.31
▧ Male antags	0.83	−1.20	−0.84	−0.88
▩ Female protags	−0.45	0.56	−0.21	0.39
□ Male consorts	−0.39	0.50	−0.53	0.22

Figure 6.6 Emotional responses to Austen's antagonists, female protagonists, and male consorts.

weight, but Maria's folly is freighted with good consequences for Fanny and Edmund, the protagonistic couple, and Austen keeps the central focus on their happiness. "Let other pens dwell on guilt and misery. I quit such odious subjects as soon as I can, impatient to restore everybody, not greatly in fault themselves, to tolerable comfort, and to have done with all the rest."[16] Those actually "in fault" are sacrificed to the affirmation of the principles that regulate conduct, and agonistic polarization easily brings emotional response into conformity with that sacrifice. Maria Bertram is selfish, arrogant, and vain, and Henry Crawford is vain and emotionally frivolous. Wounded by Crawford's failure to follow through on his many romantic promises to her, Maria marries a wealthy but mentally deficient young man, then abandons him and runs off with Crawford. She and Crawford are then segregated into an emotional out-group that leaves the resolution as serene as the resolutions in Austen's more purely comic novels. After Crawford abandons Maria, she is joined by her aunt Norris, the only character in the story who elicits strong and active dislike. The emotional world thus segregates itself into protagonistic and antagonistic spheres. "Misery" is shunted off into the antagonistic sphere, and "guilt" sanctions the elimination of empathy from that sphere.

Emotional Responses to Individual Female Protagonists

We can divide Austen's female protagonists into the four who produce little emotional ambivalence in readers and the three who are more problematic (figures 6.7 and 6.8).

In respect to emotional response, as in other respects, Elizabeth Bennet is the paradigmatic Austen protagonist. She receives very low scores on Dislike and high scores on both Interest and Root For; and she is at the low end of the scale on Sorrow. Readers are emotionally absorbed in her story; they like her, wish her to succeed, and rejoice in her success. Catherine Morland of *Northanger Abbey* receives scores on emotional response very similar to those received by Elizabeth, but readers are less interested in her. She is the least developed of Austen's protagonists. She is an ingénue, a straight man (or woman) for Austen's satire on gothic fiction. Anne Elliot has a sweet and gentle nature, quiet, affectionate, and calm, intelligent but not assertive. She is the most sympathetic listener among Austen's protagonists, thus giving occasion for fine comic scenes in which all the members of her extended family bring to her their querulous complaints about

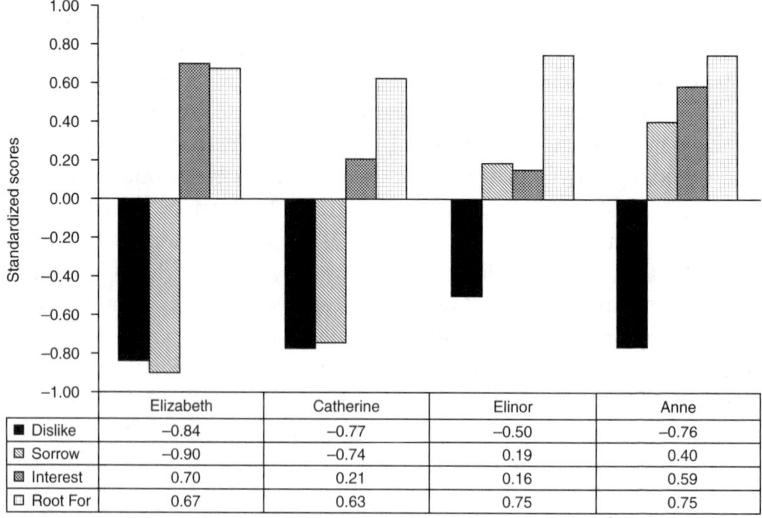

	Elizabeth	Catherine	Elinor	Anne
■ Dislike	–0.84	–0.77	–0.50	–0.76
▧ Sorrow	–0.90	–0.74	0.19	0.40
▩ Interest	0.70	0.21	0.16	0.59
□ Root For	0.67	0.63	0.75	0.75

Figure 6.7 Emotional responses to Austen's less agonistically problematic female protagonists.

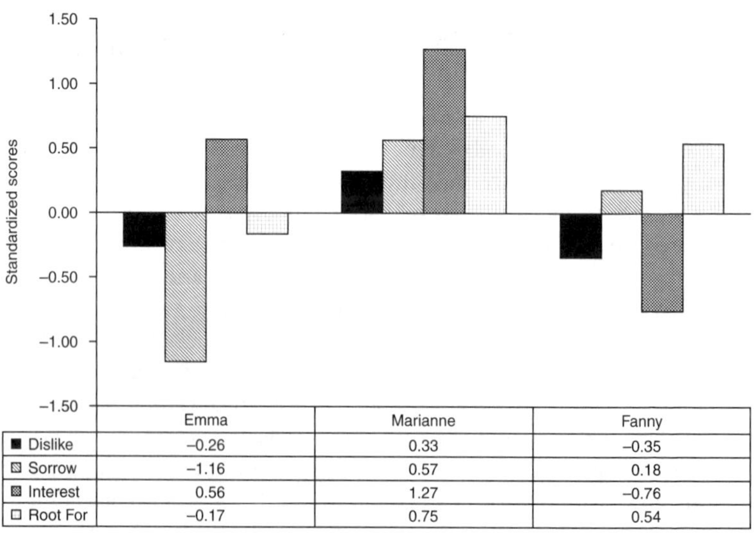

	Emma	Marianne	Fanny
■ Dislike	–0.26	0.33	–0.35
▧ Sorrow	–1.16	0.57	0.18
▩ Interest	0.56	1.27	–0.76
□ Root For	–0.17	0.75	0.54

Figure 6.8 Emotional responses to Austen's more agonistically problematic female protagonists.

each other. As an introvert, though, she is a less dynamic and engaging character than Elizabeth.

Marianne Dashwood and Anne Elliot excite the most Sorrow, but Marianne also scores unusually high, for a protagonist, on Dislike, almost within the antagonistic range. Her score on Dislike is counterbalanced by her extremely high score on Interest. She is a figure of romantic passion, and readers are excited by her, even though they do not like her. (The same scoring pattern appears in emotional responses to Catherine Earnshaw in *Wuthering Heights.*) The contrast between the kind of emotional appeal exercised by Elinor and Marianne is exaggerated in the contrast between Fanny and Marianne. Fanny receives a low score on Dislike, but she also receives a very low score—the lowest in the group—on Interest. Many readers have been frustrated by the discrepancy between the interest she excites and the moral authority with which she is ultimately invested. Readers who relish the frank assertiveness of Austen's extraverted protagonists often react with irritated impatience at Fanny's timid and conventional disposition. They seem annoyed that she gradually assumes a position of commanding influence on all the people who surround her.[17] Other readers, though, have felt that *Mansfield Park* displays a depth of feeling and a seriousness of ethical vision nowhere else equaled in Austen's work.[18] Again, such differences in evaluative response, though often rationalized on formal or ideological grounds, seem at bottom to reflect differences in the personality and temperament of the critics. It might be true that there is no disputing matters of taste. Empirical study can nonetheless illuminate the reasons for evaluative judgments.

Six of the seven protagonists score well above average on Root For. Emma is the one exception. Most of her actions in the course of the story are ill-judged and inadvertently destructive, and she is less agreeable than any other female protagonist except Marianne. Austen anticipated that many of her readers would not like Emma, and indeed she scores higher on Dislike than any female protagonist except Marianne.

If readers tend not to like Emma so much as they like other Austen protagonists, and if they do not, through most of the novel, wish her to succeed, why is it that *Emma* runs a close second to *Pride and Prejudice* in popularity with Austen's readers? We think that the popularity can be accounted for, in good measure, by the quality of the relationship between Emma and Knightley. It is in important ways the least romantic, most purely companionable of all Austen's protagonistic relationships. All the other female protagonists marry men reasonably close to their own age. Emma marries a man 16 years older than she is—old enough biologically, if not socially, to be her father. Knightley recalls holding Emma when she was a baby. In important ways, psychologically, he replaces her father, an infantile valetudinarian. Throughout the novel, even when they are most at odds, Emma and Knightley conspire to coddle Mr. Woodhouse as if he were their baby. Their understanding on this point forms a companionable bond like that shared by parents. Emma scores relatively high on Nurture (.52), but Knightley scores even higher (.93). By marrying Emma, Knightley gives a permanent legal sanction to his role as her surrogate father. He is thus doubly a parent, both a surrogate father to Emma, and as her consort, a father to her infantile father. Emma too occupies a dual family role. She is a daughter to her husband and a mother to her father. By occupying these two roles, she achieves family intimacy while avoiding a specifically sexual relationship. Through her filial relation to Knightley and her maternal relation to her father, she occupies both ends of the reproductive cycle, completing the cycle from daughter to mother while skipping the sexual middle link—enacting thus a sort of imaginative virgin birth. The scores on motives and mating across the whole body of Austen's novels point in this direction: family intimacy without specifically sexual interest. *Emma* goes farthest in that direction.

Conclusion: Reader Response in the Circle of Privilege

Austen's novels are all love stories, but love stories of a peculiar kind. They are romances devoid of sex. The scenes in which female protagonists and their male consorts achieve intimacy are not scenes of passion. They are conversations, civil, lucid, poised, even when heated by underlying indignation or transient distress. The male consorts are less motivated by erotic passion than by the need for companionable society and family partnership. In this crucial respect, they are scarcely distinguishable from the female protagonists.

By muting sexual passion while also eliminating Sorrow from her emotional register, Austen runs a serious risk of being bland. By so successfully evading this danger, she demonstrates how much dramatic interest can be vested in agonistic structure even when it is isolated from other sources of emotional power. Sex and death, it would seem, are unnecessary.

In all of Austen's novels, antagonists who value only Social Dominance are placed in conflict with protagonists who value the qualities of mind and character that evoke admiration and liking in readers. In *Northanger Abbey*, *Pride and Prejudice*, *Sense and Sensibility*, and *Mansfield Park*, protagonists who embody personal merit are set at a disadvantage in relation to antagonists who possess greater wealth and power. In *Emma*, this basic conflict is displaced onto Jane Fairfax, who is in important ways more like a standard protagonist than is Emma herself. The central problem situation in *Persuasion* is that Anne Elliot is pressing toward the end of the nubile age range, but she finds herself in this precarious position precisely because early in life she had rejected a suitor who was not sufficiently wealthy. In all the novels, merit and privilege are set in tension with one another, and in all the novels, the resolutions of the plot resolve this tension.

If the political views of our respondents are at all representative of contemporary students and teachers of literature—and we have no reason to suppose they are not—they are probably to the left of the center point in the political spectrum. Nonetheless, when the respondents read Jane Austen, they slip easily and comfortably into the ideological norms that characterize the stance of a privileged elite. Whatever political theses our respondents might formulate about the novels, their scores on Root For and Dislike reveal that they participate vicariously in the emotional resolutions that Austen provides for her characters.

The ease with which most readers accept social privilege in Austen's novels can be explained, we think, by the closed social circle in which her characters live. In the novels of Dickens and Eliot, the egalitarian ethos manifests itself in a scathing critique of class differences. In Austen's novels, the same ethos operates by suppressing dominance within the single class to which she devotes her attention. Austen defines that class primarily through "manners," a word that denotes a personal style distinguished by intelligence, poise, cultivation, and a courteous regard for the feelings of others. People who exemplify that style belong to the "gentry." Whether or not they possess a country estate, they are "ladies" and "gentlemen." When Lady Catherine de Bourgh is trying to persuade Elizabeth not to marry Darcy, she says, "If you were sensible of your own good, you would not wish to quit the sphere, in which you have been brought up." Elizabeth responds, "In marrying your nephew, I should not consider myself as quitting that sphere. He is a gentleman; I am a gentleman's daughter; so far we are equal" (3:14).

In Austen's world, possessing gentle manners depends heavily on birth and wealth, but Austen discriminates sharply between two possible attitudes toward birth and wealth. Her antagonists typically regard birth and wealth as necessary, sufficient, and exclusive criteria for status as gentlefolk. Her protagonists and their consorts, in contrast, regard manners as the decisive criterion. One crucial test for Darcy is whether he can make that distinction. Austen's uncle and aunt Gardiner live on Mr. Gardiner's income as a merchant. Their class identity is thus borderline. They nonetheless pass the test of manners. By recognizing that the Gardiners pass this test, Darcy himself passes a crucial test. He moves decisively into the protagonistic field. Lady Catherine, of course, despite her birth and wealth, fails the test of manners. The climactic scene in which Elizabeth trounces Lady Catherine in debate provides readers the kind of pleasure that is specific to suppressing dominance. By identifying with Elizabeth, modern readers participate vicariously in a world of high social rank while nonetheless remaining true to the egalitarian ethos.

It is little wonder, then, that Austen is so perennial a favorite. She is a shrewd, penetrating psychologist, and she is caustic enough to gratify malice, but her tonal trajectory remains resolutely focused on an ultimate felicity. She invites her readers to participate vicariously in the satisfactions of a companionable pair bond untroubled by conflicting male and female sexual needs. If they follow her prompts, Austen's readers also join a fictional community populated exclusively by members of a privileged elite but governed internally by an egalitarian ethos. With sexual and social conflict thus contained, readers need fear no distressing appeals to their compassion, their tolerance, or their powers of endurance. They need only luxuriate in an imaginary world regulated by high qualities of character, illuminated by wit, graced by elegance of style, and blessed by good fortune.

Chapter 7

Indifferent Tragedy in *The Mayor of Casterbridge*

The Incoherence of the Critical Tradition on *Mayor*

For the novels of Jane Austen, quantitative methods provide new evidence on disputed issues, offer opportunities for confirming and refining the best insights of traditional criticism, and provide a deeper and more systematic understanding of her underlying designs. For *The Mayor of Casterbridge*, quantitative analysis gives occasion for a more radical intervention in the critical tradition. On the thematic and tonal structures of Jane Austen's novels, critics have reached a very high degree of consensus. Most major differences arise only at the highest level of thematic reduction—the level at which common observations are located within global theoretical paradigms. In Austen's case, global theories have little impact on the analytic summary that constitutes the bulk of most criticism. *The Mayor of Casterbridge*, in contrast, presents a major interpretive puzzle.

Virtually all the previous criticism on *Mayor* has tried to interpret the novel by invoking one of three standard models of tragedy: retributive justice, Promethean revolt, and redemptive transformation. These three models are incompatible with one another, and none of them accords well with the demonstrable, quantifiable facts—the attributes of the characters and the emotional responses of readers. The critical tradition has failed to produce a consensus because none of the three models gives a satisfactory account of how the novel works. Each model leaves too much out, or distorts too much of what it tries to take in. Successfully reinterpreting *Mayor* would demonstrate that quantitative methods can solve problems that have baffled traditional methods. In this chapter, we first give an exposition of our results, then examine the critical tradition on the novel, contrasting the traditional models with the implications of the data produced by our respondents.

In *Mayor*, Hardy fundamentally disrupts the agonistic structures that typically govern reader response. We had 62 respondents providing scores for the main character, Michael Henchard. A large majority (54) identify Henchard as a protagonist, but the scores they give him on motivations and personality are overwhelmingly those that usually characterize antagonists. In previous chapters, we have described several agonistically borderline characters—Becky Sharp, Dorian Gray, Catherine Earnshaw, Kurtz, and Marianne Dashwood. In each of those cases, we trace out predictable correlations among the agonistically mixed attributes of the character (motives and personality) and the emotional responses of readers. Problematic personalities produce dissonant emotional responses, and so it is also with Henchard. But the disruptions in the pattern of emotional response run still deeper in *Mayor*. The two characters who have protagonistic profiles, Farfrae and Elizabeth-Jane, are not designated as protagonists by our respondents. Henchard himself scores just at average on the emotional response factor Interest, and every other character scores far below average on Interest. Hardy has designed the novel in such a way as to disconnect readers emotionally from the events of the story.

These findings suggest two alternative interpretive approaches. If we were to assume that readers should be emotionally invested in the outcome of the story, we would have little choice but to declare the novel a failure. The alternative would be to ask what other psychological functions the novel might fulfill for the reader. Declaring the novel a failure would run up against its canonical standing as one of Hardy's major works. The fact that Hardy is the author would not in itself be sufficient to confer canonical status. Hardy's unevenness—his similarity to the little girl with a curl in the middle of her forehead—is notorious. How many literary scholars would claim major canonical standing for *A Pair of Blue Eyes* or *Two on a Tower*? It seems unlikely, then, that the novel is simply a failure. Here, we take the second approach, offering a new interpretation by identifying a different kind of psychological function that we think the novel fulfills.

The critics' failure to achieve consensus on *Mayor* runs deeper than might at first appear. It is not just that one set of critics disagrees with another set. Each set disagrees with itself. More than two-thirds of the 85 respondents on *Mayor* had published on some aspect of Hardy's work, and nearly one-third (25) had published directly on *Mayor*. In using the data to demonstrate the inadequacy of the standard interpretive models, we thus turn the readers' observations against their own interpretations. The interpretive models do not fit the facts, and the facts are the particular observations made by the critics using the models. This situation might seem a little shocking, but disparities between particular observations and larger interpretive models are a common fact of everyday life. If they seem particularly disturbing in an interpretive, scholarly tradition, that is only because we wrongly assume that professional scholarly training eliminates conceptual incoherence. Such training usually produces high levels of fluency and acuity in arguing a case, but that sort of proficiency guarantees no ultimate conceptual coherence, either in theoretical vision or in practical criticism.

A Separate Website for *Mayor*

We set up a separate website for *Mayor* and solicited respondents separately from the solicitations for the other novels in this study. We wanted to collect enough data on enough characters to give a thorough quantitative analysis of at least one novel. We chose *Mayor* because it is relatively compact, has only a few major characters, and has unusual agonistic and tonal features that make it particularly inviting for comparative analysis—that is, for comparing scores on individual characters with average scores from the larger data set. The six characters we listed from *Mayor* are Michael Henchard; his wife Susan; his stepdaughter Elizabeth-Jane; his rival Donald Farfrae; Lucetta Templeman, the woman for whose favors Henchard and Farfrae enter into competition; and Newson, the sailor who, at the beginning of the novel, buys Henchard's wife and daughter from him.

The website questionnaire for *Mayor* differed from that of the larger data set in only one respect. For the website using a single questionnaire of 2,000 characters, we could not ask questions about romantic relationships between specific characters. The questionnaire had to be applicable to any character selected from the list. For the characters in *Mayor*, we could ask readers to identify the mate-selection criteria that each individual character uses in selecting another specific character for a mate.

We solicited participation in the *Mayor* study by directly contacting scholars who had published on Hardy and particularly on *Mayor* and on other Hardy novels. We also advertised the study on the website of the Thomas Hardy Association and listservs associated with the study of Victorian literature. Using information on age, sex, level of education, when and why the novel was read, and the publishing history of the respondents, we determined that a total of 85 individual coders responded to the survey. Fifty-one were males, 34 females. The youngest respondent was 23, and only 8 respondents were under the age of 30. All had college degrees. Nine had a bachelor's degree, 21 a master's, and 55 a doctorate. In other words, 89 percent, nearly nine out of ten, had advanced degrees. Twenty-five had published on *Mayor*; another 23 had published on some other novel by Hardy; and another 10 had published on some other aspect of Hardy's work. Thus, a total of 58 out of the 85 (68 percent) had published on some aspect of Hardy's work. Sixty-seven respondents reported having read the novel within the past five years, and 31 within the past year. Fifty-five (65 percent) read it either for teaching a class or for "professional purposes." In sum, the respondents were well-informed, competent readers. They knew their Hardy. Several respondents completed more than one protocol. A total of 124 protocols were completed.

On scores for substantive categories such as motives and emotional responses, the respondents to *Mayor* had remarkably high intercoder reliability scores. As we note in chapter 4, in most psychological research, alpha values above .70 are considered acceptable, and alphas from .80 to .90 range are considered good. Values above .90 are normally achieved only by trained professionals. In the responses to the characters in *Mayor*, the averaged alpha values for the various categories were as follows: character success (.83); motives (.91); mate selection (.86); emotional responses (.78); and personality factors (.82). The lowest alpha values were for Newson, a relatively minor character who received only five codings. If we exclude Newson's alpha values, the averaged alpha values are as follows: character success (.87); motives (.93); mate selection (.86); emotional responses (.88); and personality factors (.91). All of these averaged alpha values are either good or very good. In other words, there was a high level of consensus among the respondents on all the substantive categories of analysis.

Clearly, the respondents converged to a high degree on their assessments of the attributes of the characters and also on their emotional responses to the characters. Role assignments are another matter. There, we find wider than usual variation (table 7.1). That variation is one of the main clues to the kind of interpretive puzzle that *Mayor* presents.

Table 7.1 Number of respondents voting for each role assignment in *Mayor*

Character	Protag	Good Minor	Antag	Bad Minor	"Other"	Sum	Consensus Rating[a]
Henchard	54	0	4	0	4	62	87%
Farfrae	1	7	9	1	3	21	43%
E-Jane	2	7	0	1	2	12	58%
Lucetta	2	3	3	1	1	10	30%
Susan	1	9	1	0	3	14	64%
Newson	0	0	3	1	1	5	60%

[a] *The consensus rating is derived by dividing the number of respondents voting for the majority role assignment by the total number of respondents.*

Consensus ratings on Role Assignments

Respondents largely agree that Henchard is the protagonist. They are strongly divided about the roles to be assigned to Farfrae, Elizabeth-Jane, Lucetta, Newson, and Susan. All except Lucetta are in some ways more attractive or more typically "good" than Henchard, but their role assignment is defined in relation to him. If we add the total number of respondents for all the characters who agree on role assignment, and divide that number by the total number of respondents, the total consensus rating on role assignment for *Mayor* is 69 percent. The comparable consensus rating for all 206 multiply coded characters in the larger data set website is 81 percent.

"Interest" as a Key to the Tonal Structure of *Mayor*

Had we started with *Mayor*, and studied it alone, we could never have derived a clear idea of the standard agonistic structure of the novels of the period. The consensus level for assigning characters to roles in *Mayor* is low, and the assignment of roles puts strong pressure on the standard agonistic logic articulated in the relations among personality, motives, mate-selection criteria, and emotional responses. Henchard is a protagonist with an antagonistic profile, and he comes into sharp conflict, in one way or another, with Farfrae and with Newson. As a result, those two characters are identified as antagonists, but their scores on motive factors and personality factors are not like those of standard antagonists. Newson's profile is that of a good minor character. In motive factors, Farfrae's profile combines protagonistic and antagonistic features, but his personality profile is emphatically that of a protagonist.

Elizabeth-Jane has a profile that is clearly that of a female protagonist, but she is identified as a good minor character. Moreover, her score on Main Feature (–.11) indicates that the success or failure of her hopes and efforts is not a main feature in the outcome of the story. She nonetheless has an important function in the story. She provides a point of view wider and more comprehensive than that of any of the other characters. As several of the best critics of the novel have observed, her perspective on the success or failure of other characters is very similar to Hardy's own. The attitude implicit in her motives and personality thus offers a guide to the emotional and tonal quality of the story as Hardy himself conceives it.

All novels perform some kind of psychological work. They activate the emotions and imaginative responses of readers and lead the readers through an integrated emotional process culminating in some kind of conclusion or point of rest ("resolution"). Most of the novels in our data set seek in a fairly simple and direct way to involve the reader in the story, to engage the reader's sympathy for one or more main characters. That sort of involvement is registered in part through the emotional response factor "Interest." This factor has moderate positive loadings from Admiration and Liking, but the main element in Interest is a strong negative loading from Indifference. Characters who score low on Interest typically receive very high scores on Indifference. That is, the readers indicate that they are highly indifferent to the character. A high score on Interest suggests that the readers care what happens to the character, though not always in a positive way. Count Dracula scores as high in Interest as Dorothea Brooke. Readers do not want Dracula to succeed, but they do care whether he succeeds or not. They want him to fail. (His score on Root For is –.88.) Interest is qualitatively distinct from the evaluatively charged response of Dislike, which constitutes a measure of positive or negative emotional valence. Otherwise, they would not be separate factors. Interest is qualitatively distinct also from Sorrow, which constitutes a measure of sympathy or compassion.

In one of the earliest published responses to *Mayor*, an anonymous critic observed that the novel "does not contain a single character capable of arousing a passing interest in his or her welfare."[1] As the scores on Interest in our study indicate, this critic's observation of the fact is correct, but the inference that the critic draws from that fact is erroneous. The critic presupposes that some sort of passional involvement with characters is an indispensable requirement in all novels, so that the absence of interest is merely a defect, and a large one. Passional involvement is indeed a common way in which novels work, but it is not the only possible way, and it is not the way *Mayor* works. What Hardy is after in this novel is something fairly unusual, peculiar to Hardy, and perhaps more fully exemplified in this particular novel than in any other novel by Hardy. What Hardy is after is in fact something like the reverse of Interest. The kind of psychological work that Hardy accomplishes in *Mayor* is that of gaining a reflective detachment from the story that he depicts. He seeks himself to achieve a defensive, stoic stance against both passion and the vagaries of circumstance. Within the story itself, as a participant observer, Elizabeth-Jane embodies that stance.

The actions in the plot of *Mayor* are like a roller coaster ride of wildly changing fortunes—especially the fortunes of Henchard, Susan, and Lucetta. In the opening chapter, Henchard is 21 years old. Embittered at being held back and burdened by family responsibilities, he gets drunk and sells his wife and infant daughter at a country fair. Within the next 20 years, he becomes a wealthy and respected corn merchant and is elected mayor of the market town Casterbridge. Meanwhile, his wife Susan has lived with Newson, the man who bought her. Her child from the marriage with Henchard has died, but she has another child with Newson. Both children are named Elizabeth-Jane. Newson is lost at sea, and Susan returns to Henchard, deceiving him by telling him that Newson's child, now grown, is his child. He remarries her, but she dies soon after. Shortly after her death, Henchard tells Elizabeth-Jane that she is his daughter and asks her to take his name, but almost immediately after that he discovers that Elizabeth-Jane is not in fact his daughter. He does not tell her that he had been deceived in believing himself her father, but he becomes cold and hostile toward her. Since her arrival in Casterbridge, Elizabeth-Jane has been romantically interested in Henchard's young protégé Farfrae, who had come to Casterbridge without place or prospect. Farfrae loses interest in Elizabeth-Jane and takes up instead with Lucetta, who previously, unbeknownst to him, was Henchard's mistress. Henchard began his relationship with Farfrae by being overbearingly friendly, but he becomes jealous of Farfrae's popularity. Henchard becomes bitterly antagonistic to Farfrae, and they become competitors in business. After Susan's death, Henchard also becomes Farfrae's rival for Lucetta, and her preference for Farfrae embitters Henchard still further. Farfrae and Lucetta marry. Henchard attempts to kill Farfrae by throwing him out of a hay loft, but relents and breaks down in remorse. Lucetta becomes pregnant with Farfrae's child, but her past with Henchard is made public. She becomes hysterical, has a seizure, and dies through complications with the pregnancy. In the period of just a few years after Susan's return, Henchard's fortunes decline drastically, and Farfrae's fortunes steadily rise. Henchard eventually loses both his wealth and his social position and is compelled to work as a lowly employee for Farfrae, who now dominates the corn trade and also becomes the new mayor of Casterbridge. Having lost his worldly position, Henchard seeks solace in establishing a bond with Elizabeth-Jane. They live together companionably for a while, but Elizabeth-Jane secretly renews her romantic relations with Farfrae, and then her biological father Newson reappears. Fearing to lose her, Henchard tells Newson that Elizabeth-Jane is dead. When his lie is about to be discovered, Henchard leaves Casterbridge to take up laboring work in a far district. He returns for Elizabeth-Jane's wedding, but she rejects him. He falls into despair, declines to eat, and dies.

Hardy worried about having cluttered the serial publication of the novel with sensational events, and he pruned and simplified the plot in the book version (Mallett xiv–xv). Even in its chastened form, the pace of the story is such that the rapidly shifting fortunes and love entanglements are like a spectacle seen through the wrong end of a telescope, a fantasmagoria of passion and folly, tinged with absurdity and futility.

To get a comparative sense of the level of interest, we can line up the Interest scores for the 48 most frequently coded characters in the larger data set, add the six characters from *Mayor* to the list, and then sort the scores in descending order (high to low). Out of the 54 characters, the four lowest scores on Interest are all from *Mayor* (Newson, Farfrae, Susan, and Lucetta). Henchard, though he excites strong emotional responses in Dislike and in Sorrow, nonetheless occupies the thirty-seventh position in the Interest scale, and Elizabeth-Jane, though she excites feelings of Admiration and Liking, occupies the forty-second position. Because the scores in the data set for the multinovel website are standardized, the average score for all characters is zero. For the 48 most frequently coded characters, the average score on Interest is .17. For the six characters in *Mayor*, the average Interest score is –.81—nearly a standard deviation lower than the average for the most frequently coded characters. Given the proportions of the normal curve, about 79 percent of all characters in the multinovel website—major and minor together—have Interest scores higher than the average score for the six main characters in *Mayor*. If it is true that Hardy is seeking to damp down excitement, to discourage the emotional involvement of readers, he has evidently succeeded.

Achieving reflective, stoic detachment—gaining a calm and distant perspective on the transient ambitions and passions of human life and the changes of fortune—is not the most common kind of psychological work that a novel accomplishes, but it is a common strategy for coping with life, and it is altogether consistent with Hardy's melancholy and philosophical temperament. Late in life, Hardy wrote a poem titled "For Life I Had Never Cared Greatly." The sentiment declared in the title was untrue, but it did reflect one of Hardy's persistent philosophical ambitions. He felt this ambition as an exceptionally keen need, because for life he had always cared very much, and he was thus vulnerable to all its travails.

Most commentators on the generic structure of *Mayor* have assumed that the novel operates along the usual lines of passional involvement with the protagonist, and they have often inferred that the protagonist must therefore evoke some strongly positive imaginative response in the reader. As our data indicate, in the case of *Mayor* these assumptions are erroneous and misleading. By examining the connections between the scores on the attributes of the characters, the emotional responses of readers, and agonistic role assignments, we can illuminate the way in which the false assumptions about passional involvement and positive emotional response obscure the actual tonal and perspectival structure of the novel.

Character Success

Farfrae, Henchard, and Susan all score fairly close to average on Root For; Lucetta scores far below average (–1.08) (figure 7.1). Only Elizabeth-Jane scores within the normal range for protagonists (.65), but Elizabeth-Jane is clearly a minor character and scores below average (–.11) on Main Feature (figure 7.1).

Henchard is very decidedly a Main Feature in the story, more so than any other character. As Hardy remarks in the General Preface for the Wessex edition of the novel, "The story is more particularly a study of one man's deeds and character than, perhaps, any other of those included in my Exhibition of Wessex life."[2]

In respect to the tonal structure of *Mayor*, the scores on Achieves Goals can best be understood by observing their relation to Root For. The correlation between Root For and Achieves Goals is a concise measure of "poetic justice," the plot pattern in which everyone gets his or her just deserts. For all 435 characters in the multinovel website, the correlation between Root For and Achieves Goals is .44, a moderately high correlation. In novels that are designed particularly

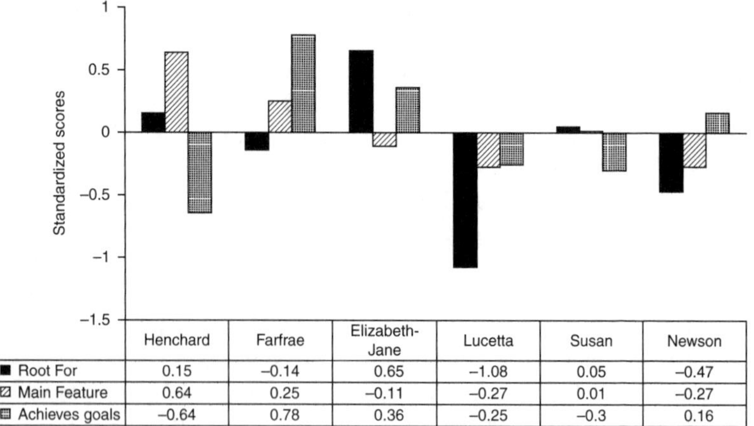

	Henchard	Farfrae	Elizabeth-Jane	Lucetta	Susan	Newson
Root For	0.15	−0.14	0.65	−1.08	0.05	−0.47
Main Feature	0.64	0.25	−0.11	−0.27	0.01	−0.27
Achieves goals	−0.64	0.78	0.36	−0.25	−0.3	0.16

Figure 7.1 Character success in *Mayor of Casterbridge*.

to fulfill the readers' hopes and wishes, the correlation between Root For and Achieves Goals is very high. For the 17 Austen characters included in the 48 most frequently coded characters, the correlation between Root For and Achieves Goals is .77. For the four most frequently coded characters in *Jane Eyre*, the correlation is .92. For the six characters in *Mayor*, the correlation between Root For and Achieves Goals is .15—a very weak correlation. The low correlation between Root For and Achieves Goals in *Mayor* indicates that in this novel Hardy systematically disrupts any distinct pattern in the relation between the readers' sympathetic engagement with characters and the outcome of the story.

The issue of poetic justice is given a decisive priority in the culminating internal reflections on the meaning of the story. The last two paragraphs of the novel are devoted to summarizing Elizabeth-Jane's matured views on life, from her later perspective, and her final thoughts include reflections on the meaningless vagaries in the relations between merit and reward. "Her strong sense that neither she nor any human being deserved less than was given, did not blind her to the fact that there were others receiving less who had deserved much more."

Achieves Goals, Poetic Justice, and the 1880 Divide

To put Hardy's treatment of poetic justice into historical context, we compared scores for Root For and Achieves Goals before and after

1880. The period around 1880 forms a distinct historical watershed, a change in historical phase—the passing of the generation of the mid-Victorians, and the emergence of a new generation that was to be dominated creatively by James, Hardy, and Conrad. George Eliot died in 1880 and Anthony Trollope in 1882. (Thackeray had died in 1863 and Dickens in 1870.) On the basis of simple observation, a literary historian can recognize differences in the tone or mood of fiction in the mid-Victorian and later Victorian period. By scanning the plot outcomes for the major novelists of the later period, counting the number of happy and unhappy endings, and comparing these outcomes with outcomes in the works of the earlier major novelists such as Austen, Dickens, or Thackeray, one can readily enough see the difference. Austen, Dickens, and Thackeray have no endings for protagonists like those which occur for Hardy's protagonists Michael Henchard, Tess Durbeyfield, and Jude Fawley, for Decould in Conrad's *Nostromo*, Edwin Reardon in Gissing's *New Grub Street*, or Dorian Gray in Wilde's *The Picture of Dorian Gray*.

To gain a more precise sense of this difference, and assess its general validity across all the novelists represented in this study, we divided the novelists into those who flourished before 1880 and those who published most or all of their work after 1880, and we conducted a statistical test (one-way ANOVA) to compare the scores of the earlier and later protagonists on Character Success.

The total set of 435 characters in the multinovel website contains 128 protagonists—84 in novels by authors who flourished before 1880, and 44 in novels by authors who published all or most of their works after 1880. The protagonists of the two generations display no statistically significant differences on Root For or Main Feature, but they do display a statistically significant difference on Achieves Goals. (The protagonists of the earlier generations score .41 on Achieves Goals, and those of the later generation score –.05 [$p = .007$].) The protagonists of the later generation are simply not as successful, overall, in life.

Emotional Response Factors

There is a good deal of Sorrow in the story—for Henchard, Elizabeth-Jane, Lucetta, and Susan—but the low scores on Interest suggest a low level of intensity in emotional response (figure 7.2).

Henchard is unequivocally the protagonist, but he scores high on Dislike. Farfrae and Newson come into conflict with Henchard or present obstacles to him, and they are thus assigned roles as

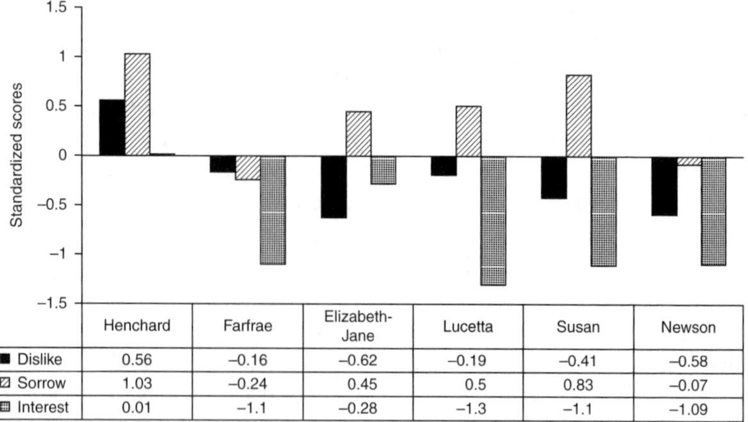

	Henchard	Farfrae	Elizabeth-Jane	Lucetta	Susan	Newson
Dislike	0.56	−0.16	−0.62	−0.19	−0.41	−0.58
Sorrow	1.03	−0.24	0.45	0.5	0.83	−0.07
Interest	0.01	−1.1	−0.28	−1.3	−1.1	−1.09

Figure 7.2 Emotional responses to characters in *Mayor of Casterbridge*.

antagonists, but neither scores in the antagonistic range on Dislike. In the scores for the larger data set, Root For correlates strongly and negatively with Dislike ($r = -.67$). For *Mayor*, the correlation is only −.03—essentially no correlation. The confounding of normal agonistic role assignments disrupts the usual relationship between liking or disliking characters and becoming emotionally invested in the outcome of the story. This disruption evidently helps neutralize emotional responsiveness in readers and thus contributes to the low scores on Interest.

Motive Factors

The disruption in the normal correlations between Root For and Emotional responses works itself out in the attributes of characters: motives, the criteria for selecting mates, and personality. Henchard is the lynch pin. For the novels in the period as a whole, both before and after 1880, the most distinctive feature in the motivational profile of antagonists is Social Dominance. Henchard is unequivocally the protagonist, and yet he scores in the antagonistic range on Dominance (figure 7.3).

The typical expectations of readers are thus deeply disturbed, and the disturbance reverberates through the emotional responses to all the other characters. Farfrae and Lucetta also score high on Dominance, thus alienating readers from three of the four main characters. Only Elizabeth-Jane scores in the protagonistic range on

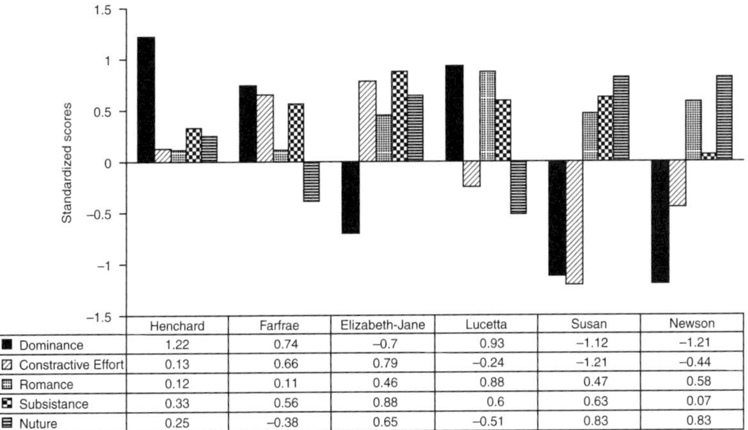

	Henchard	Farfrae	Elizabeth-Jane	Lucetta	Susan	Newson
Dominance	1.22	0.74	–0.7	0.93	–1.12	–1.21
Constractive Effort	0.13	0.66	0.79	–0.24	–1.21	–0.44
Romance	0.12	0.11	0.46	0.88	0.47	0.58
Subsistance	0.33	0.56	0.88	0.6	0.63	0.07
Nuture	0.25	–0.38	0.65	–0.51	0.83	0.83

Figure 7.3 Motive factors in *Mayor of Casterbridge*.

Dominance, and she is a minor character. Only Elizabeth-Jane and Farfrae score within the protagonistic range on Constructive Effort, and Farfrae, though his role assignment is equivocal, is definitely not a protagonist.

Henchard has a volatile personality and goes through more profound changes of phase in motivation than most characters in novels. In assessing his motives, our respondents had to weigh the different phases of his life and decide what motives had the most weight for his life as a whole. By choosing Social Dominance as his central motive, they are evidently acknowledging that the desire for wealth, power, and prestige are the overmastering passions in the central portion of his adult life. He sells his wife and child because they are holding him back, and when he is free to pursue his own course, he single-mindedly sets about achieving wealth, power, and prestige. We see nothing of him in this period, but we know from his own report that he has been emotionally isolated. After Lucetta's death, Henchard seems to turn away from Social Dominance and fixates on creating a bond with Elizabeth-Jane, but when that also fails him, and he chooses to die, his final act of renunciation, his scrawled testament, has itself the appearance of a strangely inverted effort of dominance. He gives directions for the disposal of his remains, and the directions are intended, so far as possible, to obliterate his memory from the minds of men—Elizabeth-Jane not to be told of his death and not to mourn for him, not to be buried in consecrated ground, no sexton to toll the bell, no one to view the body, no mourners, no flowers on the grave. The will concludes with the explicit command "that no man remember me."[3] If he cannot command as an acknowledged leader, he can still assert his power to control the image of himself in the minds of others. Rather than the image of a lowly and defeated man, better no image at all.

Sexual Romance in Casterbridge

When we listed relationships and asked respondents to identify the criteria by which characters selected each other as mates, we did not ask about Henchard's choice of Susan or Susan's of Henchard. We hear nothing about their motives in their first marriage, and we know that their motives in their second marriage are not a matter of choosing a person, for the sake of qualities in that person, but of dealing with a situation; Susan seeks a home for Elizabeth-Jane, and Henchard seeks to make reparation for a past misdeed. We asked about each of the relations involving Henchard, Farfrae, Lucetta, and Elizabeth-Jane. Except for the first episode between Henchard and Lucetta, all these relationships involve efforts at long-term mating. Accordingly, we standardize the mate-selection scores for *Mayor* relative to those for long-term mating in the larger data set (figure 7.4).

The scoring pattern for long-term mate selection in *Mayor* seems to have two chief effects (figure 7.4). One effect is to blur and confuse the value structures that usually channel the readers' emotional

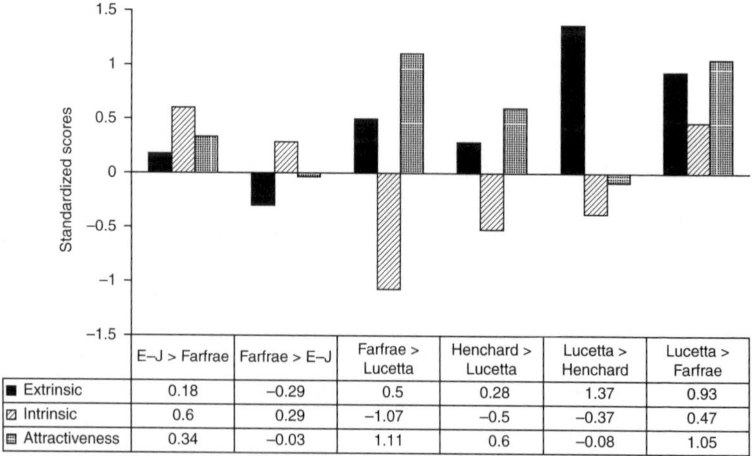

	E–J > Farfrae	Farfrae > E–J	Farfrae > Lucetta	Henchard > Lucetta	Lucetta > Henchard	Lucetta > Farfrae
■ Extrinsic	0.18	–0.29	0.5	0.28	1.37	0.93
▨ Intrinsic	0.6	0.29	–1.07	–0.5	–0.37	0.47
▦ Attractiveness	0.34	–0.03	1.11	0.6	–0.08	1.05

Figure 7.4 Criteria for selecting mates in *Mayor of Casterbridge*.

responses to characters. The other is to create a distinct and gender-neutral vision of sexual romance—a vision in which worldly ambition and sexual excitement are mingled in an affective mix that is hectic, volatile, and emotionally disorienting. The sexual relations in the novel confound the elements of good and bad, major and minor, and male and female. In this commingling of features, the sexual relations in the novel cooperate with all the other aspects in the novel that disrupt the usual agonistic organization of characters. The reader is left bemused and detached, with little inducement to identify closely with the romantic aspirations of any character.

For the six relationships on which we obtained scores, the score on preference for Intrinsic Qualities (–.1) is about average, but both Extrinsic Attributes and Physical Attractiveness run substantially higher than average (both .5). Mating relations in *Mayor* characteristically involve both the appeal of worldly advantages and the appeal of sexual excitement. In *Mayor*, these two criteria cross the usual gender boundaries. In responding to Lucetta, Farfrae and Henchard have very similar profiles—Farfrae's being only more exaggerated—and in both profiles, the appeal of Lucetta's Extrinsic Attributes—wealth and class status—intermingles with the sexual excitement of her physical appeal. Neither Henchard nor Farfrae is at all drawn to Lucetta for her Intrinsic Qualities—for intelligence, kindness, or reliability. In her response to Henchard, Lucetta's profile is essentially that of a standard female antagonist, seeking Extrinsic Attributes and nothing else, but in her response to Farfrae, Lucetta is nearly as excited by his physical charm as he is by hers. In both her choices of men, Lucetta has a typically antagonistic female interest in Extrinsic Attributes, but in responding to Farfrae she is also attracted by his Intrinsic Qualities. In this respect, she is like Elizabeth-Jane and other female protagonists, but her emphasis on both Extrinsic Attributes and Physical Attractiveness is much higher than that of most female protagonists. In only two of the six relationships is Physical Attractiveness not an important criterion of mate selection: Lucetta's choice of Henchard, and Farfrae's choice of Elizabeth-Jane. The one culminating relationship in the story, and the only ultimately successful relationship, is that of Elizabeth-Jane and Farfrae, and from Farfrae's side, that relationship is devoid of erotic excitement.

Elizabeth-Jane's mate selection criteria are the closest to normal protagonistic criteria, but the very fact that she has chosen Farfrae casts a shadow over her personal romance. He is only weakly interested in her, and he does not respond to the deepest and best features of her identity. He has some slight interest in her Intrinsic Qualities, but his appreciation of those qualities is shallow and inadequate. Hardy refers to Elizabeth-Jane as "a subtle-souled girl" and as a "discerning silent witch" (chs. 18 and 24). Farfrae merely calls her "thrifty," and even for the thrifty Scotchman, the appeal of her domestic economy weighs very slightly in the balance against the sexual glamour that evidently emanates from Lucetta.

Elizabeth-Jane is not disappointed in her marriage with Farfrae, but the point of tonal resolution in *Mayor* is not that of her romantic fulfillment. The scores on Root For, Achieves Goals, and Interest tell us that. Readers root for her; she achieves her goals; and the readers do not much care one way or the other. If we listen to Hardy's own judgment on the trajectory of her emotional career, the point of tonal resolution for Elizabeth-Jane is that of Stoic prudence and moderation. The strongest feature in her relation with Farfrae is an attraction to his Intrinsic Qualities, and the relationship thus constituted modulates easily enough into an "equable serenity" (ch. 45). The value of that serenity, in the general economy of the book, makes itself felt in contrast to the kinds of passions that have so disturbed the other characters. All the hectic agitations of worldly ambition and sexual excitement end in disaster for Henchard and Lucetta. Farfrae too has been shocked by misfortune, and he has been saved from tragic pathos only by the relatively shallow character of his attachment to Lucetta.

Personality and the Confounding of Agonistic Role Assignments

The reversal of normal agonistic role assignments in this novel is more vividly apparent in personality than in any other category of analysis (figure 7.5).

As we argue in the chapter on Jane Austen, the factors of personality are primary thematic terms on a par with the largest thematic reductions of the various critical schools. Like Austen and indeed like most or all great novelists, Hardy is a gifted intuitive psychologist. What that chiefly means is having insight into motives, the emotions that activate motives, and the dispositions of personality that orient people toward specific motives. The profiles for personality attributes in *Mayor* cohere tightly with the scores on motives and mating. They form a unified network that is convincing in its mimetic verisimilitude but alienating in its emotional impact on readers. Hardy knows what he is doing, but what he is doing violates normal expectations in the assignment of roles.

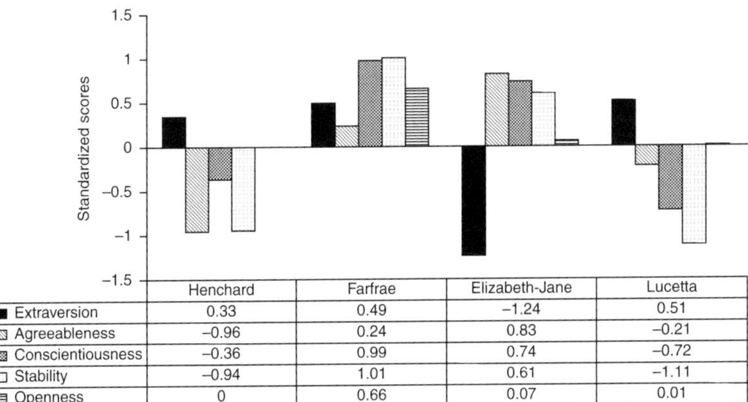

	Henchard	Farfrae	Elizabeth-Jane	Lucetta
■ Extraversion	0.33	0.49	−1.24	0.51
▧ Agreeableness	−0.96	0.24	0.83	−0.21
▩ Conscientiousness	−0.36	0.99	0.74	−0.72
□ Stability	−0.94	1.01	0.61	−1.11
⊟ Openness	0	0.66	0.07	0.01

Figure 7.5 Personality factors for four main characters in *Mayor of Casterbridge*.

So far as role assignments go, Henchard is the clearly identified protagonist, but his personality is predominantly antagonistic. Henchard scores lower on Agreeableness than any of the other five characters for whom we obtained scores, and lower than 83 percent of the characters in the larger data set. His manners are harsh and abrupt, and he is habitually careless of the feelings of others. At one point or another, he comes into sharp conflict with most of the characters in the story. Throughout his career, Henchard displays a temperament at the mercy of extreme and erratic emotional impulses, and his emotional instability takes on a specific emotional cast from a strong tendency toward clinical depression. (The word "gloom" or "gloomy" is used repeatedly to describe his mood or the atmosphere around him.) Henchard is an extremely volatile character, and his volatility combines deficiencies in Conscientiousness with deficiencies in Emotional Stability.

Farfrae, in contrast to Henchard, has an unequivocally protagonistic personality profile. With respect to personality, he is a very paragon of a male protagonist. He is right at average for male protagonists on Agreeableness, and far above average on Conscientiousness, Stability, and Openness. He is reliable in business, he is consistently cheerful and even-tempered, and he scores higher on Openness than any other character. He likes to read; he invents a process for restoring damaged wheat; and he introduces new agricultural technology into Casterbridge. And yet, nine of twenty-one respondents identified him as an antagonist; seven identified him as a good minor character; one as a bad minor character; and three said "other." Only one respondent identified him as a protagonist. Farfrae's motivational profile mixes protagonistic and antagonistic features, but his personality is overwhelmingly protagonistic. Despite his apparently appealing personality, readers are indifferent to him. He excites little Interest, and his scores on both Dislike (–.16) and Root For (–.14) are close to average.

Farfrae is a bright, cheerful, friendly, young man, ambitious and successful, but also constructive and open to new experiences. He is a fortunate person, admirable, attractive, and successful, but within the emotional economy of this novel, that particular profile has no special claims on the interest or sympathy of the reader. The novel is designed around catastrophic losses and failures—those of Susan, first, and then of Lucetta, and ultimately of Henchard. Unlike a substantial portion of nineteenth-century novels, *Mayor* is not designed to align the reader's perspective with that of a Golden Youth, to engage the reader's sympathetic identification with that youth, to fulfill the reader's expectations concerning the hopes and fortunes of that youth, and to affirm the normative and central value of the personality and motives embodied in that youth. Within the perspectival and emotional economy of this novel, the concerns of a young man like Farfrae are relegated to marginal status, and the novel occupies itself instead in coping with forms of distress that remain outside the scope of Farfrae's empathic power.

If *Mayor* had been a standard Victorian novel, Farfrae or Elizabeth-Jane would have been the protagonist and Henchard the antagonist. It is because Hardy so thoroughly disrupts these standard role assignments that critics have been driven to desperate measures in trying to invest Henchard with characteristics that qualify him for protagonistic status in accordance with the usual templates for role assignment.

Hardy's disruption of the standard role assignments is not merely capricious. Much evidence, both quantitative and textual, can be marshaled to support the contention that he has a psychologically functional aim vested in the "equable serenity" achieved by Elizabeth-Jane. Apart from the scores on Interest and the quantitative evidence of anomalous agonistic role assignments, the main quantitative evidence supporting this interpretive contention are Elizabeth-Jane's scores on personality. She is intensely introverted. She lives quietly and studiously, apart from the bustle and gossip of the town. She is highly agreeable—warm and sympathetic—and also highly conscientious and emotionally stable. (The reader is invited to compare her scores with those of Elinor Dashwood in *Sense and Sensibility* and those of Anne Elliot in *Persuasion*.) Even when she is suddenly and painfully dropped by Farfrae, she never loses her poise or her capacity for reflective detachment. Watching both Henchard and Farfrae become sexually fixated on Lucetta, she is hurt by their indifference to her, but unlike Henchard and Lucetta, she is never wholly immersed in her own emotions. "The pain she experienced from the almost absolute obliviousness to her existence that was shown by the pair of them became at times half dissipated by her sense of its humourousness" (ch. 25). As with all her experiences, her own sensations become material for reflection and ultimately eventuate in a detached curiosity about the course of human affairs.

Elizabeth-Jane's average scores on Openness reflect her anxiety not to offend against the conventional proprieties. The unseemly aspects of her parents' history make her all the more sensitive to impropriety, and in respect to intimate sexual relations, she is quite straight-laced. Being willing to violate the conventional proprieties is one aspect of Openness, but cultural curiosity is another. For this aspect of Openness, the instrument we used to obtain scores on personality does not have the level of resolution we need to obtain a clear image of Elizabeth-Jane's personality. (On this limitations in the Ten-Item-Personality Inventory, see chapter 2.)

When Susan returns to Casterbridge to reunite with Henchard, her chief motive is to provide opportunities for her daughter. Susan "had long perceived how zealously and constantly" Elizabeth-Jane's mind "was struggling for enlargement." Elizabeth-Jane's deepest desire "was indeed to see, to hear, to understand" (ch. 4). Seeing, hearing, understanding, mental expansion—all these, too, are elements of Openness to Experience, and for Hardy they are the more important features. Were Elizabeth-Jane's score on Openness actually to reflect those features, her profile would stand forth clearly as that of an exemplary female protagonist. Given the particular purposes of this novel, though, she would still not be a "passional" protagonist. She is not driven by her passions. Her fate is not centrally defined by success or failure in fulfilling the common aims of life—love, family, and friends. Within the passional plot, she is thus necessarily a minor character, but her minor status in the passional plot is merely the inverse of her major status in another dimension. She is a "perspectival" protagonist. Her chief goal is to gain a perspective adequate to comprehend the struggle and turmoil in the world around her—to comprehend it, and to rise above it.

> She had learnt the lesson of renunciation, and was as familiar with the wreck of each day's wishes as with the diurnal setting of the sun. If her

> earthly career had taught her few book philosophies it had at least well practised her in this. Yet her experience had consisted less in a series of pure disappointments than in a series of substitutions. Continually it had happened that what she had desired had not been granted her, and that what had been granted her she had not desired. So she viewed with an approach to equanimity the now cancelled days when Donald had been her undeclared lover, and wondered what unwished-for thing Heaven might send her in place of him. (ch. 25)

This lesson of equanimity before the variable possibilities of life is a lesson that Henchard never learns and that it is not in his nature to learn. He seizes on one goal at a time and concentrates all his passion on it. In the depth of his despair, he turns to Elizabeth-Jane as to "a pin-point of light" (ch. 40), but he treats of this one possible good as the only possible good. "He was developing the dream of a future lit by her filial presence, as though that way alone could happiness lie" (ch. 41). In a world of circumstances as capricious as those in Hardy's novels, no such fixation on a single source of happiness could possibly end well.

The Rustic Chorus

Restricting the analysis to six main characters eliminates no essential features of the plot in *Mayor*. With respect to a tonal analysis, the main thing that is lost by this restriction is the rustic chorus—the set of minor characters who observe the action and offer shrewd, humorous, and pithy observations on the character and behavior of the chief actors. Christopher Coney, Solomon Longways, Buzzford, Nance Mockridge, and Mother Cuxsom modulate the tragic perspective in ways similar to those of Shakespeare's clowns and court jesters—the fool in *King Lear*, or the grave digger in *Hamlet*.

Early in the story, Elizabeth-Jane listens to an exchange between Farfrae and the rustics at the Three Mariners Inn. Her response provides a basis for assessing Hardy's own relation to the three perspectives involved—Farfrae's, Elizabeth-Jane's, and that of the rustic chorus:

> She admired the serious light in which [Farfrae] looked at serious things. He had seen no jest in ambiguities and roguery, as the Casterbridge toss-pots had done; and rightly not—there was none. She disliked those wretched humours of Christopher Coney and his tribe; and he did not appreciate them. He seemed to feel exactly as she felt about life and its surroundings—that they were a tragical rather than a

> comical thing; that though one could be gay on occasion, moments of gaiety were interludes, and no part of the actual drama. It was extraordinary how similar their views were. (ch. 8)

Elizabeth-Jane is quite mistaken about Farfrae, and Hardy understands her mistake. Tragedy is outside the scope of Farfrae's imagination. Elizabeth-Jane projects onto Farfrae her own depth of feeling and her own meditative seriousness. At this point in the story, she is only about 19, and her experience hitherto has been narrow and rather somber. As her mind expands and her experience broadens, she gains more understanding of the "humorousness" of things. She sees for instance the comical side of the sexually overwrought attentiveness Henchard and Fafrae fix on Lucetta. Still, the tone of her mind remains fundamentally serious. Hardy's own tonal range takes in more of the jest and roguery of Christopher Coney and his tribe, and his humanity is thus broader and more complete than hers. Hardy nonetheless shares with her an emotional conviction that life is a tragical rather than a comical thing, and so far as this story is concerned, he agrees with her that interludes of gaiety are no part of the actual drama.

Models of Tragedy in the Interpretive History of *Mayor*

The three models of tragedy commonly used to interpret *Mayor*—retributive justice, Promethean Romantic heroism, and redemptive change—have retained their basic structural character through many theoretical metamorphoses: old fashioned humanism, New Criticism, Archetypalism, Marxism, psychoanalysis, Deconstruction, Feminism, and the various hybrid blends of postmodernism. In the late seventies and early eighties, literary studies underwent profound changes in theoretical and ideological orientation. The models used to interpret *Mayor* survived those changes with only superficial alterations of critical idiom. The models evidently function at imaginative levels deeper than the various fashions through which they have persisted, but none of the models is sufficiently deep and general to give a decisively superior account of the tonal and perspectival structure of *Mayor*. The models overlap in some ways but conflict in others, and the inadequacies of each help to explain the persistence of its rivals.[4]

Each of the three models depends on philosophical preconceptions that have their origins outside of Hardy's own structure of meanings, and they each seek emotional resolution in some form different from that which is revealed in the structure of data from our study. All three models presuppose passional involvement with a protagonist as a central feature in the tonal structure of the novel, and they all seek resolution in some ultimately affirmative condition in the protagonist's own mind. Retributive justice eliminates the element of chance in Hardy's vision of the world and adopts a stance of vindictive satisfaction incompatible with Hardy's tolerant humanity. Promethean Romantic heroism glamorizes Henchard's character and strikes a note of vainglorious triumphalism incompatible with Hardy's shrewd irony. Redemptive change blurs the essential continuity of Henchard's character and posits a sentimental resolution that is alien to Hardy's tragic austerity. In all three models, the preemptive necessity of an affirmative resolution located in the protagonist's own mind sorts ill with the violence and bitterness of self-repudiation in Henchard's final will and testament.

John Paterson offers a transcendental version of the model of retributive justice. In his view, tragedy depends on "moral and religious universals" and reaches resolution in vindicating "the existence of a moral order, an ethical substance, a standard of justice and rectitude, in terms of which man's experience can be rendered as the drama of his salvation as well as the drama of his damnation." The role of the tragic protagonist in this scheme is that of acknowledging this transcendent ethical order. Henchard offends against the cosmic order, which destroys him, but he also "stands for the grandeur of the human passions." He is thus the tragic agent of a "heroic imagination."[5] J. Hillis Miller offers an equally cosmic but nihilistic and emotionally negative version of this transcendental vision. In Miller's version, the baffling of all Henchard's desires constitutes "one of Hardy's most dramatic demonstrations of a condition of existence in his universe." In a less cosmic version, the model of redemptive justice requires neither the affirmation nor the negation of a transcendent ethical order; it requires only that the protagonist be "obsessed by guilt and so committed to his own destruction."[6] Invocations of self-destructiveness as a primary, irreducible motive internalize the idea of retributive justice. The protagonist has violated some absolute ethical principle; he achieves tragic consciousness in acknowledging the lethally numinous character of that principle. This internalized version of the retributive model has usually been lodged within a Freudian context.

Like the model of retributive justice, the Promethean Romantic model focuses on the assertion of heroic though destructive grandeur. George Levine, for example, identifies "the romantic hero" as a figure of "large aspirations" and "uncontrollable energies that destroy with the force of an Alpine torrent." These heroic figures "desire beyond the limits of nature" and they thus exemplify qualities that are "quintessentially human." The tragic hero achieves "a new freedom of imagination" and represents "a new conception of human dignity." In the Romantic model, defiance is heroic because the universe itself is "imperfect." Defiance is equated with the assertion of spiritual idealism. Adapting his view of Henchard to this Romantic notion, Keith Wilson declares that Henchard is "tortured by the lack of correspondence between the world as it is and the world as it should be." In the Romantic model, as in the retributive model, the tragic hero is one of "the supremely conscious." Henchard thus stands as "the type of the exceptional human being who experiences, recognizes and accepts the inevitability of suffering" (xxvii). In a politicized version of this model, Michael Valdez Moses argues that heroic tragedy is not possible within a modern bourgeois context but that "the peculiarly unmodern characteristics" of Casterbridge lend "heroic grandeur and tragic dignity to what would otherwise remain a typical novelistic tale of bourgeois life."[7]

In contrast both to the model of retributive justice and to the Promethean Romantic model, the model of redemptive change deprecates the idea of heroic passion and emphasizes instead the deplorable and contemptible aspects of the protagonist's career. Advocates of the redemptive model, like advocates of retributive justice, require that the protagonist feel contrition for his various misdeeds. As R. H. Hutton conceives it, Henchard's "tragic career of passionate sin, bitter penitence, and rude reparation" serves ultimately to bring him "to a better and humbler mind." In this model, the purpose of tragedy is to exemplify the way in which "circumstance" can serve "to chasten and purify character." Hutton was Hardy's contemporary, and his version of redemptive change seems typically Victorian in its commitment to the idea of human amelioration. Elaine Showalter offers a modern feminist version of the redemptive model. In her reading, Henchard undergoes a transformation "from a romantic male individualism to a more complete humanity." By becoming less male, Henchard becomes more fully human, and he thus becomes "capable of tragic experience." In Pamela Dalziel's simpler version of this model, "Henchard's journey towards self-knowledge is a journey towards love."[8]

Each of these three models appeals to some historically conditioned articulation of a fundamental disposition in human nature. The model of retributive justice has an affinity with the ethos of the

Old Testament, and its proponents are wont also to cite antecedents from Greek tragedy. The model of redemptive change, with its emphasis on salvation through moral transfiguration, has an obvious affinity with the Christian ethos. Like the model of retributive justice, the Promethean Romantic model operates in a cosmic sphere, but it repudiates the justice of the cosmic order and, like the redemptive model, locates its resolution within the affirmation of specifically human qualities. As its name suggests, the Romantic model is closely associated with the spiritual defiance of a certain phase of Romanticism, a phase identified more closely with Byron and Shelley than with Wordsworth or Keats. Each model appeals to a specific emotional range and finds its resolution in the gratification of some deep emotional need—the desire for justice, the claim for self-abnegating affiliation, or the assertion of individual power. The assertion of power and the claim for affiliation constitute the two basic forms of human social interaction. Justice mediates between these two forms.

In invoking one or another of the three models of tragedy, Hardy's critics have been like the blind men touching the elephant—each describing just one part of the elephant and generalizing from that one part. The critics have selected one or another of three principles of social interaction—power, affiliation, and justice—generalized that aspect as a matrix principle for a model of tragedy, and used that model as a template for organizing the details of the narrative in *Mayor.* Because it is overgeneralized, each template is itself imperfect, and each correlates poorly with some important aspect of the novel. The templates are Procrustean beds, each stretching and distorting the novel, in different and irreconcilable ways, to make the novel fit the model.

At about the time that he was writing *Mayor*, Hardy wrote a note formulating a concept of tragedy that contains none of the distorting assumptions in the three models typically invoked to account for the thematic and tonal structure of *Mayor.* "Tragedy. It may be put thus in brief: a tragedy exhibits a state of things in the life of an individual which unavoidably causes some natural aim or desire of his to end in a catastrophe when carried out."[9] This definition covers a broad spectrum of works typically regarded as tragic, and it is fully adequate to account for Henchard's fate in *Mayor.* It involves no commitment to a principle of poetic justice, transcendental or internalized; it does not derive affirmations of human nobility from the struggles of a tragic protagonist; nor does it presuppose a morally uplifting transformation in the tragic protagonist.

As many critics of the novel have recognized, Hardy identifies closely with the perspective of Elizabeth-Jane, and for Elizabeth-Jane, the spectacle of Henchard's career culminates in a state of compassionate, detached meditation. That also is a form of resolution, but it is a form different from that of passional involvement with the protagonist, and it does not require that we locate resolution within some affirmative state of the protagonist's own mind. Critics who deploy models of heroic tragedy have sometimes characterized Elizabeth-Jane as an embodiment of conventional propriety—prim, cold, and imperceptive.[10] Similar terms of indictment have been leveled at her from a postmodern perspective programmatically hostile to all affirmations of normative authority.[11] Bernard Paris, reading the novel within a framework of values derived from Karen Horney, describes Elizabeth-Jane as "fearful," "rigid," and "self-imprisoned."[12]

Depicting Elizabeth-Jane as merely a personification of bourgeois propriety conflicts fundamentally with Hardy's own presentation of her, and treating her as a case study in stunted emotional development wrenches her violently out of Hardy's imaginative universe. Like Hardy himself, Elizabeth-Jane combines compassionate warmth with the power of detached contemplation. In all of Hardy's work, there is no other character who so completely occupies a position of interpretive authority on a level with his own. Hardy not only acknowledges her concern for propriety, excusing it as a reflex of her shadowed past, but he also unequivocally affirms her humanity and rectitude, her modesty, her self-effacing generosity, her perceptiveness, her resilience, balance, and fortitude, and the depth, scope, and wisdom in her general view of life.

One might anticipate that feminist critics would respond favorably to a female character invested with exceptional powers of observation and reflection, but with respect to Elizabeth-Jane, that is not the case. Writing from a feminist perspective, Pamela Dalziel observes that "in the recent proliferation of feminist readings of Hardy," Elizabeth-Jane "has been largely invisible." Dalziel observes that *Mayor* has not been a favored topic for feminist criticism and that in the one most prominent feminist reading, Elaine Showalter's, the focus is on the male protagonist. Comparing the depiction of Elizabeth-Jane in the original serial publication of the novel and the book version, Dalziel argues that in the serial version Elizabeth-Jane is more appealingly aggressive and self-assertive. In the revisions for book publication, Dalziel thinks, she has been reduced to "the bland consistency of stereotypical womanliness."[13]

From Hardy's own perspective, aggressive self-assertion is neither peculiarly male nor particularly admirable. One of Hardy's most perceptive critics, Lord David Cecil, observes that while Hardy had rejected Christian beliefs, his ethos remained deeply imbued with Christian values. "The Christian virtues—fidelity, compassion, humility—were the most beautiful to him."[14] In *Mayor*, those virtues are most fully exemplified by Elizabeth-Jane. In other Hardy novels, they are exemplified by both male and female characters, and more often by male than by female characters—for instance, by Gabriel Oak in *Far from the Madding Crowd*, Diggory Venn in *The Return of the Native*, John Loveday in *The Trumpet Major*, Giles Winterborne in *The Woodlanders*, and Tess in *Tess of the d'Urbervilles.* Hardy himself regards all of these characters with affectionate respect, but because he has more developed powers of reflective contemplation, he also stands apart from them, and above them. In the final chapter of *Mayor*, Hardy evokes Elizabeth-Jane's most matured perspective, intermingling indistinguishably with Hardy's own. She also stands apart from the action and above it, and she is thus not herself a passional protagonist. So far as the passional drama is concerned, she is only a good minor character. So far as the perspectival drama is concerned, she is the central character. It is in her mind, and not in that of the protagonist, that Hardy locates his own sense of resolution.

Some of the best critics of *Mayor* have registered the importance of Elizabeth-Jane's perspective in modulating the tone of the story and in providing a medium for Hardy's own interpretive reflections on the events of the story. Ian Gregor observes that "the developed consciousness of Elizabeth-Jane" is part of the meaning of the resolution in the final chapter of the novel. Michael Millgate observes that "her role is an extraordinarily interesting one, without a close parallel elsewhere in Hardy's work." Millgate points out that Hardy repeatedly uses Elizabeth-Jane "as the point of view from which events are viewed." She is thus "kept constantly before the reader even during the stretches of the action in which she has no substantial part to play... She gradually establishes herself for the reader as much the most acute and reliable intelligence within the novel, the one whose judgments are most to be trusted. In a real sense, she becomes the reader's representative within the novel's world." She becomes the reader's representative, because she is the author's representative. Robert Langbaum observes that through much of the book Elizabeth-Jane "acts as a surrogate for the author." He comments perceptively on "the contrast between the serenity of her perceiving mind and the passionate material perceived." The contrast between serenity and passion is the central dynamic in the tonal organization of the novel.[15]

Even though they recognize the interpretive authority invested in Elizabeth-Jane, Gregor, Millgate, and Langbaum all still fall under the sway of the Promethean Romantic model. The Romantic model presupposes that the tragic protagonist must necessarily be a "hero," that the hero must exemplify human "grandeur" and "dignity," and that the story as a whole must produce sublime affects that confirm some essential human nobility. Gregor declares that "for Henchard life has been tragic but never at any time has it lost dignity." Millgate acknowledges the faults of Henchard's character but declares that "Hardy nonetheless compels us to recognize in Henchard a man of almost superhuman grandeur, of great if uncontrollable passions, a tragic hero." Langbaum too refers to Henchard as "a tragic hero." He claims that "Henchard's display of imaginative and emotional resources too large for success in life makes him tragic."[16]

In contrast to his critics, Hardy seems to have felt no obligation to conform to the Romantic model of tragedy. He refers once to Elizabeth-Jane as "our poor only heroine" (ch. 43). He nowhere uses the words "hero" or "heroic" to refer to Henchard. The structure of Henchard's motives is not a generic expression of romantic passion. His failures are not simply the manifestation of "resources" too great for "success in life." Henchard seeks wealth, power, and prestige, forms a transient friendship with Farfrae, is briefly excited into a competitive sexual interest in Lucetta, and then forms a companionable bond with his stepdaughter. None of these desires go "beyond the limits of nature," And there is nothing particularly "superhuman" about them.[17] Henchard is strong willed and energetic, but he is also emotionally unstable, and as a result he is erratic and violent. Subsuming these various qualities under the general term "grandeur" would place an unusual strain on the connotative force of that word, and it is a word that Hardy does not himself use with respect to Henchard. In invocations of the Romantic model, the words "grandeur" and "dignity" are often linked, but Hardy does not identify dignity as one of Henchard's signal characteristics. It would be strange if he did. Henchard often behaves recklessly and foolishly. He is more than once publicly humiliated, and performs acts of which he is himself deeply ashamed. Getting drunk at a fair and auctioning off one's wife is not an act that can be conducted with dignity. Nor is he dignified when he bellows in public rage at hearing of Fafrae setting up a business on his own, when he competes eagerly and unsuccessfully for the favors of a fickle woman, when he is ejected drunk from an official public ceremony, when he crumples in sobbing remorse after trying to fling Farfrae out of a loft, or when confronted by Newson seeking his daughter, he speaks "mad lies like a child" (ch. 41).

We need not accept any of the main assumptions that have animated the standard tragic models used to interpret *Mayor*—that the novel must elicit passional involvement with a heroic protagonist, that the protagonist must achieve an adequate interpretive perspective on his experience, that the events of the story must affirm a morally meaningful order, that the story must culminate in the production of sublime affects, that it must exemplify moral improvement, or that it must provide some reassuring image of human goodness or nobility. The evidence will not support any of these assumptions.

Insofar as our respondents feel anything for Henchard, it is detached distaste, not passionate responsiveness. They recognize that he is the protagonist, but his motives and personality offer little for them to admire, and he excites strong feelings of Dislike. Our respondents' feelings are quite distinct, but their scores on Interest and Root For clearly indicate that they are not much absorbed, emotionally, in Henchard's story. Attaining an adequate interpretive perspective requires emotional maturity and implies a power of introspective meditation. Hardy tells us explicitly that Henchard is not introspective. All the evidence of the story confirms that judgment. Henchard's final will and testament indicate that his ultimate perspective does not remotely approach to the equable serenity that Hardy commends in Elizabeth-Jane, and indeed, a character with such low scores on Emotional Stability could hardly be expected to achieve serenity. Hardy's explicit declarations indicate that he admires Elizabeth-Jane's perspective and regards it as adequate to encompass the events of the novel. In temperament, as indicated by scores on personality, Elizabeth-Jane and Henchard could hardly be more different. Not only is she agreeable, conscientious, and emotionally stable, but her introversion, coupled with her other traits, also produces a profoundly meditative perspective. Nonetheless, she is not a protagonist.

The scores on Root For and Achieves Goals indicate the implausibility of claims that the story reveals a morally meaningful order. Elizabeth-Jane gets what she deserves, sort of, if Farfrae can be considered a prize. With respect to the other main characters, our respondents evidently concur with Elizabeth-Jane's opinion that the people in this imagined world end up being hurt and disappointed in ways that could not possibly correspond with any faults of their own, no matter how grievous those faults might be. "Hap" is a keynote poem in Hardy's poetic repertory. His whole body of philosophical poetry dedicates itself to the contemplation of the curious fact that terrible things happen, and keep happening, in an evidently random way. The lack of correlation between Root For and Achieves Goals in *Mayor* indicates that "Hap" could also be the poetic anthem for *Mayor*.

The scores on motives and personality in *Mayor* are not compatible with sublime effects. An ambitious, violent, and unstable protagonist; and an ambitious, stable, but thrifty and prudent antagonist—these are not the materials for epic or tragic grandeur. If there were sublime effects, those effects would have to be realized in readers' responses. The scores on emotional response indicate that readers dislike all the main characters except Elizabeth-Jane. What is more, they are indifferent to *all* the main characters, including Elizabeth-Jane. If there are sublime effects occurring in the story, they are not being registered by our respondents. Our own judgment is that the respondents give us a reliable account and that the critics who have argued for sublime effects have lost touch with the actual subjective reactions elicited by the story—even their own subjective responses. They have been carried away by an idea, and that idea does not correspond to the actual experience that most qualified readers have had in reading the novel.

Henchard does display some degree of moral improvement toward the end of the story—some dimly reflected illumination from the mental state he glimpses in Elizabeth-Jane. That illumination is clearly not sufficient to save him from bitter despair and self-destruction, conditions not typically included in stories culminating in redemption. Standing back and taking Henchard in the sum of his whole life-trajectory, our respondents identify the central phase of his life, seeking and attaining Social Dominance, as the defining phase. In this respect, the respondents and Hardy seem to concur. After Henchard leaves Casterbridge, Hardy observes that externally nothing prevents Henchard from starting over and "achieving higher things" than in his first career. But, Hardy says, by this time, Henchard's disappointments have deprived him of the energy needed for starting over. "He had no wish to make an arena a second time of a world that had become a mere painted scene to him." (ch. 44). The turning toward Elizabeth-Jane and affection come too late, bulk too small, and have too little motivating force to define the trajectory of the story.

If we reject the various assumptions animating the standard tragic models, we can avoid romanticizing or sentimentalizing the tragic protagonist. Henchard is a powerful, commanding personality, deeply flawed, often misguided, inadvertently self-destructive, and ultimately pathetic. The scores on motives, personality, and emotional responses support this specific characterization without difficulty, and one can affirm all of this without affirming any of the standard patterns of tragedy. On the basis of his explicit declarations about Henchard and other characters, we can say with some confidence that Hardy does not himself feel that Henchard's career is a sublime or ennobling spectacle. On the basis of the respondents' scores, we can definitely affirm that our respondents, in any case, do not feel that way. By correlating Hardy's explicit statements on the characters with scores in multiple categories, and especially with scores on Interest, we can draw a firm interpretive conclusion: the spectacle of "The Life and Death of the Mayor of Casterbridge"—the full main title of the novel—challenges Hardy to devise a perspective adequate to the contemplation of destructive passions and the mischances of life. Henchard himself can attain to no such perspective. He is not a reflective man, and to achieve a philosophic view of his experience would require powers of detachment and of generalization that are alien to his nature. It is alien also to Lucetta's nature; and to Farfrae's nature, it is simply irrelevant. It is not alien to Elizabeth-Jane's nature.

In a thoughtful recent essay on *Mayor*, J. Hillis Miller describes Hardy's perspective in terms of his "narrative voice." He characterizes that voice as "grave and compassionate, but at the same time objective, dry, ironic, quizzical, detached." A "voice" articulates values and attitudes—a stance toward a given subject. More than half a century ago, Cecil gave a finely nuanced description of the stance that Hardy adopts toward Henchard. As Hardy sees him, Cecil claims, Henchard "is a pathetic figure, born with an unfortunate disposition but genuinely longing to do right, tortured by remorse when he does wrong, and always defeated by some unlucky stroke of Fate."[18] Unlike the accounts that emerge from the three models of tragedy, these characterizations of Hardy's stance do not force Henchard into a mould out of keeping with his actual behavior, nor do they force Hardy's tone into a register out of keeping with his own actual statements. Hardy does not seek resolution in affirming that Henchard got what was coming to him, that he manifests some supremely conscious form of human nobility, or that he achieves salvation through a moral transfiguration. Putting the elements of thematic and tonal structure into quantitative form makes it possible to measure the distance between these strained interpretive models and the actual content and emotional character of the novel.

Conclusion: The Point of Point of View

Our data indicate that the agonistic structure of *Mayor* is very different from that of the average Victorian novel. It is not surprising, then, that *Mayor* has presented an especially difficult challenge to interpretive criticism. By quantifying the elements of tonal analysis, we can break up the prefabricated affective and conceptual structures that have shaped criticism on this particular novel. Reducing affective structures to their component parts can render interpretive analysis more flexible and more precise. Advances in flexibility and precision can refine common perceptions of exceptionally accessible authors such as Jane Austen, and they can also help to solve intractable interpretive problems in exceptionally difficult novels such as *Mayor*.

Adopting a quantitative approach need not render a critic less sensitive to nuances of character and tone. Quite the contrary. It can free us from distorting preconceptions, making it possible to see an old and familiar text with eyes newly opened. Many of the particular observations that we make in this chapter converge closely with those of Hardy's other critics. It could hardly be otherwise. The questions in the questionnaire are couched in the common language and appeal to the common understanding. The data on which we base our conclusions have been contributed largely by professional scholars intimately familiar with Hardy's work. These scholars have not simply been blind to the attributes of the characters. They have only been unable to combine their particular observations and emotional responses into a coherent picture of the novel as a whole. Quantifying agonistic structure makes it possible to construct an interpretive model that corresponds more closely to the total structure of meaning in Hardy's work.

The organization of characters in *Mayor* does not invite readers to sympathize with communitarian protagonists. Nor does it merely invert the egalitarian ethos, sliding under the moral radar to seduce readers into identifying with impulses of personal power. Becky Sharp ends up rich, contented, and unrepentant. Henchard's efforts at dominance end only in humiliation, disgrace, and despair. Farfrae fulfills his modest ambitions, but his complacency seems only to put readers off, not give them emotional satisfaction. Elizabeth-Jane also achieves contentment, but readers evidently do not consider her fate a main feature of the novel. Lucetta's end is wretched, but her life is ultimately marginal, a matter of little consequence either to readers or to the other characters.

In stepping so far outside the range of ordinary empathic identification, does *Mayor* also step outside the range of psychological effects to which an adaptive function could plausibly be attributed? Possibly. It is possible that *Mayor* is idiosyncratic, an outlier, like a mutation producing maladaptive or adaptively neutral behavior. Another possibility, though, is that the peculiar agonistic structure of *Mayor* points us toward adaptive function at a level more basic and general than that manifested in morally polarized agonistic structure. The arts, including literature and its oral antecedents, help us make sense of the world, emotionally, subjectively, imaginatively. Agonistic structure in most of the novels in this study suggests just how important our need for social bonding can be. Still, dispositions for derogating dominance and affirming one's place in a social group are not the only important features of human nature. Authors are members of a community, subserving the needs of their readers, but they are also individual human beings. Every novel is an imagined world, and in every novel the author tacitly adopts a point of view, an emotionally modulated stance toward the characters and events in the story. Each individual novel necessarily reflects its author's characteristic ways of engaging the world, responding to its challenges, and giving value to experience. As we have seen, authors exercise a high degree of control over the emotional responses of readers. To become absorbed in an imagined world is to share, for the time being, its author's point of view. Each imagined world is an exercise in making meaning. For readers, each such exercise is an opportunity to see what the world looks like and feels like from a particular point of view. If nothing else, reading novels would be an access of social learning—not just learning about the characters and situations depicted in the story, but learning how things look and feel from a particular point of view. Such learning is intrinsically valuable. It extends our natural, adaptive dispositions for gossip, dialogue, and social observation. It also provides us with a repertory of possible attitudes toward the circumstances of our own lives—toward sexual desire, jealousy, love, hatred, loneliness, confusion, disappointment. Experiences at this level are universal. They transcend particular situations and give us access to stories from every culture and every period.

Assessing thematic and tonal structure in a novel inevitably leads us back to the world view of the author who creates that structure. To evoke Hardy's total world view, we shall have to register qualities of style and authorial temperament that are not part of the data we gathered for this particular study. Our descriptive terms for those qualities can, though, be closely integrated with the categories on which we gathered data.

The organization of tonal and thematic elements in *Mayor* is unusual, but the elements themselves are common and familiar. They can be located on a continuum with the imaginative qualities in Hardy's other works. Hardy's distinctive qualities include a sensually rich lyricism scarcely equaled in English outside the poetry of Shakespeare, Milton, and the Romantics. Hardy also has an extraordinarily high capacity for registering emotional pain. In his treatment of Tess, his proclivity for negative affect combines with tenderness and strength of mind. The result is a sublime elegy. In much of *Jude*, Hardy's sensitivity to pain degenerates into neurasthenia, pure depressive affect of the sort monstrously personified in Jude's son "Father Time." *Jude* is written from a point of view morbidly fixated on the spectacle of sensitive human matter caught and mangled in destructive circumstance. Nonetheless, Jude's renunciation of life, at the end, has a ghastly magnificence that transcends self-pity. He passes beyond the reach of torment and achieves a final stage of utter indifference. In *Mayor*, Elizabeth-Jane succeeds in achieving a detached but compassionate perspective that does not involve losing all capacity for pleasure and all interest in life. In the final paragraphs of the novel, Hardy's perspective merges almost completely with that of Elizabeth-Jane. He commends her wisdom, and invites the reader to do the same. Few critics have been able to elucidate the kind of psychological work that Hardy accomplishes in *Mayor*, for himself or for them. But emotions can be powerfully active even when they are not fully understood or explained. Hardy's stance in *Mayor* has almost certainly exercised an emotional influence operating apart from critical efforts to explain it. Still, criticism is most satisfying when it both evokes and explains—evokes the feelings we have in reading a novel, and also stands apart from those feelings, analyzes them, and locates them within broader networks of explanation.

Conclusion

Recapitulation

After two long chapters devoted to one novelist each, it would perhaps not come amiss to recall that our chief findings have reference to novels covering the whole period from Austen through Forster. The large conclusions that we drew in chapters 2 through 5 are based on statistical results from questionnaires on 435 characters from 143 novels. (For a complete list, see appendix 2.) As we note in the chapter on *The Mayor of Casterbridge*, had we studied that novel alone, we could never have derived the large-scale patterns that form the heart of our findings on agonistic structure. Austen's novels are more nearly "average" than *Mayor*, but a similar principle applies. If we had studied Austen alone, and had tried to generalize from her work, we would have drawn some very strange conclusions about the representation of male sexuality in the novels. The larger patterns produced by the whole body of novels provides a base line against which we can register the peculiarities in Austen's novels and in *Mayor*. In this respect, our procedure formalizes a process that is at work also in more traditional methods of research. Scholars and critics typically read any particular novel in the context of other novels—with expectations and standards of value that have been, in part, shaped by those other novels.

The large general patterns derived from the whole body of novels do not just form a background to individual novels. The whole body of novels is itself a distinct object for the imagination of scholars. Consider the way in which social historians regard a nation or an empire not just as a set of disparate individuals but as a whole thing, a collective entity: England, France, the Roman Empire, the Han Dynasty. In a similar way, literary scholars regard a distinct group of works as a single phenomenon, an object for the imagination: the medieval mystery plays, Jacobean drama, Romantic poetry, the

Victorian novel. By using statistics to illuminate the agonistic organization of characters across the whole body of these novels, we hope to have made a productive difference in our readers' imagination. We hope to have altered, clarifying and enriching, the readers' impression of the novels as a total cultural phenomenon.

"Agonistic structure" is not just a bit of loose descriptive terminology occupying the borderland between folk concepts and scholarly discourse: it is a robust, empirically confirmed feature in the organization of individual novels and in the norms and conventions that constrain the depiction of individual characters in these novels. Moreover, those norms and conventions are not arbitrary products of a particular cultural episteme. They are rooted in the evolutionary history of human social organization. They seem to fulfill an important adaptive function: providing a medium for a group dynamic that regulates the distribution of social power.

Sex and gender are important in the novels, but less important than many scholars and critics have supposed. Our findings indicate that differences of sex are radically subordinated to moral differences between protagonists and antagonists. Males and females have differences of interest, but they have much stronger commonalities of interest. The forces that unite them into a community are stronger than the forces that divide them into politically conscious factions within that community. The pressure of differing male and female interests makes itself felt, statistically, in the contrasts between female protagonists by male and female novelists. In those contrasts, we can discern the forces of social history that have gradually reduced the limitations imposed on the social roles of women. In the contrasts between protagonists and antagonists, we can discern the even deeper forces that have made men and women partners in the evolutionary history of the human race.

If protagonists are young, attractive, and prosocial, that clearly says something about the values that prevail in the culture that produced these novels. But then, being young, attractive, and prosocial also have universal appeal. The role that these features play in the agonistic organization of the novels reflects major features of an evolved and adapted human nature. Evolutionary psychologists have not been slow in identifying the adaptive function of youth and beauty in the psychology of mating, nor have they neglected to analyze the evolutionary grounds for prosocial dispositions. They have sometimes been less alert to the desire for knowledge or the impulses that lead us to invent and discover things, but these too are part of human nature.

The findings from this study are dependent on two main sources: the categories we chose to include, and the responses of our participants. The categories ground themselves in a model of human nature derived from evolutionary psychology. The responses ground themselves in the good sense of our participants. Getting clear-cut results across a large body of novels from a large number of respondents gives support to our belief that the categories are meaningful. But the whole study would have failed had the readers not brought informed judgment to bear on assigning numerical values to attributes of individual characters.

The clear-cut nature of our results has important implications for the determinacy of meaning in literature. Characters have definite attributes on which competent readers agree, and those attributes produce predictable emotional responses from readers. The combination of attributes and responses reflects cultural norms rooted in human nature. This is of course not the last word on the determinacy of meaning in literature. But it could provide a new starting point for further research. It opens an opportunity for further empirical inquiry and could thus offer an alternative to discursive repetition based on untested speculative ideas, to say nothing of ideas that have already been tested and that have been empirically invalidated.

Global Positioning

In subsequent sections, we compare our ideas and methods with those of other critical schools in six areas. After contrasting our perspective on social power with that of Foucauldian cultural critique, we explain why evolutionary psychology should inform all cultural critique, and we suggest ways in which evolutionary concepts of human nature can correct, supplement, or replace forms of psychology currently active in literary study. Comparing the research in *Graphing Jane Austen* with empirical work that does not have a specifically evolutionary cast, we argue that empirical research, to be fruitful, must lodge itself within a theoretical structure. In considering the relation between our own research and evolutionary psychology, we argue that interdisciplinary work in the human sciences and in the humanities can and should be a two-way street, with both disciplines making real contributions to the other. Finally, responding to criticisms from literary humanists, we evaluate the charge that literary Darwinism is "reductive," formulate an ideal of a complete, comprehensive interpretive account of literary texts, and measure this study against that ideal.

An Evolutionary Perspective on Social Power

The dominant theoretical framework for current literary study is Foucauldian cultural critique. The central concept in this school is "power." For nearly three decades now, literary scholars have been heavily preoccupied with examining the way in which actual social power shapes fictive depictions. Feminists are concerned particularly with the gendered aspect of power—with male structures of political and social domination. Queer theorists are concerned with "compulsory heterosexuality" as an assertion of power in the field of sexual preferences. Marxists are concerned with social class as a primary dimension in the relations between strong and weak, between oppressors and oppressed, exploiters and exploited. Postcolonial and ethnic critics have focused on relations of ethnic and racial domination. In contemporary cultural critique, all historical and current power relations are typically measured against a norm of universal cooperative behavior—a world that is free of competing interests, and free of conflict. The utopian norm is a world in which "power," the differential exercise of force in social relations, no longer exists. Measured against the utopian norm, all historical and actual exercises of power are necessarily forms of gratuitous oppression.[1]

Our view of social power in the novels is rather different from that in most contemporary cultural critique. From an evolutionary perspective, conflicting interests are an endemic and ineradicable feature of human social interaction. Consequently, in this study we have not morally evaluated historical structures of power relative to the norm of an imaginary world in which power does not exist. When reflecting on the way social power manifests itself in the novels, we seek to be analytic, not partisan. In contrast to the avowed purposes in the bulk of contemporary Cultural Critique, we do not envision the analysis of meaning structures in literary texts as subordinate to the purpose of subverting or promoting any specific social or political ideal or any specific social or political group, set, or class.

Should then all literary study be politically quietistic, rigorously avoiding judgment on the ethical qualities of the cultural values reflected in literature? That is not our view. We think criticism has a dual mission—first to understand, and second to judge. To judge without understanding is foolish; to understand without judging is heartless. In chapter 5, describing the politics of the novels, we noted that some of the most prominent novelists are committed to diminishing differences of wealth and rank, recognizing our common humanity, and thus improving conditions of life for the most vulnerable members of society. That kind of commitment did not arise out of a facile appeal to a biologically impossible norm. It arose out of wise and generous social dispositions working in harmony with a tough-minded understanding of human nature.

The Primacy of Psychology in Literary Study

Human Universals, Cultural Differences, and Individual Identity

Literary Darwinists typically invoke "human universals"—underlying regularities of thought and behavior that appear in all known cultures.[2] Like evolutionary theorists in the human sciences, the literary Darwinists aim at reducing cultural particularities to more general and basic causal principles. But they also reverse that explanatory process, analyzing the way in which elemental features of human nature articulate themselves within particular cultural ecologies. They thus often refer to their work as "biocultural critique." In contrast to the literary Darwinists, most contemporary cultural critics in the humanities concentrate exclusively on cultural differences, neglecting or explicitly rejecting the idea of human universals.

One can readily enough understand the thinking that induces critics to emphasize cultural differences. Humans are social animals. There are virtually no human beings who exist outside of culture or whose personal identities are not profoundly influenced by the culture in which they happen to live. Culture offers social roles to individuals in the way that a theater closet offers costumes to actors. Individuals adopt the roles available within their culture. Still, look a little more deeply, and one can see that social roles have never been detached from the constraints and impulses of an evolved and adapted human nature. Consequently, in company with evolutionary psychologists, we think that psychological analysis, rooted in an understanding of our evolved and adapted human nature, should inform and constrain cultural critique.[3] That is the assumption on which we have conducted this study.

Biology precedes culture. The features of physiology and the impulses conducing to survival and reproduction have been conserved in humans from ancestral organisms that precede the evolution of mammals. Like all mammals, humans are physically dependent on live birth and mother-infant bonding, and that physical dependence fundamentally influences all specifically human forms of feeling.

Specifically human dispositions for mate selection, pair-bonding, parenting, and kin association precede and constrain all specific cultural forms for the organization of marriage, family, and kinship. Humans share with social primates the elementary dispositions of affiliation and dominance, and those dispositions constrain all specific forms of social organization. The dispositions that emerge from human life history constitute the building blocks of culture. Cultures vary in their forms of organization, but all forms of cultural organization consist of arrangements of a limited set of species-typical dispositions operating within specific ecological conditions. All forms of cultural imagination—religious, ideological, artistic, and literary—are imbued with the passions derived from the evolved and adapted dispositions of human nature. Literature and the other arts derive their deepest emotional force from those dispositions.

Humans are adaptively organized to construct cultures and to assimilate cultural information. Through "gene-culture coevolution," the development of the capacity for advanced cultural organization has fundamentally altered the human genome.[4] Virtually all human interactions are organized within cultural systems, and cultural systems profoundly influence all individual human experience. All experience is, nonetheless, individual. We can postulate collective entities and endow them, metaphorically, with the powers of experience—"the experience of a century," "the American tradition," or "the Western mind." On the literal level—the level at which "experience" correlates with neurological events—all such collective entities instantiate themselves in individual minds. No physical, neurological entity corresponding to a transcendent collective mind—a mind existing outside and independently of individual minds—has ever been identified. Individuals can exist without cultures—individual organisms, and even individual human beings, as in the case of feral children. Cultures cannot exist without individuals. If all individual human beings became extinct, human culture would cease to exist.

Full, Focused Psychological Subjects

By affirming that an evolved and adapted human nature fundamentally informs particular cultural configurations, we run counter to the characteristic poststructuralist idea that individual human beings are merely empty vessels for the circulation of cultural energy. That contrast in the conception of individual identity has important implications for thinking about characters in fiction. In a celebrated Foucauldian study of Victorian novels, D. A. Miller observes that within the poststructuralist episteme "full, focused psychological subjects" are routinely "emptied out and decentered." Accordingly, poststructuralist critics typically regard depictions of identity in Victorian novels as "a doomed attempt to produce a stable subject in a stable world." Expanding on this conception, Miller envisions "a subject habituated to psychic displacements, evacuations, reinvestments, in a social order whose totalizing power circulates all the more easily for being pulverized."[5]

In contrast to poststructuralist conceptions of individual identity, but in concord with the depictions of characters in Victorian novels, a biological perspective suggests that in basic ways individual persons are indeed stable entities within a stable world. The world changes constantly, even if it were only the weather, but beneath those changes the human body and mind are adaptively oriented to massive regularities encapsulated in folk physics, folk biology, and folk psychology. Some features of our environment, especially those of physics, are so stable that we have evolved exquisitely complex organs adapted to detect minute variations in them: eyes to register variations in light waves; ears to register variations in sound waves. Humans universally, in all known cultures, develop similar categories for analyzing the phenomena of the natural world: space, time, motion, mass, energy, living things, plants, and animals.[6] All normally developing children come to recognize, at a predictable age, that other individual persons are intentional agents with an inner life consisting of perceptions, thoughts, beliefs, feelings, and goals.[7] We recognize, in ourselves and others, basic motives, emotions, and social dispositions.[8] To be sure, individuals undergo significant changes. They respond to the changing conditions of the world around them and also change over time, growing or aging. Moreover, they experience conflicting impulses and sometimes find themselves torn between incompatible forms of cultural identity. Even so, they are not "empty," and within their own perspectives, they remain stubbornly central.[9]

In several obvious and basic ways, the biologically grounded individual human being is the central organizing unit in human life and in novels. Humans are physically discrete. Individual persons are bodies wrapped in skin with nervous systems sending signals to brains that are soaked in blood and encased in bone. Each individual human brain contains a continuous sequence of thoughts, feelings, and memories forming a distinct personal identity. People engage in collective activities and share experiences, but when an individual person dies, all experience for that person stops. Motivations, actions, and interpretive responses all originate in the neurological events in individual brains. Thoughts, feelings, and memories are lodged in individual brains, and individual persons form the central organizing units in narrative depictions. Novelists and readers are individual persons, and characters in fiction are fictive individual persons. Because experience is individual, the analysis of fictional narrative is always, necessarily, psychological analysis. Characters are individual agents with goals. Novelists are individual persons who construct intentional meanings about those characters, and readers are individual persons who interpret those meanings. It is not possible to speak of depicted narrative events without at least tacitly identifying agents and goals, and virtually all literary commentary makes at least indirect reference to the intentions of authors and the imputed responses of readers.

In this study, we neither deprecate the idea of individual identity nor simply take it for granted, as part of common sense. Instead, we break human life history down into basic motives and link those motives with personality factors. All these elements, commingling with differences of sex, combine in different individual characters to produce distinct individual identities. The chief unit of analysis in this study is the individual character. When our respondents opened the questionnaire, after giving their own demographic information and selecting a novel, the first thing they had to do was to select a character—a single, named individual character. In ticking off numerical ratings for the attributes of characters and their own emotional responses to the characters, the respondents (perhaps inadvertently) were helping us to build a bridge between the elements of human nature and the organization of those elements into the distinct configurations that make up individual identities. In the degree to which we have succeeded in producing meaningful results, we have also tacitly affirmed the validity and importance of the full, focused psychological subject.

Alternative Forms of Psychological Literary Study

Novels originate in psychological impulses, depict human psychology, and fulfill the psychological needs of readers. In all critical commentary, some form of psychological theory, implicit or explicit, is always at work. Literature itself embodies an intuitive folk psychology at its highest level of articulation, and impressionistic literary commentary draws freely on that collective body of folk insights. In commenting on literature—on characters, authors, and readers—literary critics often also make explicit appeal to fundamental underlying principles of psychological causation. In this study, our own appeals have been delineated in models of human nature and of literature. In this section, we consider the relation between those models and the kinds of psychology that are currently active in literary study.

In seeking explanatory reductions, literary scholars have made far more use of Freudian depth psychology than of any other form of psychological theory. For generations now, literary scholars who have had some intuitive conviction about the psycho-symbolic structure of literary figuration have been drawn, as if by a fatal necessity, into the vortex of Freudian critique. The attractive force exercised by Freud has in good part been a force exercised in a vacuum. Freud offers a comprehensive, internally coherent, and provocatively sensationalistic explanation of the structure of the psyche, the most intimate bonds of family life, sexual identity, and the phases in the development of the individual personal identity. He sketches out a rudimentary theory of literature as a form of wish-fulfillment fantasy projection,[10] but that theory has been far less influential than the theory of psycho-symbolic figuration articulated in *The Interpretation of Dreams*. For much of the twentieth century, if one wished to explore psychosexual development and psycho-symbolic figuration, and to do so in a systematic and theoretically consequent way, there were few alternatives outside the work of Freud.

Within the field of psychology proper, Freud's theories have drifted steadily into the backwaters of obsolete speculative notions. Those notions were systematically developed, but their distinctive character depended more on the peculiar stamp given to them by the personality of their originator than by any claim they might have had to empirical validity. The subjects of Freud's speculations—human family relations, sexual identity, the structure of the psyche, and the phases of individual development—are essential components of human experience and thus of literary meaning. The account that Freud and the Freudians give of those subjects, though, is radically flawed. The Oedipal theory is at the very center of Freud's thinking on human development and on the psychological foundations of culture. One of the display pieces of a specifically evolutionary understanding of human psychology is the decisive demonstration that the Oedipal theory is quite simply mistaken.[11]

Freud is still cited respectfully by literary critics, but he no longer serves, very often, as a primary, unmediated source. Most postmodern literary criticism has at least a tinge of psychoanalytic thinking about it, and much of it is dyed through and through with psychoanalytic thinking, but most practical psychoanalytic criticism is derived from second- and third-generation Freudian theorists. Overwhelmingly, for literary study, the most important such later Freudian theorist is Jacques Lacan. One hears now very seldom of the ego and the id, and even less often of anal and oral stages of development, but one still hears frequently of the Phallus and The Mirror Stage of Development. Such theories, like those of Freud himself, have an obvious suggestive appeal, but like Freud's theories they also contain much that is simply false and mistaken. Moreover, Lacan's Freudian ideas are bound up with poststructuralist linguistic ideas, and Lacan's theories thus extend psychology still further into the region of speculation divorced from empirical constraint.

In the early and middle parts of the twentieth century, the one chief alternative to Freud, for psychological theory relevant to literary study, was that of Freud's apostate disciple, Jung. Freud was himself concerned chiefly with what Jung describes as "the personal unconscious," and Jung, in his own understanding of his work, was concerned with a broader and deeper subject—that of the collective unconscious of the whole human race.[12] Jungian archetypal theory provided a major stimulus to the comprehensive taxonomical effort of Frye's *Anatomy of Criticism*, and Frye was widely recognized as one of the most creative and commanding intellects in literary study in the twentieth century. Nonetheless, in the early 1980s, archetypal criticism quietly faded out of existence, and Frye's taxonomy has produced no substantial fruits within at least the past two decades.

In a formulation that has become a standard point of reference for Darwinian psychology, the Dutch ethologist Niko Tinbergen identifies four areas in which research into animal behavior should seek integrated answers: phylogeny, ontogeny, mechanism, and adaptive function.[13] Phylogeny concerns the evolutionary history of a species and ontogeny the individual development of an organism within that species. Jung's chief range of interest was that of phylogeny, and Freud's that of ontogeny. We now have means for exploring both these areas in scientifically fruitful ways that were not available to Jung and Freud. Evolutionary psychology operates both on the scale of conserved ancestral psychic structures envisioned by Jung and also on the scale of individual development on which Freud concentrated his attention. By integrating research in these fields with research into psychological mechanisms, and by locating all three forms of explanation within an evolutionary understanding of complex functional structures, we can replace the speculative theories of Jung and Freud with theories that involve the same range of universal human concerns but that can produce empirically valid results.[14]

Within the range of psychological theory now available to literary study, only one distinct group of researchers has concentrated on the analysis of psychological mechanisms—the group oriented to cognitive science.[15] Research in cognition is clearly contiguous with evolutionary research into the production and consumption of literary meaning, but most research in cognitive literary study has thus far not envisioned the necessity of linking its analysis of mechanism with the three other components of an ethological analysis—phylogeny, ontogeny, and adaptive function. As a consequence, the analytic structures of "cognitive rhetoric" or "cognitive poetics" have for the most part remained formalistic, local, and fragmentary.[16] No cognitivist literary theorist has yet sought to produce an integrated model of human nature, and none has yet produced ideas on a level with that of Frye's theory of archetypal symbolism or Freud's theories of psycho-symbolic figuration.[17]

In its early phases, research in cognitive science typically operated in the discursive mode of formalistic speculative philosophy, and it was much preoccupied with models of the mind derived from analogies with computers. In recent years that kind of discourse has steadily been giving place to research that is more tightly integrated with cognitive and affective neuroscience—research into how the brain actually works.[18] Findings in these areas intersect in important ways with evolutionary findings on motives, emotions, and social interaction. We thus anticipate that in coming years cognitive neuroscience, evolutionary social science, and evolutionary literary study will form a network of interdependent research programs.

Empirical Method and the Necessity of Theory

Outside of the context of evolutionary thinking, various efforts have been made to introduce quantitative, empirical methods into literary study.[19] We are of course strongly in sympathy with the desire to investigate literary topics by using empirical methods. Whatever substantive concepts are involved, any use of empirical methods involves a fundamental commitment to fact, evidence, and reason. Any use of empirical methods thus necessarily invokes an organon radically different from that which governs the poststructuralist mode of discourse that has prevailed for so long in the humanities. Fredric Jameson identifies the central features of this organon. He observes that "its fundamental law would seem to be the exclusion of substantive statements and positive philosophical propositions." Jameson is himself one of the most renowned practitioners of "Theory." As he himself describes it, a central challenge for such practitioners is "to advance the argument without actually saying anything."[20] In practice, such discourse consists chiefly in improvising ambiguous rhetorical formulations on themes from speculative philosophy and obsolete forms of social science. Tacitly segregating themselves from such practices, scholars who adopt empirical methods commit themselves to making substantive statements. They say something, and they invoke standards and principles that allow them to test the validity of what they say.

In comparison with the practice of making self-cancelling verbal gestures in a purely discursive field, almost any effort at empirical analysis has, in our view, some degree of epistemological merit. Even so, we do not think that adopting an empirical methodology is in itself sufficient to produce substantial advances in literary knowledge. To produce substantial advances, empirical data must have a bearing on theoretical issues of wide import; those theoretical issues must be systematically integrated within a comprehensive theory of human nature and of literature; and those theoretical models must be consilient with the larger body of knowledge about the evolved and adapted character of the human psyche.

The relation between empirical study and the use of larger theoretical models can be illustrated by an episode in the history of geology and biology. In a letter of 1861, Darwin reflected on the inconsequentiality of empirical research that lacks an organizing conceptual design:[21]

> About thirty years ago there was much talk that geologists ought only to observe and not theorise; and I well remember some one saying that at this rate a man might as well go into a gravel-pit and count the pebbles and describe the colours. How odd it is that anyone should not see that all observation must be for or against some view if it is to be of any service!

The dates registered in Darwin's letter and his reference to "thirty years ago" are pregnant with meaning. The period of 30 years ago to which he refers is the period just before Charles Lyell produced the first edition of his *Principles of Geology* and thus produced the first real and workable paradigm for geology as a science. Darwin took Lyell's newly published first volume with him on his nearly five-year voyage on the *Beagle*. (Volumes two and three reached him in the course of the voyage.) The paradigmatic synthesis produced by

Lyell was an essential precondition for Darwin's own production of a theory that would unite all the scattered fragments of information produced by the energetic but diffuse and disorganized activity of naturalists in his generation.[22]

Darwin's theory of adaptation by means of natural selection is itself now firmly established as a paradigm within evolutionary biology. That paradigm is the framework within which all evolutionary social science operates. By constructing a comprehensive theory of human nature and of literature, evolutionary literary study can itself produce a paradigm within which empirical analysis contributes to genuine advances in knowledge. Within that paradigm, we need lose nothing of value from earlier forms of psychological literary study. In place of Jungian archetypal myth criticism, we can use evolutionary anthropology and evolutionary psychology as the basis for research into myths, folk tales, and epics. In place of Frye's suggestive but speculative accounts of genre, we can construct accounts of genre that integrate models of basic emotions, basic motives, and personality. In place of Freud's theories about the structure of the psyche, human development, and the relations of family, we can make appeal to human life history theory. All the elements of personal and social identity can be integrated with a biologically informed understanding of symbolic figuration. Cognitive and affective neuroscience will in all likelihood provide us with ever more subtle and precise ways of understanding the psychological functions of specific formal features and figurative modes.[23]

Quantitative Literary Hermeneutics

Research that uses a purely discursive methodology for evolutionary literary study remains passively dependent on the knowledge generated within an adjacent field. The methodological barrier that separates discursive literary study from the evolutionary program in the social sciences limits the scope and significance of both literary study and the evolutionary human sciences. The production and consumption of literature and its oral antecedents is a large and vitally important part of our specifically human nature. An artificial barrier that leaves evolutionary literary scholars as passive consumers of knowledge also leaves evolutionary social scientists cut off from any primary understanding of one of the most important and revealing aspects of human nature. Literature and its oral antecedents derive from a uniquely human, species-typical disposition for producing and consuming imaginative verbal constructs. Removing the methodological barrier between humanistic expertise and the expertise of the social sciences can produce results valuable to both fields.

In the statement of purpose that we included on our website, along with the questionnaire, we listed a set of questions that we hoped our research would help us to address, and the final question we posed was this: "Can literary works be mined as rich sources of data for formal psychological studies?" In our view, the answer is unequivocally yes. For instance, in analyzing the different ways in which male and female authors construct male and female characters, we are conducting a formal psychological study. That study operates in a field similar to that occupied by Ellis and Symons in their study of pornography and romance novels, though we are using dead people (nineteenth-century authors) as our subject pool.[24] As it happens, dead people serve very well as subjects of research, so long as they leave records behind them. They work just as well as the authors of romance novels, even if the authors are still living. The people who make up our respondent pool were all live subjects (and we sincerely hope they all still are—our warmest thanks to them for their participation). We conducted formal psychological studies on them, too. To what do they respond emotionally? Which personality factors and motives excite which specific basic emotions in them? Does the sex of a respondent significantly influence responses? All questions that bear on the model of literature as a medium of social interaction are questions simultaneously of literary study and of research in the social sciences. In that sense, every analysis we have conducted in this study is a "formal psychological study."

We do not envision a form of research in which men and women in white lab coats produce nothing, with respect to literary texts, except tables of numbers and mathematical equations. In this current study, we have ourselves sought to integrate the forms of expertise that are particular to a humanistic training with the forms of expertise that are particular to a training in the social sciences. We constructed our questionnaire on the basis of our models of human nature and of literature as a mimetic and communicative medium, and we also drew freely on our knowledge of how fictional prose narratives tend to work. On the basis of research into both human nature and the novels in this period, we made predictions about the scoring patterns in the character sets. The responses to the questionnaire produced data from which we drew inferences about the population of the novels. Some of the most important and far-reaching of the generalizations thus produced were ideas that we had not ourselves foreseen. In reflecting on our findings, we drew connections among seemingly disparate concepts in different disciplinary fields—in the study of emotions, personality, motives, mate selection, literary history, and literary theory. This analytic and reflective process broadened and deepened our understanding of the novels. We make no claim that the results reported here exhaust the possibilities of meaning in these texts, or that they exemplify a comprehensively adequate design of research. Our central purpose has been to contribute to a body of knowledge that can be, and should be, empirical, cumulative, and progressive.

Centrifugal and Centripetal Forms of Literary Study

Research in all fields displays antithetical but complementary forms of movement: centrifugal and centripetal. In centrifugal movement, research moves toward phenomenal particularity. In the centripetal, it moves toward reductive consolidation in explanatory principle.[25] Both literary Darwinism and quantitative methodology have strong centripetal tendencies. Whether adopting empirical or discursive methods, literary Darwinists aim at identifying basic traits of human nature and "deep structures" of literary meaning. Like evolutionary social scientists, they tend to focus on "human universals." Quantitative methodology takes this tendency toward "reduction" one step further. By reducing categories to numbers, social scientists seek to eliminate ambiguity and polysemy. To use a phrase Jonathan Gottschall develops in *Literature, Science, and a New Humanities*, quantitative methodology aims at "shrinking possibility space." It aims, that is, at reducing the range of possibly valid conclusions. Reducing that range is an indispensable condition for producing cumulative, progressive knowledge.

Many literary scholars believe that literary studies are and should be essentially centrifugal. For instance, William Deresiewicz, contrasting literary study with the social sciences, declares that literary study "is not concerned with large classes of phenomena of which individual cases are merely interchangeable and aggregable examples. It is concerned, precisely, with individual cases, and very few of them at that: the rare works of value that stand out from the heap of dross produced in every age." Frederic Crews adopts a similar perspective. Resisting the Darwinist drive toward generalization and explanatory reduction, he argues that "there is nothing trivial about trying to make sense of single works, or single careers, or single moments in literary history, that strike the common understanding as representing a pinnacle of insight and skill." Turning from resistance to attack, he rejects the literary Darwinists' "reduction to the most primordial level," a level at which, he believes that "perceived factors tend to be banal common denominators that aren't helpful for the particular instance." In a more extreme version of this charge against explanatory "reduction" in literary Darwinism, Eugene Goodheart maintains that literary study should occupy itself only with particular cases divorced from any larger explanatory context. "Reductionism in the natural sciences is no vice; on the contrary, it enables one discipline (for instance, physics) to explain another (chemistry). In the humanities, however, it subverts the uniqueness and complexity of works of art." What the Darwinists propose, he thinks, "is the dissolution of the individuality of a work (the very reason we enjoy and value it) into large generalizations that remove all of its distinctive features and vitality."[26]

These affirmations of a centrifugal critical ethos imply a necessary conflict between explanatory principles and a sensitivity to particular features in individual works of art. That implication is misconceived. Literary Darwinists invoke explanatory principles from evolutionary psychology, but they have nonetheless produced many good essays in interpretive literary criticism.[27] In our own critiques of Jane Austen and *The Mayor of Casterbridge*, we have used a universal model of human nature to produce highly particular commentaries on the specific meanings and effects in individual works of literature. In the case of *Mayor*, comparing the novel with patterns in the novels of the period as a whole makes it possible to see much more clearly the truly singular, individual character of that one novel.

Not only is sensitivity to particulars compatible with explanation; all particular criticism inescapably entails general explanatory ideas. Even when they try to avoid invoking ideas derived from recognizable theoretical systems, humanist critics such as Deresiewicz, Crews, and Goodheart must necessarily appeal to a complex of common-sense notions that M. H. Abrams designates the "humanist literary paradigm." As Abrams describes it, the humanist paradigm consists of the belief that individual authors convey intentional meanings to readers in a shared actual world. This common-sense belief is part of an intuitive theory of the world; it is part of our evolved "folk psychology." Nonetheless, it is highly vulnerable to skeptical critique. Abrams argues that poststructuralist theory can be most concisely characterized as a concerted attack on all the basic elements in the humanist paradigm: authorial intention, communication, determinate meanings, and a correspondence between signs and actual things. Abrams is not sympathetic to poststructuralism, but Jonathan Culler, one of its spokesmen, concurs with Abrams about its essential character. "The main effect" of poststructuralist theory, he says, "is the disputing of 'common sense': common-sense views about meaning, writing, literature, experience." Poststructuralists try "to show that what we take for granted as 'common sense' is in fact a historical construction, a particular theory that has come to seem so natural to us that we don't even see it as a theory." Most literary Darwinists would affirm the validity of the folk epistemology embodied in the humanist literary paradigm, but they would lodge that epistemology within a larger explanatory system: modern evolutionary theory.[28]

By appealing to a general explanatory system, literary Darwinism joins company with other theoretical schools such as psychoanalysis and Marxism. Strange as these bedfellows might seem, we can spread at least one common coverlet over them—the desire for explanatory depth. Though seriously mistaken in its conception of human developmental psychology, Freudian psychology enables critics to abstract psychologically charged themes from literary texts. Freudian psychology gets at partial truths about literary texts, though inevitably distorting them in the process. So also, Marxist social psychology gets at social themes that do in fact exist, though the inadequacies of Marxist views of human social psychology inevitably distort the themes that Marxist theory serves to isolate. Similar observations could be made about deconstruction, feminism, Bakhtinian dialogics, and all the other standard elements in contemporary critical theory. None is absolutely wrong. Otherwise, it could not have had large persuasive appeal to intelligent literary scholars who sincerely wish to understand their subject. But we need not stop short with partial and distorted versions of explanatory systems for which better alternatives already exist. If the evolutionary human sciences can provide a comprehensive understanding of the mind, Darwinist ideas about literature should be able to incorporate the valid elements from other literary theories.

In its most complete forms, Darwinist literary criticism would construct continuous explanatory sequences linking "inclusive fitness"—the "ultimate" causal principle in evolution—to particular features in an evolved and adapted human nature and to particular structures and effects in specific works of art. A comprehensively adequate interpretive account of a given work of art would take in, synoptically, its phenomenal effects (tone, style, theme, formal organization), locate it in a cultural context, explain that cultural context as a particular organization of the elements of human nature within a specific set of environmental conditions (including cultural traditions), identify an implied author and an implied reader, examine the responses of actual readers (for instance, other literary critics), describe the sociocultural, political, and psychological functions the work fulfills, locate those functions in relation to the evolved needs of human nature, and link the work comparatively with other artistic works, using a taxonomy of themes, formal elements, affective elements, and functions derived from a comprehensive model of human nature.

In the study reported in this book, how far have we succeeded in approximating to this ideal of a complete critical account of the texts we discuss? We can identify specific areas in which we fall short of it. We did not aim at a universal, exhaustive explanation of the novels. We focused on only one specific large-scale element in the organization of characters: agonistic structure differentiated by sex. We did not construct a complete taxonomy of formal elements. More particularly, we did not incorporate ways of operationalizing some of the concepts that form the subject matter of Narratology: for instance, the distinction between *syuzhet* and *fabula* or distinctions among different types of narrators. Insofar as we are concerned with quantifying features in individual texts, the main gap in our research design is probably the absence of any means for registering verbal "style": diction, syntax, rhythm, metaphors, motifs, and figures of speech.

Commenting on Austen and Hardy, we have sometimes made observations about their literary style, blending those observations with the inferences that we drew from the data produced by the questionnaires. From an absolutist methodological perspective, blending social science methods with judgments based on literary experience falls short of creating a questionnaire so comprehensive that it could integrate all aspects of the texts and reduce them to data. In practical reality, there are limitations to what can be done with any given protocol. At least one of us (Gottschall) concedes that certain kinds of literary problems might never be fully amenable to a quantitative methodology. At least one other of us (Carroll) believes that all mental phenomena, including those involved in the production and reception of novels, consist of states of the brain and are hypothetically susceptible to quantification. But here we enter the realm of science fiction—a genre that deliberately erases the boundaries between "reality" and what is only "hypothetically" possible.

If any such science-fiction scenario could be realized, it still would not render the personal, subjective aspect of literary study obsolete. "Meaning" and "effect" are crucial elements of literary phenomenology, and meaning is always meaning *for* someone, some particular person; effect is always an effect *on* some particular person. Literary scholars explain their subjects, or try to, but they also register the value and significance of their subjects. Identifying large-scale patterns of meaning in the novels need not reduce our appreciation of the value and significance of the novels. Quite the contrary. The better we understand how the novels work, the more keenly we can appreciate their effects. True enough, when scholars succeed in narrowing the range of possibly valid conclusions, they reduce the sense of vaguely infinite potential in the world of literary response, but they also open up new possibilities for actual discovery—for deeper levels of explanation, more complete understanding.

Glossary

We include here the chief terms through which we have organized and analyzed the data in the study. More detailed explanations of statistical procedures are provided in chapter 1 and in appendix four.

Achieves Goals Achieves Goals provides a score derived from the question: "Does [Character Name] accomplish his or her main goals?"

Agonistic Structure The structure resulting from the polarization of Valence (good and bad characters) and Salience (major and minor characters).

Agreeableness One of the five personality factors. (The other four are Extraversion, Conscientiousness, Emotional Stability, and Openness to Experience.) Agreeableness consists of a pleasant, friendly disposition and tendency to cooperate and compromise.

Alpha reliability estimates A measure of the degree to which different coders agree in scoring the same items.

Antagonist A character identified by a majority of respondents as an antagonist; a character with a negative rating in Valence and "major" status in Salience.

Bad character A character identified by a majority of respondents as either an antagonist or a friend or an associate of an antagonist.

Bad minor character A character identified by a majority of respondents as a friend or an associate of an antagonist.

Conscientiousness One of the five personality factors. (The other four are Extraversion, Agreeableness, Emotional Stability, and Openness to Experience.) Conscientiousness refers to an inclination toward purposeful planning, organization, persistence, and reliability.

Constructive Effort One of the five motive factors. (The other four are Social Dominance, Romance, Nurture, and Subsistence.)

Constructive Effort is produced chiefly by positive scores on seeking education or culture, seeking friends and alliances, helping nonkin, and building, creating, or discovering something.

Correlation A measure of the degree to which two sets of scores vary in relation to one another, either positively (high scores with high scores) or negatively (high scores with low scores).

Dislike One of the three emotional response factors. (The other two are Sorrow and Interest.) Dislike is constituted chiefly by a cluster of negative emotions—anger, fear-of, disgust, and contempt—and by relatively low levels of admiration and liking.

Dominance See "Social Dominance."

Emotional response factors Three factors (Dislike, Sorrow, Interest) produced by analyzing correlations among ten constituent emotions.

Emotional Stability One of the five personality factors. (The other four are Extraversion, Agreeableness, Conscientiousness, and Openness to Experience.) Emotional stability reflects a temperament that is calm and relatively free from negative feelings such as anger, anxiety, and depression.

Extraversion One of the five personality factors. (The other four are Agreeableness, Conscientiousness, Emotional Stability, and Openness to Experience.) Extraversion describes assertive, exuberant activity in the social world. Introversion, in contrast, describes a tendency to be quiet, withdrawn, and disengaged.

Extrinsic Attributes One of the three mate-selection factors in both the long and short term. (The other two factors are Intrinsic Qualities and Physical Attractiveness.) A preference for Extrinsic Attributes in a mate is produced chiefly by a preference for power, wealth, and prestige.

Factor A category in which certain variables correlate with one another. For an example, see Dislike in this glossary.

Factor Analysis A statistical procedure that identifies clusters of variables that correlate with one another. Variables that cluster together produce a "factor."

Good character A character identified by a majority of respondents as either a protagonist or a friend or an associate of a protagonist

Good minor character A character identified by a majority of respondents as a friend or an associate of a protagonist.

Interest One of the three emotional response factors. (The other two are Dislike and Sorrow.) Interest is produced chiefly by a high negative score on indifference and by moderately positive scores on admiration and liking.

Intrinsic Qualities One of the three mate-selection factors in both the long and short term. (The other two factors are Extrinsic Attributes and Physical Attractiveness.) A preference for Intrinsic Qualities in a mate is produced chiefly by a preference for intelligence, kindness, and reliability.

Long-term mate selection Seeking a romantic partner with a commitment over the long term. (See Mate-selection factors.)

Main Feature Main Feature provides a score derived from the question: "In your opinion, is the success or failure of [Character Name]'s hopes or efforts a main feature in the outcome of the narrative?"

Major character A character identified by a majority of respondents as either a protagonist or an antagonist.

Mate-Selection Factors Three factors produced by analyzing correlations among seven criteria for selecting mates. The three factors are preferences for Intrinsic Qualities, Extrinsic Attributes, and Physical Attractiveness. Mate-selection is subdivided into seeking mates for the long term and the short term. (The factors are the same for the long and short term.)

Minor character A character identified by a majority of respondents as a friend or an associate of either a protagonist or antagonist.

Motive factors Five factors produced by analyzing correlations among 12 constituent motives. The five motive factors are Social Dominance, Constructive Effort, Romance, Nurture, and Subsistence.

Nurture One of the five motive factors. (The other four are Social Dominance, Constructive Effort, Romance, and Subsistence.) Nurture is produced chiefly by a high positive score on helping kin, a moderate score on helping nonkin, and by a moderately high negative score on short-term mating.

Openness to Experience One of the five personality factors. (The other four are Extraversion, Agreeableness, Conscientiousness, and Emotional Stability.) Openness references a disposition that is imaginative, intellectual, creative, and complex.

Personality factors Five factors used to categorize the traits of personality—sometimes referred to as the Five-Factor System or the Big Five.

The five factors are Extraversion, Agreeableness, Conscientiousness, Emotional Stability, and Openness to Experience.

Physical Attractiveness The term physical attractiveness has two distinct referents. It is a characteristic on which our respondents rated characters. (How attractive is the character?) Physical Attractiveness is also one of the three mate-selection factors in both the long and short term. (The other two factors are Extrinsic Attributes and Intrinsic Qualities.) In contrast to the other mate-selection factors, which are composites of correlated preferences, a preference for Physical Attractiveness in a mate is produced by the single criterion of seeking physical attractiveness.

Protagonist A character identified by a majority of respondents as a protagonist; a character with a positive rating in Valence and "major" status in Salience.

Romance One of the five motive factors. (The other four are Social Dominance, Constructive Effort, Nurture, and Subsistence.) Romance is produced chiefly by high scores on long-term mating and short-term mating and by a moderate score on seeking wealth.

Root For Root For provides a score derived from the question: "On the whole, do you want [Character Name] to achieve his or her goals?"

Salience One of the three "quasi-independent variables" used to organize the character sets. Salience divides characters into "major" and "minor" sets. Major characters are protagonists and antagonists. Minor characters are associates of protagonists and antagonists. (The other two quasi-independent variables are Valence and Sex.)

Sex One of the three "quasi-independent variables" used to organize the character sets. Sex divides characters into "male" and "female" sets. (The other two quasi-independent variables are Valence and Salience.)

Short-term mate selection Seeking a romantic partner with no anticipation of engagement or marriage. (See Mate-selection factors.)

Social Dominance One of the five motive factors. (The other four are Constructive Effort, Romance, Nurture, and Subsistence.) Social Dominance is produced chiefly by high positive scores on seeking wealth, power, and prestige and by a moderately low score on helping nonkin. We sometimes refer to "Social Dominance" simply as "Dominance."

Sorrow One of the three emotional response factors. (The other two are Dislike and Interest.) Sorrow is produced chiefly by positive scores on fear-for and sadness and by a negative score on amusement.

Standardized scores Raw scores that have been transformed into scores that reflect the position of one character or character set relative to the average for all scores. The average score is set at zero. The unit of measurement in standardized scores is the standard deviation—the average distance from the average score. A score of "1" in standardized scores = one standard deviation.

Statistical Significance A difference between two scores that is so large that it is unlikely to have arisen by chance as a result of sampling error.

Subsistence One of the five motive factors. (The other four are Social Dominance, Constructive Effort, Romance, and Nurture.) Subsistence is produced chiefly by high positive scores on survival and on performing routine tasks to earn a living.

Valence One of the three "quasi-independent variables" used to organize the character sets. Valence divides characters into "good" and "bad" sets. Good characters are protagonists and their associates. Bad characters are antagonists and their associates. (The other two quasi-independent variables are Salience and Sex.)

Appendix 1

A Link to the Questionnaire

When a respondent entered the site containing the questionnaire, the first screen that appeared introduced the study, requested acknowledgement of informed consent from respondents, and gave links to pages that described the purpose of the study and the criteria through which we had selected novels and characters. A subsequent screen asked for personal information about the respondent (age, sex, level of education, and how the respondent had heard of the site). After answering these questions, respondents were given a list of novels, arranged alphabetically by author and title, and asked to select a novel. Once a respondent had selected a novel, she or he was asked to select a character from the novel. The remaining questions were about that specific character or about the respondent's responses to that character. In order to proceed from one page to the next, respondents had to answer the questions on a given page.

We have placed a copy of the questionnaire on a single page so that our readers can see what the questionnaire looked like. (The form is no longer active and will not be used to collect data.)

http://www-personal.umich.edu/~kruger/carroll-survey.html

On the sample copy available through this link, in order to provide a character thread for the questions, we have selected a character (Emma from Jane Austen's *Emma*) from the list of possible selections.

Appendix 2

Characters for Whom Protocols Were Completed

These 435 characters are grouped by sex and role assignment, and within roles, alphabetically by first name. The titles and authors of the books in which the characters appear are given after each character's name. Characters not assigned to character roles are included at the end of the list. (The scores of these characters are included in the correlation scores for the various categories of analysis.)

Female Protagonists

Agnes Grey, *Agnes Grey*, Anne Brontë
Alice, *Alice in Wonderland* and *Through the Looking Glass*, Lewis Carroll
Alice Vavasor, *Can You Forgive Her?*, Anthony Trollope
Amelia Sedley, *Vanity Fair*, William Makepeace Thackeray
Anna Tellwright, *Anna of the Five Towns*, Arnold Bennet
Anne Elliot, *Persuasion*, Jane Austen
Baroness Eugenia of Silberstadt-Schreckenstein, *The Europeans*, Henry James
Belinda, *Belinda*, Maria Edgeworth
Catherine Earnshaw, *Wuthering Heights*, Emily Brontë
Catherine Morland, *Northanger Abbey*, Jane Austen
Catherine Sloper, *Washington Square*, Henry James
Cathy Linton, *Wuthering Heights*, Emily Brontë
Dorothea Brooke, *Middlemarch*, George Eliot
Eleanor Harding, *The Warden*, Anthony Trollope
Elinor Dashwood, *Sense and Sensibility*, Jane Austen
Elizabeth Bennet, *Pride and Prejudice*, Jane Austen

Emily (also known as Little Em'ly), *David Copperfield*, Charles Dickens
Emma Woodhouse, *Emma*, Jane Austen
Esther Summerson, *Bleak House*, Charles Dickens
Esther Waters, *Esther Waters*, George Moore
Eustacia Vye, *Far from the Madding Crowd*, Thomas Hardy
Fanny Price, *Mansfield Park*, Jane Austen
Florence Dombey, *Dombey and Son*, Charles Dickens
Gwendolen Harleth, *Daniel Deronda*, George Eliot
Helen Graham (also known as Helen Huntingdon), *The Tenant of Wildfell Hall*, Anne Brontë
Isabel Archer, *The Portrait of a Lady*, Henry James
Jane Eyre, *Jane Eyre*, Charlotte Brontë
Jeanie Deans, *The Heart of Midlothian*, Sir Walter Scott
Kate Payton, *Griffith Gaunt*, Charles Reade
Lady Glencora McCluskie, *Can You Forgive Her?*, Anthony Trollope
Lady Verinder, *The Moonstone*, Wilkie Collins
Lilia Herriton, *Where Angels Fear to Tread*, E. M. Forster
Lilian (Lily) Dale, *The Small House at Allington*, Anthony Trollope
Lucilla Marjoribanks, *Miss Marjoribanks*, Margaret Oliphant
Lucy Honeychurch, *A Room with a View*, E. M. Forster
Lucy Snowe, *Villette*, Charlotte Brontë
Maggie Tulliver, *The Mill on the Floss*, George Eliot
Maggie Verver, *The Golden Bowl*, Henry James
Maisie Farange, *What Maisie Knew*, Henry James
Margaret Hale, *North and South*, Elizabeth Gaskell
Margaret Mackenzie, *Miss Mackenzie*, Anthony Trollope
Margaret Schlegel, *Howard's End*, E. M. Forster
Marian Halcombe, *The Woman in White*, Wilkie Collins
Marianne Dashwood, *Sense and Sensibility*, Jane Austen
Mary Barton, *Mary Barton*, Elizabeth Gaskell
Mary Douglas, *Marriage*, Susan Ferrier
Mary Lennox, *The Secret Garden*, Frances Hodgson Burnett
Maud Ruthyn, *Uncle Silas*, J. Sheridan Le Fanu
Mlle Frances Evans Henri, *The Professor*, Charlotte Brontë
Molly Gibson, *Wives and Daughters*, Elizabeth Gaskell
Princess Casamassima, *Princess Casamassima*, Henry James
Rachel Ray, *Rachel Ray*, Anthony Trollope
Rebecca (Becky) Sharp, *Vanity Fair*, William Makepeace Thackeray
Rhoda Nunn, *The Odd Women*, George Gissing
Romola de' Bardi, *Romola*, George Eliot

Sara Crewe, *A Little Princess*, Frances Hodgson Burnett
Sophia Baines, *The Old Wives' Tale*, Arnold Bennett
Tess Durbeyfield, *Tess of the d'Urbervilles*, Thomas Hardy

Male Protagonists

Adam Bede, *Adam Bede*, George Eliot
Allan Quatermain, *King Solomon's Mines*, H. Rider Haggard
Alton Locke, *Alton Locke*, Charles Kingsley
Arthur Clennam, *Little Dorrit*, Charles Dickens
Captain Tom MacWhirr, *Typhoon*, Joseph Conrad
Charles Darnay, *A Tale of Two Cities*, Charles Dickens
Christopher Newman, *The American*, Henry James
Colonel Guy Mannering, *Guy Mannering*, Sir Walter Scott
Daniel Deronda, *Daniel Deronda*, George Eliot
David Balfour, *Catriona*, Robert Louis Stevenson
David Copperfield, *David Copperfield*, Charles Dickens
Dorian Gray, *The Picture of Dorian Gray*, Oscar Wilde
Dr. Tertius Lydgate, *Middlemarch*, George Eliot
Edward Waverley, *Waverley*, Sir Walter Scott
Edwin Reardon, *New Grub Street*, George Gissing
Fitzwilliam Darcy, *Pride and Prejudice*, Jane Austen
Gabriel John Utterson, *Dr. Jekyll and Mr. Hyde*, Robert Louis Stevenson
Gabriel Oak, *Far from the Madding Crowd*, Thomas Hardy
George Rouncewell, *Bleak House*, Charles Dickens
Gerard Eliason (also known as Brother Clement), *The Cloister and the Hearth*, Charles Reade
Godwin Peak, *Born in Exile*, George Gissing
Griffin, *The Invisible Man*, H. G. Wells
Harry Coningsby, *Coningsby*, Benjamin Disraeli
Harvey Cheyne, *Captains Courageous*, Rudyard Kipling
Heathcliff, *Wuthering Heights*, Emily Brontë
Henry Esmond, *Henry Esmond*, William Makepeace Thackeray
Henry Pelham, *Pelham*, Edward George Bulwer-Lytton
Jim, *Lord Jim*, Joseph Conrad
Jim Hawkins, *Treasure Island*, Robert Louis Stevenson
John Harmon, *Our Mutual Friend*, Charles Dickens
Jude Fawley, *Jude the Obscure*, Thomas Hardy
Kimball (Kim) O'Hara, *Kim*, Rudyard Kipling
Lambert Strether, *The Ambassadors*, Henry James

Ludwig Horace Holly, *She*, H. Rider Haggard
Marlow, *Heart of Darkness*, Joseph Conrad
Mowgli, *The Jungle Books*, Rudyard Kipling
Mr. Boldwood, *Far from the Madding Crowd*, Thomas Hardy
Mr. Lockwood, *Wuthering Heights*, Emily Brontë
Mr. Vane, *Lilith*, George MacDonald
Mr. Verloc, *The Secret Agent*, Joseph Conrad
Nostromo (also known as Gian' Battista), *Nostromo*, Joseph Conrad
Oliver Twist, *Oliver Twist*, Charles Dickens
Osborne Hamley, *Wives and Daughters*, Elizabeth Gaskell
Philip Hepburn, *Sylvia's Lovers*, Elizabeth Gaskell
Phineas Finn, *Phineas Finn*, Anthony Trollope
Pip (also known as Philip Pirrip), *Great Expectations*, Charles Dickens
Plantagenet Palliser, *The Prime Minister*, Anthony Trollope
Prendick, *The Island of Dr. Moreau*, H. G. Wells
Prince Amerigo, *The Golden Bowl*, Henry James
Razumov, *Under Western Eyes*, Joseph Conrad
Redmond Barry, *The Luck of Barry Lyndon*, William Makepeace Thackeray
Richard (Dick) Dewy, *Under the Greenwood Tree*, Thomas Hardy
Robert Audley, *Lady Audley's Secret*, Mary Elizabeth Braddon
Robert Walton, *Frankenstein*, Mary Shelley
Sergeant Cuff, *The Moonstone*, Wilkie Collins
Sherlock Holmes, *The Hound of the Baskervilles*, Sir Arthur Conan Doyle
Stephen Blackpool, *Hard Times*, Charles Dickens
Sydney Carton, *A Tale of Two Cities*, Charles Dickens
The Mad Hatter, *Alice's Adventures in Wonderland*, Lewis Carroll
The narrator (an unnamed scholar), *The Aspern Papers*, Henry James
The Reverend Josiah Crawley, *The Last Chronicle of Barset*, Anthony Trollope
The Reverend Micah Balwhidder, *Annals of the Parish*, John Galt
The Reverend Septimus Harding, *The Warden* and *Barchester Towers*, Anthony Trollope
The Time Traveller, *The Time Machine*, H. G. Wells
Thomas Gradgrind, *Hard Times*, Charles Dickens
Tom Brown, *Tom Brown's School Days*, Thomas Hughes
Victor Frankenstein, *Frankenstein*, Mary Shelley
Walter Hartright, *The Woman in White*, Wilkie Collins
Wilfred of Ivanhoe, *Ivanhoe*, Sir Walter Scott
William Crimsworth, *The Professor*, Charlotte Brontë

Female Friends or Associates of Protagonists

Adele Varens, *Jane Eyre*, Charlotte Brontë
Amy Edmonstone, *The Heir of Redclyffe*, Charlotte M. Yonge
Baroness Beatrix Bernstein, *Henry Esmond*, William Makepeace Thackeray
Becky, *A Little Princess*, Frances Hodgson Burnett
Biddy, *Great Expectations*, Charles Dickens
Caroline Jelly by (also known as Caddy), *Bleak House*, Charles Dickens
Carry Brattle, *The Vicar of Bullhampton*, Anthony Trollope
Catherine Arrowpoint, *Daniel Deronda*, George Eliot
Charlotte Lucas, *Pride and Prejudice*, Jane Austen
Clara Copperfield, *David Copperfield*, Charles Dickens
Daisy Miller, *Daisy Miller*, Henry James
Drusilla Clack, *The Moonstone*, Wilkie Collins
Drusilla Fawley, *Jude the Obscure*, Thomas Hardy
Edith Granger (later Edith Dombey), *Dombey and Son*, Charles Dickens
Effie Deans, *The Heart of Midlothian*, Sir Walter Scott
Eleanor Tilney, *Northanger Abbey*, Jane Austen
Elizabeth Lavenza Frankenstein, *Frankenstein*, Mary Shelley
Ellen (Nelly) Dean, *Wuthering Heights*, Emily Brontë
Ermengarde St. John, *A Little Princess*, Frances Hodgson Burnett
Fancy Day, *Under the Greenwood Tree*, Thomas Hardy
Gertrude Morel, *Sons and Lovers*, D. H. Lawrence
Gertrude Wentworth, *The Europeans*, Henry James
Ginevra Fanshawe, *Villette*, Charlotte Brontë
Grace Poole, *Jane Eyre*, Charlotte Brontë
Harriet Beadle (also known as Tattycoram), *Little Dorritt*, Charles Dickens
Harriet Smith, *Emma*, Jane Austen
Helen Burns, *Jane Eyre*, Charlotte Brontë
Helen Schlegel, *Howard's End*, E. M. Forster
Irene Heron Forsyte, *The Man of Property*, John Galsworthy
Isabella Knightley, *Emma*, Jane Austen
Isabella Linton, *Wuthering Heights*, Emily Brontë
Jane Bennet, *Pride and Prejudice*, Jane Austen
Jane Fairfax, *Emma*, Jane Austen
Julia Mannering, *Guy Mannering*, Sir Walter Scott
June Forsyte, *The Man of Property*, John Galsworthy

Lady Carbury, *The Way We Live Now*, Anthony Trollope
Lady Delacour, *Belinda*, Maria Edgeworth
Lady Honoria Dedlock, *Bleak House*, Charles Dickens
Lady Russell, *Persuasion*, Jane Austen
Laura Fairlie, *The Woman in White*, Wilkie Collins
Lottie Legh, *A Little Princess*, Frances Hodgson Burnett
Lucy Steele, *Sense and Sensibility*, Jane Austen
Lucy Westenra, *Dracula*, Bram Stoker
Lydia Bennet, *Pride and Prejudice*, Jane Austen
Madame Marie Max Goesler, *Phineas Finn* and *Phineas Redux*, Anthony Trollope
Maria Gostrey, *The Ambassadors*, Henry James
Maria Temple, *Jane Eyre*, Charlotte Brontë
Martha Sowerby, *The Secret Garden*, Frances Hodgson Burnett
Mary Garth, *Middlemarch*, George Eliot
Millicent Henning, *The Princess Casamassima*, Henry James
Mina Murray, *Dracula*, Bram Stoker
Miss Bates, *Emma*, Jane Austen
Miss Betsey Trotwood, *David Copperfield*, Charles Dickens
Miss Flite, *Bleak House*, Charles Dickens
Miss Marchmont, *Villette*, Charlotte Brontë
Molly, *Great Expectations*, Charles Dickens
Mrs. Bennet, *Pride and Prejudice*, Jane Austen
Mrs. Croft, *Persuasion*, Jane Austen
Mrs. Dashwood, *Sense and Sensibility*, Jane Austen
Mrs. Errol, *Little Lord Fauntleroy*, Frances Hodgson Burnett
Mrs. Flora Finching, *Little Dorritt*, Charles Dickens
Mrs. Gardiner, *Pride and Prejudice*, Jane Austen
Mrs. Georgiana Maria Gargery (Mrs. Joe), *Great Expectations*, Charles Dickens
Mrs. Jennings, *Sense and Sensibility*, Jane Austen
Mrs. Weston, *Emma*, Jane Austen
Mrs. Wilfer (Bella Wilfer's mother), *Our Mutual Friend*, Charles Dickens
Penelope (Pennyloaf) Candy, *The Nether World*, George Gissing
Polly Mary Home de Bassompierre, *Villette*, Charlotte Brontë
Rosalie Murray, *Agnes Grey*, Anne Brontë
Shirley Keeldar, *Shirley*, Charlotte Brontë
Sue Bridehead, *Jude the Obscure*, Thomas Hardy
Susan Sowerby, *The Secret Garden*, Frances Hodgson Burnett
The Beech Tree, *Phantastes*, George MacDonald

The Red Queen, *Through the Looking Glass*, Lewis Carroll
The White Queen, *Through the Looking Glass*, Lewis Carroll
Weena, *The Time Machine*, H. G. Wells
Winifred Dartie, *The Man of Property*, John Galsworthy

Male Friends or Associates of Protagonists

Abel Magwitch (also known as Mr. Provis), *Great Expectations*, Charles Dickens
Adam Verver, *The Golden Bowl*, Henry James
Admiral Croft, *Sense and Sensibility*, Jane Austen
Alan Breck Stewart (also known as Mr. Thomson), *Kidnapped*, Robert Louis Stevenson
Alan Campbell, *The Picture of Dorian Gray*, Oscar Wilde
Angel Clare, *Tess of the d'Urbervilles*, Thomas Hardy
Arthur Holmwood, *Dracula*, Bram Stoker
Austin Ruthyn (Maud Ruthyn's father), *Uncle Silas*, Joseph Sheridan Le Fanu
Bagheera, *The Jungle Books*, Rudyard Kipling
Barkis, *David Copperfield*, Charles Dickens
Basil Hallward, *The Picture of Dorian Gray*, Oscar Wilde
Ben Weatherstaff, *The Secret Garden*, Frances Hodgson Burnett
Bob Jakin, *The Mill on the Floss*, George Eliot
Captain Benwick, *Persuasion*, Jane Austen
Captain William Dobbin, *Vanity Fair*, William Makepeace Thackeray
Chadwick (Chad) Newsome, *The Ambassadors*, Henry James
Colin Craven, *The Secret Garden*, Frances Hodgson Burnett
Colonel Brandon, *Sense and Sensibility*, Jane Austen
Dickon Sowerby, *The Secret Garden*, Frances Hodgson Burnett
Diggory Venn, *The Return of the Native*, Thomas Hardy
Disko Troop, *Captains Courageous*, Rudyard Kipling
Dolly Longstaffe, *The Way We Live Now*, Anthony Trollope
Dr. John Watson, *The Hound of the Baskervilles*, Sir Arthur Conan Doyle
Dr. Seward, *Dracula*, Bram Stoker
Dr. Van Helsing, *Dracula*, Bram Stoker
Edmund Bertram, *Mansfield Park*, Jane Austen
Edward (Teddy) Ponderevo, *Tono-Bungay*, H. G. Wells
Edward Rochester, *Jane Eyre*, Charlotte Brontë
Edward Weston, *Emma*, Jane Austen

Ezra Jennings, *The Moonstone*, Wilkie Collins
Ezra Lapidoth (also known as Mordecai), *Daniel Deronda*, George Eliot
Felix Young, *The Europeans*, Henry James
Frank Churchill, *Emma*, Jane Austen
Freddy Honeychurch, *A Room with a View*, E. M. Forster
Frederick Lawrence, *The Tenant of Wildfell Hall*
Frederick Winterbourne, *Daisy Miller*, Henry James
Fred Vincy, *Middlemarch*, George Eliot
Gabriel Betteredge, *The Moonstone*, Wilkie Collins
George Arthur, *Tom Brown's Schooldays*, Thomas Hughes
George Emerson, *A Room with a View*, E. M. Forster
George Knightley, *Emma*, Jane Austen
George Osborne, *Vanity Fair*, William Makepeace Thackeray
George Ponderevo, *Tono-Bungay*, H. G. Wells
Giovanelli, *Daisy Miller*, Henry James
Henry Tilney, *Northanger Abbey*, Jane Austen
Henry Wilcox, *Howard's End*, E. M. Forster
Henry Woodhouse (Emma's father), *Emma*, Jane Austen
Herbert Pocket, *Great Expectations*, Charles Dickens
James Steerforth, *David Copperfield*, Charles Dickens
Jarvis Lorry, *A Tale of Two Cities*, Charles Dickens
Jem Wilson, *Mary Barton*, Elizabeth Gaskell
Joe Gargery, *Great Expectations*, Charles Dickens
John Grey, *Can You Forgive Her?*, Anthony Trollope
John Jarndyce, *Bleak House*, Charles Dickens
John Knightley, *Emma*, Jane Austen
John Thornton, *North and South*, Elizabeth Gaskell
John Wemmick, *Great Expectations*, Charles Dickens
Leonard Bast, *Howard's End*, E. M. Forster
Little Father Time, *Jude the Obscure*, Thomas Hardy
Lord Dorincourt, *Little Lord Fauntleroy*, Frances Hodgson Burnett
Lord Henry Wotton, *The Picture of Dorian Gray*, Oscar Wilde
Lord John Roxton, *The Lost World*, Sir Arthur Conan Doyle
Monsieur Paul Emanuel, *Villette*, Charlotte Brontë
Morris Townsend, *Washington Square*, Henry James
Mr. Bennet, *Pride and Prejudice*, Jane Austen
Mr. Bingley, *Pride and Prejudice*, Jane Austen
Mr. Cheyne, *Captains Courageous*, Rudyard Kipling
Mr. Emerson (George Emerson's father), *a Room with a View*, E. M. Forster
Mr. Hunsden, *The Professor*, Charlotte Brontë
Mr. Jaggers, *Great Expectations*, Charles Dickens

Mr. Weston, *Emma*, Jane Austen
Mr. Wilkins Micawber, *David Copperfield*, Charles Dickens
Nicholas Higgins, *North and South*, Elizabeth Gaskell
Ozias Midwinter, *Armadale*, Wilkie Collins
Philip Bossiney, *The Man of Property*, John Galsworthy
Ram Dass, *A Little Princess*, Frances Hodgson Burnett
Richard Carstone, *Bleak House*, Charles Dickens
Richard Phillotson, *Jude the Obscure*, Thomas Hardy
Robert Martin, *Emma*, Jane Austen
Sam Weller, *The Pickwick Papers*, Charles Dickens
Shere Khan, *The Jungle Books*, Rudyard Kipling
Sir Henry Curtis, *King Solomon's Mines*, H. Rider Haggard
Sir Peregrine Orme, *Orley Farm*, Anthony Trollope
St. John Rivers, *Jane Eyre*, Charlotte Brontë
Stephen Guest, *The Mill on the Floss*, George Eliot
Stewart Ansell, *The Longest Journey*, E. M. Forster
The Cheshire Cat, *Alice's Adventures in Wonderland*, Lewis Carroll
The English Professor, *Under Western Eyes*, Joseph Conrad
The Red Lama, *Kim*, Rudyard Kipling
The Reverend Theophilus Grantly, *Barchester Towers*, Anthony Trollope
The White King, *Through the Looking Glass*, Lewis Carroll
The White Knight, *Through the Looking Glass*, Lewis Carroll
Umbopa, *King Solomon's Mines*, H. Rider Haggard
William Dorrit (Amy Dorrit's father), *Little Dorrit*, Charles Dickens

Female Antagonists

Augusta Elton, *Emma*, Jane Austen
Bertha Rochester, *Jane Eyre*, Charlotte Brontë
Caroline Bingley, *Pride and Prejudice*, Jane Austen
Fanny Dashwood, *Sense and Sensibility*, Jane Austen
Gagool, *King Solomon's Mines*, H. Rider Haggard
Lady Bertram, *Mansfield Park*, Jane Austen
Lady Catherine de Bourgh, *Pride and Prejudice*, Jane Austen
La Signora Madeline Vesey Neroni, *Barchester Towers*, Anthony Trollope
Lydia Gwilt, *Armadale*, Wilkie Collins
Madame Beck, *Villette*, Charlotte Brontë
Madame Merle, *Portrait of a Lady*, Henry James
Madame Thérèse Defarge, *A Tale of Two Cities*, Henry James
Mary Crawford, *Mansfield Park*, Jane Austen

Maria Minchin, *A Little Princess*, Frances Hodgson Burnett
Miss Havisham, *Great Expectations*, Charles Dickens
Mrs. Clay, *Persuasion*, Jane Austen
Mrs. Norris, *Mansfield Park*, Jane Austen
Mrs. Proudie, *Barchester Towers*, Anthony Trollope
Mrs. Reed, *Jane Eyre*, Charlotte Brontë
Rosa Dartle, *David Copperfield*, Charles Dickens
She (also know as She-Who-Must-Be-Obeyed), *She*, H. Rider Haggard
The Queen of Hearts, *Alice's Adventures in Wonderland*, Lewis Carroll
Winifred Hurtle, *The Way We Live Now*, Anthony Trollope

Male Antagonists

Alec d'Urberville, *Tess of the d'Urbervilles*, Thomas Hardy
Austin Sloper, *Washington Square*, Henry James
Bradley Headstone, *Our Mutual Friend*, Charles Dickens
Burgo Fitzgerald, *Can You Forgive Her?*, Anthony Trollope
Cecil Vyse, *A Room with a View*, E. M. Forster
Charles Wilcox, *Howard's End*, E. M. Forster
Count Dracula, *Dracula*, Bram Stoker
Count Fosco, *The Woman in White*, Wilkie Collins
Daniel Quilp, *The Old Curiosity Shop*, Charles Dickens
District Manager, *Heart of Darkness*, Joseph Conrad
Dolge Orlick, *Great Expectations*, Charles Dickens
Ebenezer Balfour (David Balfour's uncle), *Kidnapped*, Robert Louis Stevenson
Edward Hyde, *Dr. Jekyll and Mr. Hyde*, Robert Louis Stevenson
Fagin, *Oliver Twist*, Charles Dickens
Ferdinand Lopez, *The Prime Minister*, Anthony Trollope
Frederick Fairlie, *The Woman in White*, Wilkie Collins
Geordie Robertson (also known as George Staunton), *The Heart of Midlothian*, Sir Walter Scott
George Vavasor, *Can You Forgive Her?*, Anthony Trollope
Gerald Scales, *The Old Wives' Tale*, Arnold Bennett
Godfrey Ablewhite, *The Moonstone*, Wilkie Collins
James Durie, *The Master of Ballantrae*, Robert Louis Stevenson
John Chester, *Barnaby Rudge*, Charles Dickens
John Dashwood, *Sense and Sensibility*, Jane Austen
Kurtz, *Heart of Darkness*, Joseph Conrad
Long John Silver, *Treasure Island*, Robert Louis Stevenson
Mr. Brocklehurst, *Jane Eyre*, Charlotte Brontë

Mr. Camperdown, *The Eustace Diamonds*, Anthony Trollope
Mr. Wickham, *Pride and Prejudice*, Jane Austen
Nicholas Sowerby, *Framley Parsonage*, Anthony Trollope
Reverend Jeremiah Maguire, *Miss Mackenzie*, Anthony Trollope
Reverend Philip Elton, *Emma*, Jane Austen
Robert Wringham Colwan, *Private Memoirs and Confessions of a Justified Sinner*, James Hogg
Silas Wegg, *Our Mutual Friend*, Charles Dickens
Sir Brian de Bois-Guilbert, *Ivanhoe*, Sir Walter Scott
Sir Thomas Bertram, *Mansfield Park*, Jane Austen
Sir Willoughby Patterne, *The Egoist*, George Meredith
Stephen Hargraves, *Aurora Floyd*, Mary Elizabeth Braddon
The Monster, *Frankenstein*, Mary Shelley
The Reverend Obadiah Slope, *Barchester Towers*, Anthony Trollope
Tito Melema, *Romola*, George Eliot
Wackford Squeers, Jr., *Nicholas Nickelby*, Charles Dickens
William Elliot, *Persuasion*, Jane Austen

Female Friends or Associates of Antagonists

Anne Catherick, *The Woman in White*, Wilkie Collins
Fanny Robin, *Far from the Madding Crowd*, Thomas Hardy
Jacky Bast, *Howard's End*, E. M. Forster
Laura Edmonstone, *The Heir of Redclyffe*, Charlotte Yonge
Marie Melmott, *The Way We Live Now*, Anthony Trollope
Rachel, *Hard Times*, Charles Dickens
Sairey Gamp, *Martin Chuzzlewit*, Charles Dickens
Sophronia Lammle, *Our Mutual Friend*, Charles Dickens
The Duchess, *Alice's Adventures in Wonderland*, Lewis Carroll

Male Friends or Associates of Antagonists

Captain Frederick Tilney, *Northanger Abbey*, Jane Austen
James Vane, *The Picture of Dorian Gray*, Oscar Wilde
Linton Heathcliff, *Wuthering Heights*, Emily Brontë
Mr. Mason, *Jane Eyre*, Charlotte Brontë
Mr. Venus, *Our Mutual Friend*, Charles Dickens
Robert Acton, *The Europeans*, Henry James
Russian traveler, *Heart of Darkness*, Joseph Conrad
The Caterpillar, *Alice's Adventures in Wonderland*, Lewis Carroll
The King of Hearts, *Alice's Adventures in Wonderland*, Lewis Carroll

Female Characters Not Assigned to Agonistic Roles

(characters who received only one coding and no assigned role or multiple codings and a tie vote on role assignment; the scores of these characters are included in correlation figures)

Arabella Donn, *Jude the Obscure*, Thomas Hardy
Blanche Ingram, *Jane Eyre*, Charlotte Brontë
Charlotte Stant, *The Golden Bowl*, Henry James
Clare Hyacinth Kirkpatrick Gibson, *Wives and Daughters*, Elizabeth Gaskell
Cynthia Kirkpatrick, *Wives and Daughters*, Elizabeth Gaskell
Estella, *Great Expectations*, Charles Dickens
Flora MacIvor, *Waverly*, Sir Walter Scott
Hester (Hetty) Sorrel, *Adam Bede*, George Eliot
Isabella Thorpe, *Northanger Abbey*, Jane Austen
Justine Moritz, *Frankenstein*, Mary Shelley
Kate Croy, *The Wings of the Dove*, Henry James
Kurtz's fiancée, *Heart of Darkness*, Joseph Conrad
Lizzie Eustace, *The Eustace Diamonds*, Anthony Trollope
Louisa Gradgrind, *Hard Times*, Charles Dickens
Lucie Manette, *A Tale of Two Cities*, Charles Dickens
Lucy Graham, *Lady Audley's Secret*, Mary Elizabeth Braddon
Mrs. Elinor Cadwallader, *Middlemarch*, George Eliot
Mrs. Herriton, *Where Angels Fear to Tread*, E. M. Forster
Mrs. Sparsit, *Hard Times*, Charles Dickens
Olive Chancellor, *The Bostonians*, Henry James
Rosamond Vincy Lydgate, *Middlemarch*, George Eliot
Sibyl Vane, *The Picture of Dorian Gray*, Oscar Wilde

Male Characters Not Assigned to Agonistic Roles

(characters who received only one coding and no assigned role or multiple codings and a tie vote on role assignment; the scores of these characters are included in correlation figures)

Archibald Craven, *The Secret Garden*, Frances Hodgson Burnett
Arthur Huntingdon, *The Tenant of Wildfell Hall*, Anne Brontë
Bill Sikes, *Oliver Twist*, Charles Dickens
Captain Wentworth, *Persuasion*, Jane Austen
Dr. Henry Jekyll, *Dr. Jekyll and Mr. Hyde*, Robert Louis Stevenson

Edgar Linton, *Wuthering Heights*, Emily Brontë
Festus Derriman, *The Trumpet Major*, Thomas Hardy
George Talboys, *Lady Audley's Secret*, Mary Elizabeth Braddon
Gilbert Markham, *The Tenant of Wildfell Hall*, Anne Brontë
Hareton Earnshaw, *Wuthering Heights*, Emily Brontë
Harold Skimpole, *Bleak House*, Charles Dickens
Humpty Dumpty, *Through the Looking Glass*, Lewis Carroll
Inspector Bucket, *Bleak House*, Charles Dickens
Jo, *Bleak House*, Charles Dickens
John Barton, *Mary Barton*, Elizabeth Gaskell
John Willoughby, *Sense and Sensibility*, Jane Austen
Jonathan Harker, *Dracula*, Bram Stoker
Joseph, *Wuthering Heights*, Emily Brontë
Little Nell's grandfather, *The Old Curiosity Shop*, Charles Dickens
Mr. Alfred Jingle, *The Pickwick Papers*, Charles Dickens
Mr. Redgauntlet, *Redgauntlet*, Sir Walter Scott
Rawdon Crawley, *Vanity Fair*, William Makepeace Thackeray
Richard Swiveller, *The Old Curiosity Shop*, Charles Dickens
Richard the Crookback, Duke of York, *The Black Arrow*, Robert Louis Stevenson
Sir Walter Elliot, *Persuasion*, Jane Austen
Soames Forsyte, *The Man of Property*, John Galsworthy
The March Hare, *Alice's Adventures in Wonderland*, Lewis Carroll
The White Rabbit, *Alice's Adventures in Wonderland*, Lewis Carroll
Tom Tulliver, *The Mill on the Floss*, George Eliot
Tweedledum/Tweedledee, *Through the Looking Glass*, Lewis Carroll
William Collins, *Pride and Prejudice*, Jane Austen

Appendix 3

The Distribution of Characters in Sets

Codings per Character

Out of the 1,470 protocols completed on the website, 206 characters received multiple codings, and a total of 435 characters were coded (not counting the six from *The Mayor of Casterbridge*). The distribution of codings for individual characters is displayed in table A.1:

A little over half of the characters (53 percent) received only one coding. A little over one-third (36 percent) received between two and six codings, and 48 characters (11 percent) received seven or more codings.

Assigning Multiply Coded Characters to Sets

Because of the characters who were coded multiple times, the total number of characters (435) is only about 30 percent the total number of protocols that were completed (1,470). Respondents were asked to assign characters to agonistic roles (protagonist, antagonist, or friend or associate of protagonist or antagonist). For role assignments, respondents were also given the option of checking "I don't remember" or "other." For 22 characters who received only one coding (about 10 percent of the 229 singly coded characters), the respondents checked "other" and thus declined to assign the character to a role. Those 22 characters are not included in the character sets. For characters who received codings from more than one respondent, we assigned roles on the basis of majority vote. If a character received a tie vote—for instance, two respondents identified the character as a protagonist, and two as a good minor character—that character was not assigned a role. From among the 206 characters who received multiple codings, 29 characters (14

Table A.1 Distribution of codings among characters

Number of codings per character	Number of characters
1	229
2	86
3–6	72
7–19	38
20–35	7
36–81	3

percent) received tie votes, and they were not included in the character sets. For instance, two respondents filled out questionnaires on Lucy Manette from Dickens' *A Tale of Two Cities*. One respondent identified her as a protagonist and one as the friend or associate of a protagonist. Since the vote was a tie, she was not assigned to a character set. In comparison, Miss Havisham from Dickens' *Great Expectations*, received 9 codings. Four respondents identified her as an antagonist, three as the friend or associate of a protagonist, one as a protagonist, and one as a friend or an associate of an antagonist. The number of respondents identifying her as an antagonist was greater than the number identifying her in any other role, and that is the character set to which she was assigned. (Two characters each received only two votes, both "other," and they also were not assigned to character sets.)

Out of the total of 435 characters who were coded, 53 characters (12 percent) were not included in character sets—the 22 characters who were singly coded and not assigned a role, the two characters who received two "other" codings, and the 29 characters who tied in role assignments. The remaining 382 characters (88 percent of 435) were assigned to character sets. (For a listing of the characters in each character set, see appendix 2.)

The Number of Characters in Each Category of Analysis

In any given category of analysis—motives, for example, or attractiveness—cases can be missing because respondents check "I don't remember" to a given question. The number of characters in the character sets thus varies from category to category. For mate selection, the numbers vary most, since not all characters are identified as seeking or finding mates. Table A.2 gives the total numbers of characters assigned to character roles in each category of analysis.

Table A.2 Numbers of characters within each category of analysis

Category of analysis	Number of characters for whom data was collected
Salience	382
Personality Factors	382
Emotional Response Factors	381
Motive Factors	377
Attractiveness	357
Age group	354
Long-Term Mate-Selection Factors	181
Short-Term Mate-Selection Factors	105

Table A.3 Number and percentage of characters in the agonistic character sets, and the unassigned characters

Character sets	Number of characters	Percentage of total of 435 characters
Good minor males	94	22%
Good minor females	77	18%
Male protagonists	70	16%
Female protagonists	58	13%
Unassigned Characters	53	12%
Male antagonists	42	10%
Female antagonists	23	5%
Bad minor females	9	2%
Bad minor males	9	2%

The Number and Percentage of Characters in the Character Sets

Each of the three character set pairs (male/female, good/bad, major/minor) divides the total number of 382 characters into two parts. In each pair, the proportions of the two parts are somewhat different. There are 215 males and 167 females; 299 good characters and 83 bad characters; and 193 major and 189 minor characters. Males constitute 56 percent and females 44 percent of the total population of characters. Good characters constitute 78 percent and bad characters 22 percent. Major characters constitute 51 percent and minor characters 49 percent.

The six variables in these three pairs combine in eight different ways to constitute character sets. (See table A.3.)

Minor character sets are both the largest and the smallest sets. The good minor males and good minor females together constitute nearly half of all the characters. But the bad minor males and bad minor females add only another 4 percent to that proportion. Among the major characters, the male protagonists and male antagonists together constitute more than a quarter of the total population. The female protagonists and antagonists together constitute a little less than a one-fifth of the total population.

The good males together (major and minor) form 38 percent of the total population. The good females together form 31 percent. The bad males form 12 percent, and the bad females 7 percent. The protagonists (males and females together) form 29 percent and the antagonists 15 percent. The characters not assigned to roles form 12 percent of the total population.

These proportions are not necessarily representative of the proportions within the larger population of characters in the novels. Indeed, it is not at all probable that they are representative. Our respondents were less likely to take the time and trouble to fill out questionnaires on bad major characters than on good major characters, and were least likely to take the time and trouble to fill out questionnaires on bad minor characters. The actual proportions of the characters who could reasonably be assigned to the eight character sets is an issue that this study was not designed to discover. We await with interest the results of any study that can provide this information. Meanwhile, any possible disproportionate representation in the character sets would have

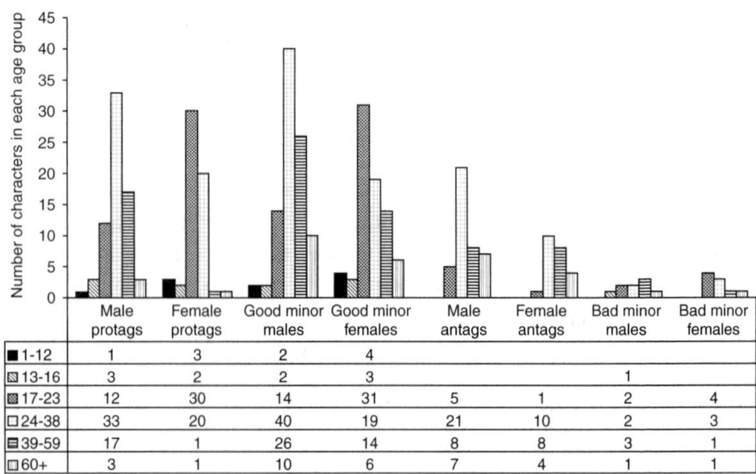

	Male protags	Female protags	Good minor males	Good minor females	Male antags	Female antags	Bad minor males	Bad minor females
1-12	1	3	2	4				
13-16	3	2	2	3			1	
17-23	12	30	14	31	5	1	2	4
24-38	33	20	40	19	21	10	2	3
39-59	17	1	26	14	8	8	3	1
60+	3	1	10	6	7	4	1	1

Figure A.1 Numbers of characters in each agonistic set in each age group.

Table A.4 48 Characters with seven or more codings each

# of Codings	Name	Role	Novel	Author
81	Elizabeth Bennet	protag	*Pride and Prejudice*	Jane Austen
74	Emma Woodhouse	protag	*Emma*	Jane Austen
68	Jane Eyre	protag	*Jane Eyre*	Charlotte Brontë
35	Edward Rochester	good minor	*Jane Eyre*	Charlotte Brontë
33	Anne Elliot	protag	*Persuasion*	Jane Austen
30	Fitzwilliam Darcy	protag	*Pride and Prejudice*	Jane Austen
26	Dorian Gray	protag	*The Picture of Dorian Gray*	Oscar Wilde
26	Heathcliff	protag	*Wuthering Heights*	Emily Brontë
21	Lucy Snowe	protag	*Villette*	Charlotte Brontë
20	Dorothea Brooke	protag	*Middlemarch*	George Eliot
19	Catherine Earnshaw	protag	*Wuthering Heights*	Emily Brontë
18	Alice	protag	*Alice's Adventures in Wonderland* and *Through the Looking Glass*	Lewis Carroll
18	Fanny Price	protag	*Mansfield Park*	Jane Austen
18	Marlow	protag	*Heart of Darkness*	Joseph Conrad
17	Tess Durbeyfield	protag	*Tess of the d'Urbervilles*	Thomas Hardy
17	The Monster	antag	*Frankenstein*	Mary Shelley
15	George Knightley	good minor	*Emma*	Jane Austen
12	Count Dracula	antag	*Dracula*	Bram Stoker
12	Mary Lennox	protag	*The Secret Garden*	Frances H. Burnett
11	Lucy Graham	not assigned	*Lady Audley's Secret*	Mary Braddon
11	St. John Rivers	good minor	*Jane Eyre*	Charlotte Brontë
11	Mr. Collins	not assigned	*Pride and Prejudice*	Jane Austen
10	Catherine Morland	protag	*Northanger Abbey*	Jane Austen
10	Isabel Archer	protag	*Portrait of a Lady*	Henry James

Continued

Table A.4 Continued

# of Codings	Name	Role	Novel	Author
10	Jane Fairfax	good minor	*Emma*	Jane Austen
9	Jane Bennet	good minor	*Pride and Prejudice*	Jane Austen
9	Jude Fawley	protag	*Jude the Obscure*	Thomas Hardy
9	Miss Havisham	antag	*Great Expectations*	Charles Dickens
9	Pip	protag	*Great Expectations*	Charles Dickens
9	Sara Crewe	protag	*A Little Princess*	Frances H. Burnett
9	Victor Frankenstein	protag	*Frankenstein*	Mary Shelley
8	Captain Wentworth	not assigned	*Persuasion*	Jane Austen
8	Helen Graham	protag	*The Tenant of Wildfell Hall*	Anne Brontë
8	Henry Woodhouse	good minor	*Emma*	Jane Austen
8	Lucy Honeychurch	protag	*A Room with a View*	E. M. Forster
8	Becky Sharp	protag	*Vanity Fair*	William Thackeray
7	Augusta Elton	antag	*Emma*	Jane Austen
7	Bertha Rochester	antag	*Jane Eyre*	Charlotte Brontë
7	Charlotte Lucas	good minor	*Pride and Prejudice*	Jane Austen
7	Kurtz	antag	*Heart of Darkness*	Joseph Conrad
7	Lord Henry Wotton	good minor	*The Picture of Dorian Gray*	Oscar Wilde
7	Paul Emmanuel	good minor	*Villette*	Charlotte Brontë
7	Mr. Bennet	good minor	*Pride and Prejudice*	Jane Austen
7	Mrs. Norris	antag	*Mansfield Park*	Jane Austen
7	Rosamond Vincy	not assigned	*Middlemarch*	George Eliot
7	Sherlock Holmes	protag	*Hound of the Baskervilles*	Arthur C. Doyle
7	The Cheshire Cat	good minor	*Alice's Adventures in Wonderland*	Lewis Carroll

no bearing on either the internal constitution of the sets themselves or the conceptual relations among them.

The Distribution of Characters across Age Groups

For the distribution of characters across age groups, see figure A.1. Protagonists are on average younger than antagonists. Female protagonists cluster in the nubile age groups (17–38). Male protagonists are on average older than female protagonists.

The Most Frequently Coded Characters

We average the scores of characters who receive multiple codings. This principle of averaging is at the heart of all descriptive and inferential statistics. Most of the characters who receive only one or two scores receive scores that, in our own judgment, look perfectly sensible. Inevitably, though, as in all such statistical studies, there are a few "outliers"—scores that most reasonable people would not consider reasonable. As we explain in chapter 1, after seven codings, increasing the number of coders does little to increase the reliability of results. For the purposes of illustration, we have in most cases used characters from the group of 48 characters who received seven or more codings. See table A.4.

Among the 48 most frequently coded characters, 17 are from novels by Jane Austen—with six each for *Pride and Prejudice* and *Emma*. Charlotte Brontë follows Austen in popularity, as a distant second, with the next two most frequently coded characters, and with a total of six characters from two novels (*Jane Eyre* and *Villette*). From novels by all three Brontë sisters together, there are nine characters.

Appendix 4

Notes on Statistical Procedures

For readers from the humanities who wish a better understanding of the statistical techniques used in this study, we here provide brief explanations of statistical significance, correlation, factor analysis, and *t*-tests and ANOVA (analysis of variance). We also give a more detailed account of the procedures that we use in part III to compare male and female characters by male and female authors.

Statistical Significance

Tests for statistically significant differences determine the level of probability that a difference in scores could arise by chance as a result of sampling error—that is, as a result of an unrepresentative distribution within a sample taken from a whole population. Our data are samples in two separate respects. First, the 435 characters for whom protocols were completed represent a sample of all the characters in all the canonical novels written in this period. The second respect in which our data constitutes a sample is that the respondents who completed questionnaires represent a sample of all potential respondents.

Significance levels are by convention registered at the .05 and .01 levels. These are known as alpha levels. An alpha level of $p < .05$ means that there is less than a 5 percent chance that the observed difference in scores between two sets arose as a result of unrepresentative sampling. (The letter "*p*" stands for "probability.") A significance level of $p < .01$ means that there is less than a 1 percent chance that the observed difference in scores between two sets arose as a result of unrepresentative sampling

Three components enter into testing significance levels: sample size, variability, and the magnitude of the difference in scores. The larger the sample, the smaller the variability within each group, and the larger the difference between means, the easier it is to detect statistically significant differences in scores. With sufficiently large samples, if within-group variability is not too great, even relatively slight differences in scores can be determined to be statistically significant. So also, with a sufficiently large difference in scores, even relatively small samples can be determined to display statistically significant differences. In our data, the two character sets that have the smallest number of cases are bad minor males and bad minor females (N = nine each). Despite the relatively small number of characters in these sets, in those categories in which these two sets display extreme scores, the sets display statistically significant differences from other sets.

Significance Testing in Character Sets Created from Different Numbers of Variables

Among the three character set pairs (males/females, good/bad, major/minor), significance levels can be calculated for differences between the pairs in each paired set: all male versus all female characters, all good versus all bad characters, and all major versus all minor characters. Among the agonistic character sets constituted by combinations of two or three of these variables (Sex, Valence, Salience), significance levels can be calculated only for contrasts between sets differentiated by one or two of the three variables that constitute the character sets. Contrasts involving all three variables cannot be calculated. We can for instance calculate significance levels for differences in scores between good males and bad males, and between good minor males and bad major males, but we cannot calculate significance levels for differences between good minor males and bad major females—sets differentiated by all three variables. The fact that significance levels cannot be calculated for sets differentiated by three variables does not, of course, mean that those differences are necessarily slight or negligible. The differences are often large and striking. Even in cases in which significance levels can be calculated but differences do not quite reach statistical significance, differences between sets can indicate a trend or be part of a pattern that is worth noting.

The Scoring System for Character Success

The first question—does the character achieve his or her goals—had a four-point scale for answers (yes, completely; mostly; a little; not at all). The second question (Root For) had three possible responses: yes, no, and I do not care. To convert the answers on the second question to a scale, we accorded one point to "no," two points to "I do not care," and three points to "yes." The converted scale thus constitutes a series from active hostility, through indifference, to positive good wishes. The third question—whether the character's success or failure is a main feature in the outcome of the novel—has a simple yes and no answer. For characters who received multiple codings, though, variations in response produce averaged results with decimal fractions running from one to two (for instance, 1.2, 1.5, 1.7). So, even this simple yes/no answer could be converted into a standardized score—a score for all characters with an average point of zero.

Correlation

The Pearson correlation coefficient, abbreviated with the letter r, is a number that expresses how strongly two sets of scores are related to each other. A positive correlation indicates that high scores on one attribute tend to accompany high scores on a second attribute, average scores tend to go with average scores, and low scores tend to be associated with low scores. Positive correlations can range from 0 to 1, where $r = 0$ indicates absolutely no relation between the sets of scores, and $r = 1$ means the one set of scores is perfectly predictable from the other. To give an example, in our data set, the desire for wealth correlates strongly with the desire for power ($r = .52$).

In typical behavioral research, two variables almost never correlate higher than .60. As a rule of thumb, researchers regard correlations of .10 or lower as weak, correlations around .30 as moderate, and correlations greater than .50 as strong.

Negative correlations also describe how closely two sets of scores are related, but in reverse directions. That is, a negative correlation indicates that high scores on one measure tend to be associated with low scores on a second measure. For example, in our study the motive to help nonrelatives correlated –.36 with the motive for wealth and –.30 with the motive for power. These moderate negative correlations indicate that characters judged to be strongly motivated by a need to help nonrelatives are also judged to have little motivation for wealth and power. Or, conversely, characters judged to have little interest in helping nonrelatives are also judged to be motivated by a relatively high need for wealth and power. A negative correlation of –.30 reflects an association between two sets of scores that is just as strong as a positive correlation of .30. The only differences is that negative correlations describe relations where high scores are associated with low scores, while positive correlations indicate that high scores are associated with high scores on a second measure.

The concept of statistical significance applies to correlation coefficients just as it applies to the differences between means. Statistical significance depends on sample size and the magnitude of the correlation. A statistically significant correlation is any correlation that we are fairly confident is not zero. More precisely, a correlation of $r = .30$, $p < .05$ means that there is less than a 5 percent chance that a correlation of this magnitude based on this sample size arose as a result of unrepresentative sampling. The stronger the correlation (in either a positive or negative direction) and the larger the sample, the more likely it will be statistically significant.

See figure A.2 for a graph that illustrates the idea of a positive correlation. It shows the scores for ten hypothetical characters on two variables, motive for wealth and motive for power.

You will note that with one exception, characters who are highly motivated by wealth are also highly motivated by power, those with low motivation for wealth have low motivation for power, and those intermediate on one motive are also intermediate on the other. The one exception to the trend is a character with a wealth motive of

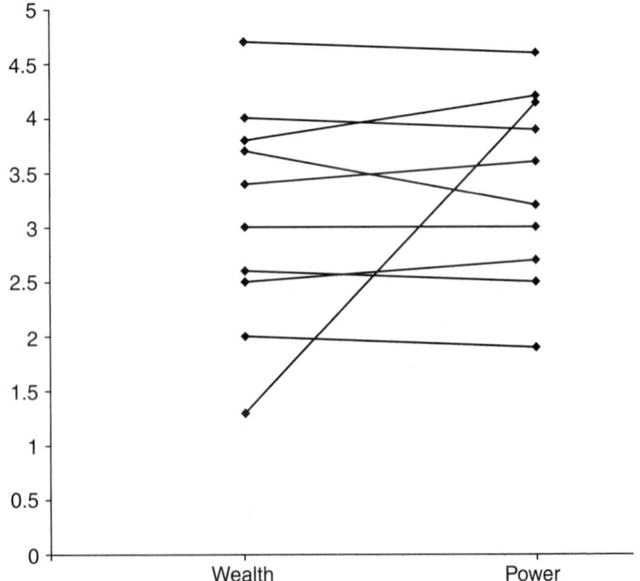

Figure A.2 A positive correlation between wealth and power.

only 1.3 but a power motive of 4.15. Without this individual, the correlation between the two motives would be r = .96. With this individual, the correlation is $r = .52$, still a strong trend, but not the nearly perfect correlation for the other nine individuals. (To recall, the actual correlation between Wealth and Power in the full set of data is $r = .52$).

Factor Analysis

Factor analysis is an extension of correlation. Instead of computing the association between two sets of scores, we compute associations among many sets of scores. The purpose of factor analysis is to identify clusters of variables that correlate with each other but that do not correlate with the other variables in the study. One purpose of factor analysis is to reduce a large number of variables to a smaller set of general themes in order to simplify subsequent analyses. Each cluster of correlated variables that defines a common theme is called a factor. In our study, for example, characters who were judged to value power in a prospective mate were also judged to value prestige and wealth, but these three highly correlated mate-selection preferences were unrelated to the value placed on reliability, kindness, intelligence, and physical attractiveness. Hence, power, prestige, and wealth defined a factor describing the importance placed on extrinsic attributes in a prospective mate. Similarly, the judgments of the importance of reliability, kindness, and intelligence correlated with each other, but not the other variables, defining a second factor, the importance placed on intrinsic qualities in a prospective mate. Physical attractiveness stood alone to define a third factor unrelated to the first two.

We summarize the factor structure of a set of variables by showing what are called the *factor loadings* of each variable on each factor. Factor loadings essentially represent the correlation between a variable and the factors. In the factor tables included in appendix 5, the relatively large loadings in each column are shown in boldface; these define the common theme of each factor.

t-tests and ANOVA

In our introduction to statistics in part II, we alluded to the use of *t*-tests and ANOVA (analysis of variance). These are the statistical tests that are used when we compare the average scores of two or more groups to see if they are significantly different, or when we would like to determine whether one group differs substantially from a given value. The *t*-test is actually a special case of ANOVA, sometimes used when we compare only two groups. Using either a *t*-test or ANOVA on the same pair of groups will yield equivalent results, so the choice of which to use is simply a matter of personal preference. For comparing more than two groups, ANOVA must be used. And, if we are comparing groups on more than one variable simultaneously (e.g., comparing character sets on five personality traits), we use a version of ANOVA called MANOVA, which stands for multivariate analysis of variance. If MANOVA showed that our character sets differ significantly in overall personality, we would then follow up by conducting separate, individual ANOVAs to see on which specific personality traits they differ. Because the *t*-test represents a special case of ANOVA, and significant MANOVAs are normally followed by ANOVAs, our discussion of testing group differences will focus on ANOVA.

ANOVA, or analysis of variance, may sound like an odd label for testing differences between group means (averages). Why don't we call it analysis of averages? The label is based on the idea that when we are testing groups to see if they differ, we need to consider both the variation within each group as well as the variation (differences) between groups. Given a specific difference between two group averages, whether or not we conclude that this difference is significant depends upon whether the variation *within* each group is small or large. If the variation within each group is small, that means that the scores of most individuals lie near the mean, such that scores between groups do not overlap much. But if the variation within each group is large, scores are more spread out and more likely to overlap between groups. The next two figures show two hypothetical scenarios where the difference between the average scores for male and female characters is exactly the same, but the within-group variances differ. See figure A.3 for a scenario in which the variation within groups is small. In this scenario you can see a relatively clear-cut difference between the groups because they do not overlap. In figure A.4, you can see that the large variation within groups causes an overlap between male and female scores, resulting in a less clear-cut difference between groups, despite the fact that the difference between the means is exactly the same as in the first scenario (1.25 versus 3.75).

To calculate whether the differences between two groups is statistically significant, ANOVA essentially looks at the ratio of the variance between groups (the difference between means) to the total variance within groups. If this ratio, called the *F* statistic, is sufficiently large (given the total sample size and the size of each group), then the difference between groups is said to be statistically significant for a

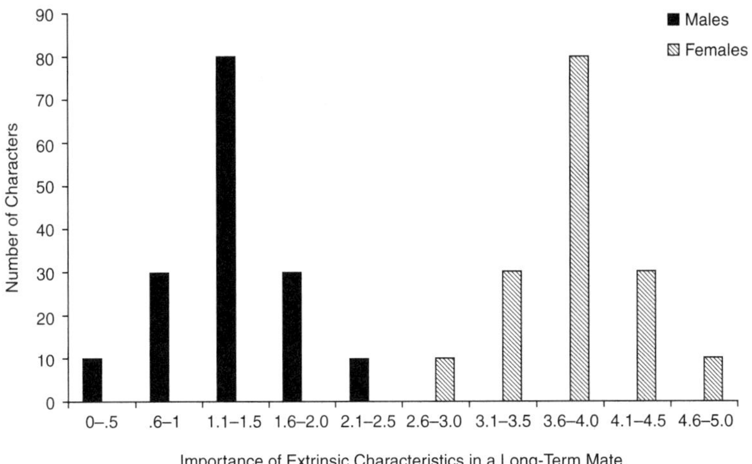

Figure A.3 Scenario with small within-group variance, little overlap, and clear-cut sex differences.

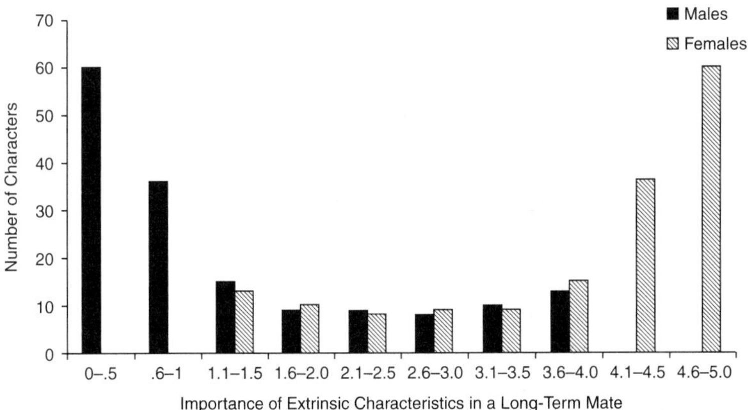

Figure A.4 Scenario with large within-group variance, significant overlap, and less clear-cut sex differences.

particular alpha level (normally at least $p < .05$). When F ratios are reported, they are accompanied by two numbers in parentheses called *degrees of freedom*, which are based on the number of groups being compared and the total number in the sample. When the data from the second hypothetical scenario above are subjected to ANOVA, the result is $F(1,318) = 362.18$, $p < .001$. So it turns out that, despite some overlap, the difference between male and female characters on this variable is statistically significant. (If we perform a *t*-test on the same data, the result is $t(318)=19.031$, $p< .001$. The value of *t* always turns out to be the square root of *F*, and the degrees of freedom is the second value in the *F* test. The two tests always give the same result.)

When an ANOVA defines groups in only one way—such as males versus females—it is called a one-way ANOVA. When we define the groups two ways—such as male/female and good/bad—the ANOVA is called a two-way ANOVA, and so forth. Each way we use to define groups is called a *factor* (not to be confused with the factors of factor analysis), and the number of groups defined by a factor are referred to as *levels* of the factor. Many of the analyses in this book are three-way ANOVAS. They employ three factors, each with two levels: character sex (male, female), valence (good, bad), and salience (major, minor).

When ANOVAs employ two or more factors, the results include three possible effects of the factors: *main effects*, *interaction effects*, and *simple main effects*. A statistically significant *main effect* means that there are significant differences between levels of one of the factors, regardless of the individuals' standing on the remaining factors. For example, if there is a main effect of character sex on importance of extrinsic characteristics in a mate (where extrinsic characteristics are more important to female than male characters), this means extrinsic characteristics are more important to female characters, regardless of whether they are good or bad, or major or minor.

A statistically significant *interaction effect* means that the effect of one factor depends on the level of another factor. If we found, hypothetically, a statistically significant interaction effect for character Sex and Valence on the importance of extrinsic characteristics in a mate, this means that the impact of Sex on this mate preference depends on whether the character is good or bad (or, alternatively, that the impact of Valence depends on whether the character is male or female). Finding a statistically significant interaction effect does not indicate exactly how the levels of the interacting factors differ; these must be investigated further by testing for simple main effects.

A statistically significant *simple main effect* indicates a significant difference between levels of one factor at a particular level of a second factor. For example, extrinsic characteristics might be more important for good female characters than for good male characters, while there is no difference for bad characters. In the most dramatic kinds of interactions, the effects are reversed for different levels of the second factor (in this example, if extrinsic characteristics were more important for good females than good males, but more important for bad males than for bad females). Again, the finding of an interaction effect by itself does not indicate which level of which factor has a higher or lower score. Tests for simple main effects reveal these specific differences.

The Independence of Sex from Valence and Salience

We can describe the independence of Sex from Valence and Salience statistically by conducting independent samples *t*-tests comparing male and female characters with respect to Valence and Salience. (We assign the number 1 to positive Valence and 2 to negative Valence; and we assign 1 to major status and 2 to minor status.) The mean for male characters with respect to Valence is 1.24 (*SD* .43), and the mean for female characters is 1.19 (*SD* .4); $t(380) = 1.02$, $p = .31$. The mean for male characters with respect to Salience is 1.48 (*SD* .5), and the mean for female characters is 1.52 (*SD*); $t(380) = -.8$, $p = .43$. We can also check this result by calculating the correlations between Sex, Valence, and Salience. Character Sex displays no significant correlation with either Valence ($r = -.05$) or Salience ($r = .04$).

Comparison of Scores for Male and Female Coders

In order to compare male and female coders, we isolated a set of 117 characters in which each character was rated by at least one male and one female coder. In cases in which there were more than one male or female coder, the scores from all respondents of either sex were averaged. We conducted two chief forms of analysis on this set of 117 characters: an analysis of variance and paired *t*-tests.

The design of the analysis of variance compared four variables: Coder Sex, Character Sex, Valence, and Salience (male and female respondents; male and female characters; good and bad characters, and major and minor characters). The result was unequivocal. Across all of the dependent variables, the sex of respondents simply did not matter. (In technical statistical terms, this was a 2x2x2x2 ANOVA, and Coder Sex had neither main effects nor interactive effects with the other independent variables.) There was one isolated exception: a possible Coder Sex versus Valence interaction effect on the question as to whether a character's success is a main feature of the story ($p = .014$), but if one adjusted for the large number of statistical tests, this would probably not be a statistically significant effect. (The greater the number of tests, the more likely one will get at least one seemingly significant result.)

The paired *t*-tests give two kinds of results. First, they show whether or not male and female coders differ on the dependent variables for the data set as a whole, regardless of whether the characters are male/female, good/bad, or major/minor. Out of all of the comparisons across dependent variables, only three statistically significant differences emerged. Male coders rated characters higher on Romance as a motive factor (.067 versus –.218, p = .001), lower on Subsistence as a motive factor (–.146 versus .061, $p < .05$), and higher on favoring Extrinsic Attributes (wealth, power, and prestige) in a long-term mate (.252 to –.093, $p < .05$). The second result is a set of correlations between male and female coders. In every case but one, male codings correlated significantly with female codings. The lone exception is a not quite significant correlation, in a small sample size, for scores on preferring Physical Attractiveness in short-term mates ($r = .37$, $p = .065$). On the whole, the significant correlations between male and female codings reinforce the view that male and female respondents were looking at the characters in a very similar way.

Statistically Significant Differences in Male and Female Characters by Male and Female Authors

We sought to determine whether scores on motives, personality, mating preferences, and emotional reactions for male and female characters differed according to whether the author was male or female. In the language of analysis of variance, Author Sex and Character Sex are independent variables. Motives, personality, mating, and emotional responses are dependent variables. We wanted to test whether there was a statistical interaction between Author Sex and Character Sex in the influence of these independent variables on the dependent variables (motives, personality, etc.). However, we also had to consider the possibility that Valence and Salience, as well as Author Sex and Character Sex, might affect the dependent variables. To focus in on the influence of Author Sex and Character Sex alone, we conducted sets of analysis of covariance (ANCOVA). (ANCOVA is a version of ANOVA that controls for the influence of variables, called covariates, that are not of primary interest.) In the first set of ANCOVAs, we wanted to eliminate variance produced by the different proportions of the agonistic character sets in novels by male and female authors, so we used Valence and Salience as covariates. This first set of analyses therefore employed a simple 2x2 design that focused on the effect of Author Sex and Character Sex. Next, we desired to add

Valence to the equation, so we conducted a second set of ANCOVAs in which Valence was a third predictor variable in a 2x2x2 design and the influence of Salience was eliminated by designating it as a covariate. We were thus able to compare the sets of all good and bad male and female characters by male and female authors. Finally, to assess the influence of all four of these variables, we used a set of regular ANOVA with a 2x2x2x2 design.

The first set of ANCOVAs, analyzing all male and female characters by male and female authors, revealed only one statistically significant interaction ($p = .003$) between the sex of authors and sex of characters. In the preference for Physical Attractiveness in short-term mate selection, male characters in male-authored novels scored much higher (.39) than male characters in female-authored novels (–.47), while female characters in female-authored novels score somewhat higher (.10) than female characters in male-authored novels (–.20). No interactive effects were found for any of the other dependent variables. The near-absence of statistically significant interactions between Author and Character Sex confirms that male and female authors portray male and female characters in fundamentally similar ways.

In the second set of ANCOVAs, comparing good and bad male and female characters by male and female authors, we found no statistically significant interactions for personality factors or long-term mating. There were a few statistically significant interaction effects across the categories of motives, short-term mating preferences, and emotional responses. We list below only the statistically significant differences between male and female authors in cases where Author Sex interacted with Character Sex:

Nurture

For good male characters: female-authored > male-authored ($p = .002$)
For bad female characters: female-authored > male-authored ($p = .023$)

Extrinsic Attributes in Short-Term Mate Preferences

For bad female characters: female authored > male-authored ($p = .01$)

Physical Attractiveness in Short-Term Mate Preferences

For good male characters: male authored > female-authored ($p = .002$)
For good female characters: female authored > male authored ($p = .038$)

Dislike

For bad female characters: female-authored > male-authored ($p < .001$)

In chapter 4 of part II, we focus on three of these differences: (1) good male characters by female authors are significantly more nurturing than good male characters by male authors; (2) good male characters by female authors give significantly less preference to Physical Attractiveness in a short-term mate; and (3) good female characters by female authors give significantly more preference to Physical Attractiveness in a short-term mate. These three differences conflict with character-sex trends in the data set as a whole and thus seem particularly relevant to the question as to whether the sex of the author biases the gender profile for characters of the other sex

Bad female characters by female authors score significantly higher on Dislike than bad female characters by male authors. That difference forms part of a pattern in which antagonistic characteristics are more extreme in female antagonists by female authors than in female antagonists by male authors.

In the full 2x2x2x2 ANOVAs, we found three statistically significant differences between character sets by male and female authors. One difference replicates the result for bad female characters and Extrinsic Attributes in short-term mating preferences given above. The other two are given below:

Nurture

For male protagonists: female-authored > male authored ($p = .006$)

Extrinsic Attributes in Long-Term Mate Preferences

For male protagonists: male-authored > female authored ($p = .034$)

The greater emphasis on Nurture in female-authored male protagonists is concordant with the ANCOVA result for all good males. With respect to seeking Extrinsic Attributes in a long-term mate, male protagonists by female authors are less demanding than male protagonists by male authors. This result is a specific instance of a general tendency: compared to authors of the other sex, authors of each sex tend to depict characters of the sex different from the author as less demanding in selecting mates.

Appendix 5

Results of Factor Analysis for Emotional Responses, Motives, and Mate Selection

Table A.5 Factor analysis of emotional responses to characters—rotated component matrix

Emotions	Dislike	Sorrow	Interest
Anger	**.85**	.11	.02
Disgust	**.90**	−.10	−.08
Contempt	**.87**	−.08	−.13
Fear-of the Character	**.71**	.00	.09
Fear-for the Character	−.26	**.78**	.17
Sadness	−.10	**.85**	.18
Admiration	**−.68**	.25	**.42**
Liking	**−.78**	.11	**.42**
Amusement	−.29	**−.65**	.28
Indifference	.04	−.07	**−.90**

Extraction Method: Principal Component Analysis. Rotation Method: Varimax with Kaiser Normalization. Rotation converged in four iterations. The three factors accounted for 72 percent of the total variance: Dislike 44.1 percent; Sorrow 18.1 percent; Interest 9.9 percent. Loadings > ±.3 in bold font.

Table A.6 Factor analysis of motives—rotated component matrix

Motives	Social Dominance	Constructive Effort	Romance	Subsistence	Nurture
Survival	.12	–.05	–.01	**.80**	–.02
Short-Term Mating	.07	.13	**.63**	–.07	**–.56**
Long-Term Mating	.02	.05	**.83**	.00	.16
Wealth	**.70**	–.27	**.38**	.22	.00
Power	**.89**	.01	–.08	.00	–.16
Prestige	**.89**	.13	.02	–.05	.02
Education or Culture	.08	**.77**	.18	.00	–.02
Friends and Alliances	.12	**.62**	.28	.01	.26
Helping Kin[a]	–.06	.11	.12	–.02	**.82**
Helping Nonkin	**–.34**	**.56**	–.06	.14	**.41**
Creating, Discovering [b]	–.10	**.73**	–.28	.13	–.10
Routine Work [c]	–.08	.20	–.01	**.76**	.05

Notes: Extraction Method: Principal Component Analysis. Rotation Method: Varimax with Kaiser Normalization. Rotation converged in seven iterations. The five factors accounted for 69 percent of the total variance: Social Dominance 21.5 percent; Constructive Effort 17.3 percent; Romance 11.3 percent; Subsistence 9.7 percent; Nurture 9.1 percent. Loadings > ±.3 in bold font.

[a] *The whole phrase in the questionnaire was "Nurturing/fostering offspring or aiding other kin."*

[b] *The whole phrase in the questionnaire was "Building, creating, or discovering something."*

[c] *The whole phrase in the questionnaire was "Performing routine tasks to earn a livelihood."*

Table A.7 Factor analysis of criteria for selecting long-term mates—rotated component matrix

Criteria	Extrinsic Attributes	Intrinsic Qualities	Physical Attractiveness
Physical Attractiveness	.01	–.04	**.98**
Power	**.89**	–.15	.05
Prestige	**.91**	–.01	.08
Wealth	**.88**	–.18	–.11
Intelligence	.01	**.78**	.14
Kindness	–.24	**.85**	–.04
Reliability	–.10	**.85**	–.20

Extraction Method: Principal Component Analysis. Rotation Method: Varimax with Kaiser Normalization. Rotation converged in four iterations. The three factors accounted for 80 percent of the total variance: Extrinsic Attributes 41.3 percent; Intrinsic Qualities 24 percent; Physical Attractiveness 14.7 percent. Loadings > ±.3 in bold font.

Table A.8 Factor analysis of criteria for selecting short-term mates—rotated component matrix

Criteria	Extrinsic Attributes	Intrinsic Qualities	Physical Attractiveness
Physical Attractiveness	.04	−.08	**.98**
Power	**.88**	−.08	.02
Prestige	**.94**	.05	.10
Wealth	**.88**	−.04	−.03
Intelligence	.15	.77	.16
Kindness	−.19	**.89**	−.09
Reliability	−.05	**.86**	−.22

Extraction Method: Principal Component Analysis. Rotation Method: Varimax with Kaiser Normalization. Rotation converged in four iterations. The three factors accounted for 81 percent of the total variance: Extrinsic Attributes 36.9 percent; Intrinsic Qualities 29.7 percent; Physical Attractiveness 14.2 percent. Loadings > ±.3 in bold font.

Appendix 6

Statistically Significant Results

Motive Factors

Social Dominance

Antagonists > protagonists ($p < .001$)
Antagonists > bad minors ($p < .001$)

Constructive Effort

Good > bad ($p < .001$)
Major > minor ($p < .05$)

Romance

Female protagonists > male protagonists ($p < .001$)
Female protagonists > female antagonists ($p < .01$)
Good minor females > good minor males ($p < .01$)

Nurture

Good > bad ($p < .01$)

Subsistence

Major males > major females ($p < .01$)
Major males > minor males ($p < .05$)

Criteria of Mate Selection

(STM = Short-term mating; LTM = Long-term mating)

Intrinsic Qualities

STMGood > bad ($p < .001$)
LTM Good > bad ($p < .001$)

Extrinsic Attributes

STMFemales > males ($p < .01$)
LTMFemales > males ($p < .001$)
STMBad females > bad males ($p < .01$)
STM Bad females > good females ($p < .05$)

Physical Attractiveness

LTMGood males > bad males ($p < .05$)
LTMGood males > good females ($p < .01$)
LTM Major males > major females ($p < .01$)
LTM Major males > minor males ($p < .05$)

Personality Factors

Extraversion

Antagonists > protagonists ($p < .001$)
Antagonists > bad minors ($p < .01$)
Good minors > protagonists ($p < .05$)

Agreeableness

Protagonists > antagonists ($p < .001$)
Good minors > bad minors ($p < .01$)
Bad minors > antagonists ($p < .001$)

Conscientiousness

Good > bad ($p < .001$)
Major females > minor females ($p < .001$)
Minor males > minor females ($p < .05$)

Emotional Stability

Good > bad ($p < .001$)

Openness

Good > bad ($p < .001$)

Emotional Response Factors

Dislike

Antagonists > Protagonists ($p < .001$)

Antagonists > bad minors ($p <. 001$)

Bad minors > good minors ($p < .05$)

Sorrow

Protagonists > antagonists ($p < .001$)

Protagonists > good minors ($p < .001$)

Interest

Female protagonists > male protagonists ($p < .01$)

Female protagonists > good minor females ($p < .01$)

Good minor males > good minor females ($p < .05$)

Good minor males > bad minor males ($p < .001$)

Good minor males > male protagonists ($p < .05$)

Male antagonists > bad minor males ($p < .001$)

Bad minor females > bad minor males ($p < .05$)

Character Success

Root For

Male protagonists > male antagonists ($p < .001$)

Female protagonists > female antagonists ($p < .001$)

Female protagonists > Good minor females ($p < .05$)

Good minor females > bad minor females ($p < .05$)

Good minor males > bad minor males ($p < .001$)

Bad minor females > bad minor males ($p < .05$)

Bad minor females > female antagonists ($p < .01$)

Main Feature

Female protagonists > good minor females ($p < .001$)
Female protagonists > female antagonists ($p < .01$)
Male protagonists > good minor males ($p < .001$)
Male antagonists > bad minor males ($p < .001$)
Good minor males > good minor females ($p < .01$)
Good minor males > bad minor males ($p < .01$)

Achieves Goals

Good > Bad ($p < .001$)
Minor males > minor females ($p < .05$)

Notes

Introduction

1. Weinberg, *Final Theory,* 10.
2. Kuhn, *Scientific Revolutions.*
3. Aronowitz, "Science Wars," 192; Dawson, "Literature and Science," 306, 308. Prominent poststructuralist critiques of science include Feyerabend, *Farewell to Reason;* Latour and Woolgar, *Laboratory Life;* Levine, *One Culture;* Peterfreund, *Literature and Science;* Rorty, *Consequences of Pragmatism;* Smith, *Scandalous Knowledge;* Woolgar, *Science.* Critiques of poststructuralist conceptions of science include Boghossian, *Fear of Knowledge;* Brown, *Who Rules in Science?*; Carroll, *Evolution and Literary Theory;* Fromm, "My Science Wars"; Fromm, "Science Wars and Beyond"; Fromm, *Being Human;* Gottschall, "Tree of Knowledge"; Gross and Levitt, *Higher Superstition;* Gross, Levitt, and Lewis, *Flight from Science;* Koertge, *House Built on Sand;* Parsons, *Science Wars;* Slingerland, *What Science Offers;* Sokal and Bricmont, *Fashionable Nonsense;* Weinberg, *Final Theory;* Weinberg, *Facing Up;* Wilson, *Consilience.*
4. Elliott and Attridge, *Theory after "Theory";* Eagleton, *After Theory;* Lopez and Potter, *After Postmodernism;* McQuillan, Purves, MacDonald, and Thomson, *Post-Theory;* Payne and Schad, *Life after Theory.*
5. "Most Cited Authors."
6. Menand, "Dangers Within," 12–13. For a critical commentary on Menand's essay, see Boyd, "Getting It All Wrong."
7. For instance, see Berubé and Nelson, *Higher Education;* Feal, *Profession; Critical Inquiry* 30 (2004); *New Literary History* 36 (2005).
8. Menand, "Dangers Within," 14.
9. Pinker, *Blank Slate,* 11. For surveys of contributions to evolutionary literary study, see Carroll, "An Evolutionary Paradigm"; Carroll, "Evolutionary Approaches." For collections of Darwinist literary theory and criticism, see Andrews and Carroll, *Evolutionary Review* 1; Andrews and Carroll, *Evolutionary Review* 2; Boyd, Carroll, and Gottschall, *Evolution, Literature, and Film;* Cooke and Turner, *Biopoetics;* Gottschall and Wilson, *Literary Animal;* Headlam Wells

and McFadden, *Human Nature;* Martindale, Locher, and Petrov, *Evolutionary and Neurocognitive Approaches.*

10. Wilson, *Consilience.*
11. For arguments on using empirical methods to renovate literary study, see Gottschall, *New Humanities;* Gottschall, "Quantitative Literary Study." For previous efforts to combine evolutionary conceptions with empirical methods in literary study, see Carroll and Gottschall, "Canonical British Novels"; Ellis and Symons, "Sex Differences in Sexual Fantasy"; Gottschall, *New Humanities;* Gottschall, "Greater Emphasis"; Gottschall, "Patterns of Characterization"; Gottschall et al., "Can Literary Study Be Scientific?"; Gottschall et al., "'Beauty Myth'"; Gottschall et al., "Are the Beautiful Good?"; Gottschall et al., "Sex Differences"; Gottschall and Nordlund, "Romantic Love"; Kruger, Fisher, and Jobling, "Proper and Dark Heroes"; Salmon, *Warrior Lovers;* Salmon and Symons, "Slash Fiction";
12. Wilson, *Darwin's Cathedral;* Wilson, *Evolution for Everyone;* Wilson, "Group-Level Evolutionary Processes"; Wilson, "Human Groups as Adaptive Units"; Wilson, "Group Selection"; Sober and Wilson, *Unto Others;* Wilson and Wilson, "Rethinking the Theoretical Foundations."
13. For historical commentaries on developments in the evolutionary human sciences, see Barrett, Dunbar, and Lycett, *Human Evolutionary Psychology,* 8–21; Buss, *Evolutionary Psychology,* 1–35; Carroll, "Human Life History"; Dunbar and Barrett, "Evolutionary Psychology"; Gangestad and Simpson, Introduction to *The Evolution of Mind;* Hagen and Symons, "Natural Psychology"; Laland and Brown, *Sense and Nonsense;* Mameli, "Evolution and Psychology"; Pinker, "Foreword to *The Handbook of Evolutionary Psychology*"; Sterelny, *Thought,* 234–35; Wilson, *Sociobiology,* v–viii. For collections that provide an overview of current thinking in the evolutionary human sciences, see Buss, *Handbook of Evolutionary Psychology;* Dunbar and Barrett, *Oxford Handbook*; Gangestad and Simpson, *Evolution of Mind.*
14. On "gene-culture co-evolution," see Barrett, Dunbar, and Lycett, *Human Evolutionary Psychology,* 351–83; Boyd and Richerson, "Cultural Adaptation"; Cochran and Harpending, *10,000 Year Explosion;* Carroll, "Human Life History"; Deacon, *Symbolic Species;* Hill, "Evolutionary Biology"; Lumsden and Wilson, *Genes, Mind, and Culture;* Lumsden and Wilson, *Promethean Fire;* Wade, *Before the Dawn;* Wilson, "Evolutionary Social Constructivism"; Wrangham, *Catching Fire.* On the adaptive function of the arts, see Wilson, *Consilience,* ch. 10; Dissanayake, *Art and Intimacy;* Tooby and Cosmides, "Does Beauty Build Adapted Minds?"; Boyd, *Origin of Stories;* Dutton, *Art Instinct.*
15. On the coevolution of intergroup rivalry and within-group cooperation, see Alexander, *Biology of Moral Systems,* 220–35; Axelrod and Hamilton, "Evolution of Cooperation"; Bingham, "Human

Uniqueness"; Boehm, *Hierarchy in the Forest;* Cummins, "Social Hierarchies"; Darwin, *Descent of Man,* 1: 70–106; Deacon, *Symbolic Species;* Eibl-Eibesfeldt, *Human Ethology,* Eibl-Eibesfeldt, "Us and the Others"; Flinn, Geary, and Ward, "Ecological Dominance"; Geary, *Origin of Mind,* 136–39, 142–44, 247–48; Katz, *Evolutionary Origins of Morality;* Kenrick, Maner, and Li, "Evolutionary Social Psychology"; Krebs, "Evolution of Morality"; Kurzban and Neuberg, "Ingroup and Outgroup Relationships"; Nesse, *Capacity for Commitment;* Premack and Premack, "Human Social Competence"; Richerson and Boyd, "Human Ultrasociality"; Richerson and Boyd, *Not by Genes Alone;* Salter, *Emotions in Command;* Schaller, Park, and Kenrick, "Human Evolution"; Smith, *Most Dangerous Animal,* 129–46; Sober and Wilson, *Unto Others,* 159–95, 329–37; Ridley, *Origins of Virtue;* Turchin, *War and Peace and War;* Wilson, *Evolution for Everyone;* Wilson, "Group-Level Evolutionary Processes"; Wilson, "Human Groups as Adaptive Units"; Wilson, "Group Selection"; Wilson and Wilson, "Rethinking the Theoretical Foundations." For an overview of Victorian debates on the existence of altruism, see Dixon, *Invention of Altruism.*

16. Miller, *Novel and the Police,* x–xi.
17. Fish, *Is There a Text in This Class?*
18. For overviews of the controversy over the adaptive function of the arts, see Boyd, "Evolutionary Theories"; Boyd, *Origin of Stories;* Carroll, "Evolutionary Paradigm" 119–28, Carroll, "Rejoinder to the Responses," 349–68.
19. Common social identity (Boyd, *Origin of Stories;* Dissanayake, *Art and Intimacy*); creativity and pattern recognition (Boyd, *Origin of Stories*); providing information (Sugiyama, "Food, Foragers, and Folklore"); game-plan scenarios (Dutton, *Art Instinct;* Pinker, *How the Mind Works;* Sugiyama, "Reverse-Engineering Narrative"; Swirski, *Literature and Knowledge*); focusing the mind on adaptively relevant problems (Dissanayake, *Art and Intimacy;* Salmon and Symons, "Slash Fiction"; Tooby and Cosmides, "Does Beauty Build Adapted Minds?"); making emotional sense (Carroll, "Evolutionary Paradigm"; Carroll, "Rejoinder to the Responses"; Deacon, *Symbolic Species;* Dissanayake, *Art and Intimacy;* Dutton, *Art Instinct;* Wilson, *Consilience*).
20. Boehm, *Hierarchy in the Forest.*
21. Anderson et al., "Violent Video Game Effects"; Iacoboni, *Mirroring People,* 204–13.
22. Brown, *Human Universals,* 136.

1 A User's Manual

1. Bower and Morrow, "Narrative Comprehension"; Woloch, *One vs. the Many.*
2. For commentaries on methods of online research in psychology, see Gosling and Johnson, *Conducting Online Behavioral Research.*

3. Barthes, *Image, Music, Text,* 142–48; Foucault, *Language, Counter-Memory, Practice,* 113–38; Wimsatt and Beardsley, "Intentional Fallacy."
4. Fish, *Is There a Text in This Class?*
5. Carroll, *Evolution and Literary Theory,* 462–65; Dworkin, "My Reply to Stanley Fish."
6. For empirical inquiries into sex and gender, see Baron-Cohen, *Essential Difference;* Baron-Cohen, Lutchmaya, and Knickmeyer, *Prenatal Testosterone;* Blum, *Sex on the Brain;* Buss, *Evolution of Desire;* Costa, Terraciano, and McCrae, "Gender Differences in Personality Traits"; Dabbs and Dabbs, *Heroes, Rogues, and Lovers;* Ellis and Symons, "Sex Differences"; Gangestad, "Reproductive Strategies and Tactics"; Geary, *Male, Female;* Goldberg, *Why Men Rule;* Gottschall, "Greater Emphasis"; Gottschall, "Patterns of Characterization"; Hrdy, *Mother Nature;* Jones, *Descent of Men;* Kimura, *Sex and Cognition;* Linden, *Accidental Mind,* ch. 6; Lippa, *Gender, Nature, and Nurture;* Low, *Why Sex Matters;* Potts and Short, *Adam and Eve;* Salmon, *Warrior Lovers;* Salmon and Symons, "Slash Fiction"; Schmitt, "Human Mating Strategies"; Symons, *Human Sexuality;* Trivers, "Parental Investment"; Vandermassen, *Who's Afraid of Charles Darwin?*
7. Johnson, et al., "Hierarchy in the Library"; Johnson et al., "Portrayal of Personality."

2 Agonistic Structure Differentiated by Sex

1. Leavis, *Great Tradition,* 19.
2. On motives as the basis of action, see McAdams, *The Person,* ch. 7; McClelland, *Human Motivation.* On the passions arising from mating, see Buss, *Dangerous Passion;* Buss, *Evolution of Desire;* Gottschall and Nordlund, "Romantic Love"; Linden, *Accidental Mind,* ch. 6. On personality traits as dispositions to act on motives, see McAdams, *Personality Psychology;* Nettle, *Personality;* Nettle and Penke, "Personality." On emotions as proximal mechanisms activating motives, see Damasio, *Descartes' Error;* Damasio, *Self Comes to Mind;* Ekman, *Emotions Revealed;* Gigerenzer, *Gut Feelings;* Linden, *Accidental Mind;* Plutchik, *Emotions and Life.* For conceptions of human nature that integrate motives, personality, and emotions, see Buss, "Personality Traits"; Brooks, *Social Animal;* Cacioppo and Patrick, *Loneliness;* Carroll, *Reading Human Nature,* 13–18; Goleman, *Emotional Intelligence;* Goleman, *Social Intelligence;* Keltner, *Born to Be Good;* Haidt, *Happiness Hypothesis;* Thagard, *Meaning of Life.*
3. Dryden, *Selected Criticism,* 25. For references to other such examples, see Carroll, *Evolution and Literary Theory,* 170; Pinker, *Blank Slate,* 404–20.

4. Boyer, "Specialised Inference Engines"; Dunbar, *Human Story;* Dunbar, "Why Are Good Writers So Rare?"; Geary, *Origin of Mind;* Mithen, *Prehistory of the Mind;* Sterelny, *Thought.*
5. On human life history theory, see Carroll, "Human Life History"; Hill, "Evolutionary Biology"; Hill and Kaplan, "Life History Traits"; Kaplan and Gangestad, "Life History Theory"; Kaplan, Gurven, and Lancaster, "Brain Evolution"; Kaplan, Hill, Lancaster, and Hurtado, "Human Life History Evolution"; Lancaster and Kaplan, "Chimpanzee and Human Intelligence"; Low, "Human Life Histories"; Low, *Why Sex Matters;* MacDonald, "Life History Theory"; Muehlenbein and Flinn, "Human Life History Evolution."
6. On the evolution of the human family, see Bellow, *In Praise of Nepotism;* Bjorklund, "Evolutionary Developmental Psychology"; Bjorklund and Pellegrini, *Origins of Human Nature;* Deacon, *Symbolic Species;* Flinn, Geary, and Ward, "Ecological Dominance"; Flinn and Ward, "Ontogeny and Evolution"; Geary, "Paternal investment"; Geary and Flinn, "Human Parental Behavior"; Gray and Anderson, *Fatherhood;* Hrdy, *Mother Nature;* Mock, *More than Kin;* Salmon and Shackelford, *Family Relationships;* Salmon and Shackelford, *Evolutionary Family Psychology;* Wrangham, *Catching Fire.* On the evolution of social cognition in humans, see Baron-Cohen, "Empathizing System"; Darwin, *Descent of Man;* Focquaert and Platek, "Social Cognition"; Gopnik, *Philosophical Baby;* Lewis, "Self-Conscious Emotions"; Paulhus and John "Egoistic and Moralistic Biases"; Premack and Premack, "Human Social Competence"; Tomasello et al., "Understanding and Sharing Intentions."
7. On the unique human capacities for culture, see Baumeister, *Cultural Animal;* Boyd and Richerson, "Cultural Adaptation"; Brown, "Human Culture"; Buss, "Personality Traits"; Carroll, "Human Revolution"; Carroll, *Reading Human Nature,* 16–18, 22–29, 42–46, 58; Deacon, *Symbolic Species;* Dissanayake, *Art and Intimacy;* Hill, "Evolutionary Biology"; MacDonald, "Dual Processing Theory"; MacDonald, "Evolution, Culture"; MacDonald, "Conflict Theory of Culture"; Mithen, *Prehistory of the Mind;* Panksepp and Panksepp, "Seven Sins"; Sterelny, *Thought;* Wade, *Before the Dawn;* Wilson, "Evolutionary Social Constructivism"; Wilson, *Consilience.*
8. On the importance of general intelligence in human evolution, see Geary, *Origin of Mind;* MacDonald, "Domain-General Mechanisms"; Mithen, *Prehistory of the Mind;* Sterelny, *Thought.* Pioneering efforts in developing an evolutionary understanding of the arts and other forms of cultural imagination include Boyd, *Origin of Stories;* Carroll, *Evolution and Literary Theory;* Carroll, *Literary Darwinism;* Carroll, *Reading Human Nature;* Dissanayake, *Art and Intimacy;* Dutton, *Art Instinct;* Gottschall, *Rape of Troy;* Tooby and Cosmides, "Does Beauty Build Adapted Minds?"; Wilson, *Consilience,* ch. 10.

9. Buss, "New Paradigm," 21; Paulhus and John, "Egoistic and Moralistic Biases," 1039, 1045. Digman ("Higher-Order Factors") has yet further examples. For a Socioanalytic perspective on the dichotomy, see Hogan, "Socioanalytic Perspective," "Socioanalytic Theory"; Hogan and Roberts, "Socioanalytic Model"; Johnson, "Criminality." For an examination of this dichotomy in the novels of Sir Walter Scott, see Jobling, "Personal Justice."
10. Buss, *Evolution of Desire;* Gangestad, "Reproductive Strategies and Tactics"; Geary, *Male, Female;* Schmitt, "Human Mating Strategies"; Symons, *Evolution of Human Sexuality.*
11. See Buss, "Social Adaptation"; Costa and McCrae, "Personality Trait Structure"; John, Angleitner, and Ostendorf, "Lexical Approach"; Johnson and Ostendorf, "Five-Factor Model"; McAdams, *The Person;* MacDonald, "Evolution, Culture"; MacDonald, "Levels of Personality"; Nettle, "Individual Differences"; Nettle, *Personality;* Nettle, "Personality Variation"; Saucier and Goldberg, "Lexical Studies"; Saucier et al. "Greek Personality Adjectives."
12. Gosling, Rentfrow, and Swann, "Very Brief Measure."
13. On literature as a form of "simulation," see Oatley, "Twice as True as Fact"; Oatley, "Story Worlds"; Tan, *Narrative Film.* On the emotionally responsive character of the reader's experience, see Feagin, "Imagining Emotions"; Hogan, *Mind and Its Stories;* McEwan, "Literature, Science, and Human Nature"; Matravers, "Paradox of Fiction"; Oatley and Gholamain, "Emotions and Identification"; Özyürek and Trabasso, "Evaluation"; Storey, *Mimesis,* 8–15; Van Peer, "Poetics of Emotion." On the parallel responses to "real" and "fictive" people, see Bower and Morrow, "Narrative Comprehension"; Grabes, "Words on the Page."
14. Ekman, "Basic Emotions"; Ekman, *Emotions Revealed.*
15. On the cognitive adaptation for perceiving goal-directed behavior, see Jellema and Perrett, "Neural Pathways"; Premack and Premack, "Human Social Competence"; Rizzolatti and Fogassi, "Mirror Neurons"; Sterelny, *Thought;* Tomasello et al., "Understanding and Sharing Intentions." For empirically grounded commentaries on goal-directed behavior in narrative, see Bower and Morrow, "Narrative Comprehension"; Heider and Simmel, "Experimental Study"; Mar, "Neuropsychology of Narrative"; Nettle, "What Happens in *Hamlet?*"; Oatley, "Taxonomy of the Emotions"; Sugiyama, "Reverse-Engineering Narrative"; Turner, *Literary Mind.* On the conceptual correlatives of agonistic structure in "folk physics"—the intuitive apprehension of causal dynamics in space and time—see Pinker, *Stuff of Thought,* 219-25.
16. On approach/avoidance as the basis of human motives and emotions, see Buss, "Personality Traits"; Haidt, *Happiness Hypothesis;* Nettle, *Personality;* MacDonald, "Evolution, Culture"; MacDonald, "Levels of Personality"; Plutchik, *Emotions and Life.*

3 Determinate Meanings

1. Kuhn, *Structure of Scientific Revolutions;* Fish, *Is There a Text in This Class?*
2. Abrams, *Doing Things with Texts;* Kolodny, "Dancing through the Minefield."
3. Carroll, *Evolution and Literary Theory,* 56–68.
4. For instances of stylometric analysis, see Martindale, *Clockwork Muse;* Sims et al., "Genome Comparison."
5. Bordwell, *Poetics of Cinema,* 46. Also see Hirsch, *Aims of Interpretation;* Hirsch, *Validity in Interpretation.*
6. Gottschall, *New Humanities,* xi–xii, 1–85.
7. Lakoff and Johnson, *Philosophy in the Flesh;* Pinker, *Stuff of Thought;* Turner, *Literary Mind.*
8. Carroll, "Pater's Figures of Perplexity."

4 Sexual Politics

1. For a scholarly account of the gynocentric ethos in this period, see Houghton, *Victorian Frame of Mind,* 341–93.
2. For a standard instance, see Butler, *Gender Trouble.* For an overview of constructivist formulations, see Vandermassen, *Who's Afraid of Charles Darwin?* 85–117.
3. Jacobus, "Difference of View," 12; Cixous, "Laugh of the Medusa," 879; Register, "American Feminist Literary Criticism," 9.
4. Spacks, *Female Imagination;* Kristeva, "Women's Time," 21; Kolodny, "Dancing through the Minefield," 98.
5. Armbruster, "Feminism and Ecology"; Dietz, "Current Controversies"; Gallop, Hirsch, and Miller, "Criticizing Feminist Criticism"; Gaard, "Ecofeminism Revisited"; Heyes, *Line Drawings;* Martin, "Methodological Essentialism"; Ridout, *Review of Third Wave Feminism'* Schor, "Essentialism"; Stone, "Genealogy of Women"; Vandermassen, *Who's Afraid of Charles Darwin?* 3–8.
6. Schor, "Essentialism," 40; Martin, "Methodological Essentialism," 632; Dietz, "Current Controversies," 407, 408; Gaard, "Ecofeminism Revisited," 27.
7. Baron-Cohen, *Essential Difference;* Baron-Cohen, Lutchmaya, and Knickmeyer, *Prenatal Testosterone;* Blum, *Sex on the Brain;* Jones, *Descent of Men;* Goldberg, *Why Men Rule;* Kimura, *Sex and Cognition;* Linden, *Accidental Mind,* ch. 6; Low, *Why Sex Matters;* Potts and Short, *Adam and Eve.*
8. For studies that examine sexual politics from an evolutionary perspective, see Buss and Malamuth, *Sex, Power, Conflict;* Gowaty, *Feminism and Evolutionary Biology;* Vandermassen, *Who's Afraid of Charles Darwin;* For evolutionary studies that take female psychology as their chief focus, see Campbell, *Mind of Her Own;* Hrdy, *Mother Nature.*

9. Linden, *Accidental Mind,* 83–86; Posner and Raichle, *Images of Mind,* 14.
10. Dawkins, *Blind Watchmaker;* Dawkins, *Selfish Gene.*
11. Buss, *Evolution of Desire;* Geary, *Male, Female;* Schmitt, *Human Mating Strategies;* Symons, *Evolution of Human Sexuality;* Trivers, "Parental Investment."

5 Adaptive Function

1. Pinker, *How the Mind Works,* 524–43. Also see Pinker, *Blank Slate* 404–20; Pinker, "Consilient Study."
2. On art as a medium for practical information or game planning, also see Dutton, *Art Instinct;* Sugiyama, "Food, Foragers, and Folklore"; Sugiyama, "Narrative Theory"; Sugiyama, "Reverse-Engineering Narrative"; Swirski, *Literature and Knowledge.*
3. Miller, *Mating Mind,* 281.
4. On sexual selection as an origin for art, also see Darwin, *Descent of Man,* 2:336–37; Dutton, *Art Instinct,* ch. 7; Voland, "Aesthetic Preferences."
5. Pinker, "Consilient Study," 169–70.
6. Wilson, *Consilience,* 224, 225, 224.
7. Damasio, *Descartes' Error;* Damasio, *Self Comes to Mind;* Ekman, *Emotions Revealed;* Gigerenzer, *Gut Feelings;* Linden, *Accidental Mind;* Plutchik, *Emotions and Life.*
8. For other arguments that human behavior is partially disconnected from stereotyped behavioral programs and that in humans the arts partially replace instinct, see Carroll, "Human Revolution"; Carroll, "*Reading Human Nature,* 20–29"; Dissanayake, *Art and Intimacy,* 73–79; Panksepp and Panksepp, "Seven Sins"; Swirski, *Literature and Knowledge,* 71–75, 85–90; Tooby and Cosmides, "Does Beauty Build Adapted Minds?"
9. Pinker, *How the Mind Works,* 528–38; Boyd, *Origin of Stories;* Tooby and Cosmides, "Does Beauty Build Adapted Minds?" 21; Dissanayake, *Art and Intimacy,* 73–82. On fostering neurocognitive adaptations, also see Dutton, *Art Instinct,* 106.
10. Deacon, *Symbolic Species,* 22.
11. On the universality of artistic practices, see D. E. Brown, *Human Universals.* On mother-infant interaction as a well-spring of aesthetic responsiveness, see Dissanayake, *Art and Intimacy;* Easterlin, "Psychoanalysis." For a commentary on the importance of the arts in childhood development, with special reference to abused children in the novels of Dickens, see Carroll, *Literary Darwinism* 63–68. For commentary that uses developmental psychology to analyze narratives aimed at children, see Boyd, *Origin of Stories.*
12. Dissanayake, *Art and Intimacy.* Also see Coe, *Ancestress Hypothesis.*
13. Boyd, "Evolutionary Theories of Art." Also see Dunbar, "Why Are Good Writers So Rare?"

14. Boehm, *Hierarchy in the Forest*. Also see Salter, *Emotions in Command*, 63–70. The similarities with Nietzsche's speculations about the psychological basis of Christian morality, as in *On The Genealogy of Morals*, should be evident.
15. On the pace and character of human evolutionary change over the past 100,000 years or so, see Cochran and Harpending, *10,000 Year Explosion;* Klein, *Dawn of Human Culture;* Mellars, *Neanderthal Legacy;* Mellars, Boyle, Bar-Yosef, and Stringer, *Rethinking the Human Revolution;* Mellars and Stringer, *Human Revolution;* Mithen, *Prehistory of the Mind;* Stringer and Gamble, *Neanderthals;* Wade, *Before the Dawn*.
16. Prominent instances of theory and criticism affirming that novels enact resistance against the dominant ideology include Bakhtin, *Dialogic Imagination;* Eagleton, *Myths of Power;* Gilbert and Gubar, *Madwoman in the Attic*.
17. Dissanayake, *Art and Intimacy;* E. O. Wilson, *Consilience*, ch. 10.

6 Jane Austen, by the Numbers

1. For instances of thematic reductions to the matrix terms of the theoretical schools, see Ahearn, *Marx and Modern Fiction;* Armstrong, Introduction to *Pride and Prejudice;* Armstrong, *Desire and Domestic Fiction;* Armstrong, "Inside Greimas' Square"; Auerbach, *Communities of Women;* Belsey, "Making Space"; Brownstein, "Jane Austen"; Fraiman, "Humiliation"; Handler and Segal, *Jane Austen;* Litvak, "Delicacy and Disgust"; Newman, "Can This Marriage Be Saved?"; Newton, *Women;* Poovey, *Proper Lady;* Smith, "Marxist-Feminist Reading;" Smith, "Oppositional Reader"; Wylie, "Dancing in Chains."
2. Goleman, *Emotional Intelligence*.
3. Austen, *Pride and Prejudice*, vol. 3, ch. 7. Hereafter references to *Pride and Prejudice* will be cited parenthetically in the text. Since there are so many editions of Austen's novels, we shall cite by volume and chapter number (3:7) rather than page number.
4. Bordwell, *Poetics of Cinema*, 46.
5. Miller, *Jane Austen*, 4; Tanner, *Jane Austen*, 130–35.
6. For empirical investigations into the constituents of pair-bonded love, see Fisher, *Why We Love;* Sternberg, "Triangulating Love." On the universality of romantic love, see Gottschall and Nordlund, "Romantic Love"; Nordlund, *Shakespeare;* Nordlund, "Problem of Romantic Love." For phenomenal accounts of the common features of romance as a genre, see Krentz, *Dangerous Men;* Snitow, "Mass Market Romance." For empirical investigations of romance within an evolutionary framework, see Ellis and Symons, "Sex Differences"; Salmon, *Warrior Lovers;* Salmon and Symons, "Slash Fiction"; Whissel, "Mate Selection."
7. Austen, *Emma*, 1:8; hereafter cited parenthetically in the text.
8. Buss, *Evolution of Desire;* Gangestad, "Reproductive Strategies and Tactics"; Schmitt, "Human Mating Strategies."

9. On the touchstone quality of the dialogues between Emma and Knightley, see Butler, *Jane Austen,* 265–66. On Austen's strategy for incorporating the reader within the privileged circle of Austen's own perspective in *Pride and Prejudice,* see Carroll, *Literary Darwinism,* 208–10.
10. Bradley, "Jane Austen"; Donovan, "Mind of Jane Austen"; Duckworth, *Improvement of the Estate;* Litz, *Jane Austen;* Wiltshire, "Mansfield Park, Emma, Persuasion."
11. Armstrong, Introduction to *Pride and Prejudice;* Brownstein, "Jane Austen"; Hinnant, "Jane Austen's 'Wild Imagination'"; Wylie, "Dancing in Chains."
12. Amodio et al., "Liberalism and Conservatism"; Eysenck, "Structure of Social Attitudes"; Eysenck and Wilson, *Psychological Basis of Ideology;* Graham, Haidt, and Nosek, "Liberals and Conservatives"; Haidt, *Happiness Hypothesis;* Haidt, "New Synthesis"; Mondak et al., "Personality and Civic Engagement."
13. Johnson, *Jane Austen,* 73.
14. For a pronominal analysis of Fanny's introversion, see Burrows, *Computation into Criticism,* 16–18.
15. On Fanny's moral intelligence, see Tanner, *Jane Austen,* 24. On the conservative ethos of *Mansfield Park,* see Butler, *Jane Austen,* 224; Moretti, *Atlas* 24–29; Said, *Culture and Imperialism,* 84.
16. Austen, *Mansfield Park,* 3:17.
17. Johnson, *Jane Austen,* 94–95; Butler, *Jane Austen,* 245–46.
18. Tanner, *Jane Austen,* 143; Trilling, "Mansfield Park."

7 Indifferent Tragedy in *The Mayor of Casterbridge*

1. Review of *The Mayor of Casterbridge,* 757.
2. Hardy, *Mayor of Casterbridge,* 3–4.
3. Hardy, *Mayor of Casterbridge,* ch. 44. All further citations to the novel will be given parenthetically in the text.
4. Interpretations invoking the model of retributive justice include Brooks, *Thomas Hardy;* Dalziel, Introduction to *The Mayor of Casterbridge;* Dalziel, "Whatever happened to Elizabeth-Jane?"; Davis, "Comparatively Modern Skeletons"; Dike, "Modern Oedipus"; Guérard, *Thomas Hardy;* Heilman, "Hardy's Mayor"; Johnson, *True Correspondence;* Karl, "New Fiction Defined"; King, *Tragedy;* Lane, *Burdens of Intimacy;* Lerner, *Tragedy or Social History?;* Miller, *Thomas Hardy;* Moore, "Death against Life"; Moore, *Descent;* Paterson, *"Mayor of Casterbridge";* Raine, "Conscious Artistry"; Ramel, "Crevice." Interpretations invoking the model of Promethean Romantic heroism include Gatrell, *Thomas Hardy;* Giordano, *Hardy's Self-Destructive Characters;* Guérard, *Thomas Hardy;* Hornback, *Metaphor of Chance;* Howe, *Thomas Hardy;* Karl, "New Fiction Defined"; Langbaum, *Thomas Hardy;* Lerner, *Tragedy*

or Social History?; Levine, *Realistic Imagination;* Millgate, *Thomas Hardy*; Moses, "Agon in the Marketplace"; Spivey, "Thomas Hardy's Tragic Hero"; Wilson, Introduction to *The Mayor of Casterbridge;* and Woolf, "Novels of Thomas Hardy." Interpretations invoking the model of redemptive change include Dalziel, Introduction to *The Mayor of Casterbridge;* Dalziel, "Whatever happened to Elizabeth-Jane?"; Gatrell, *Thomas Hardy;* Gregor, *Great Web;* Hutton, Review of *The Mayor of Casterbridge;* Langbaum, *Thomas Hardy;* Paterson, *"Mayor of Casterbridge";* Showalter, "Unmanning of the Mayor"; Spivey, "Thomas Hardy's Tragic Hero"; Wright, *Hardy and the Erotic.*

5. Paterson, *"Mayor of Casterbridge,"* 151, 152, 156, 154. For critiques of Paterson's cosmic scheme, see Draper, *"The Mayor of Casterbridge";* Edwards, *"Mayor of Casterbridge";* Schweik, "Character and Fate"; and Starzyk, "Hardy's *Mayor.*"
6. Miller, *Thomas Hardy,* 150; Guérard, *Thomas Hardy,* 146.
7. Levine, *Realistic Imagination,* 232, 232, 244, 244, 231; Wilson, Introduction to *The Mayor of Casterbridge,* xxxvii; Moses, "Agon in the Marketplace," 222.
8. Hutton, Review of *The Mayor of Casterbridge,* 138, 138–39; Showalter, "Unmanning of the Mayor," 103, 104; Dalziel, Introduction to *The Mayor of Casterbridge,* xxii.
9. Hardy, *Life and Work,* 182.
10. Gatrell, *Thomas Hardy,* 87; Heilman, "Hardy's Mayor," 282, 285; Karl, "New Fiction Defined," 206, 209; Lerner, *Tragedy or Social History?* 62–64, 78.
11. Garson, *Hardy's Fables,* 111–29; Musselwhite, *Social Transformation,* 63–64, 68–71; Neil, *Secret Life,* 77–81.
12. Paris, *Imagined Human Beings,* 169.
13. Dalziel, "Whatever Happened to Elizabeth-Jane?" 82, 85–86, 80.
14. Cecil, *Hardy the Novelist,* 222.
15. Gregor, *Great Web,* 125; Millgate, *Thomas Hardy,* 228, 229; Langbaum, *Thomas Hardy,* 129. On Elizabeth-Jane's role as observer and reflective consciousness, also see Brooks, *Thomas Hardy,* 212; Bullen, *Expressive Eye,* 157–59; Goode, *Thomas Hardy,* 78–94; Grossman, "Thomas Hardy," 619, 633–36; Hartveit, *Art of Persuasion,* 50–70; Jekel, *Hardy's Heroines,* 131–43; Vigar, *Novels,* 64–65.
16. Gregor, *Great Web,* 128; Millgate, *Thomas Hardy,* 227; Langbaum, *Thomas Hardy,* 132, 134, 136.
17. Levine, *Realistic Imagination,* 232.
18. Miller, "Speech Acts," 41; Cecil, *Hardy the Novelist,* 38–39.

Conclusion

1. For commentaries on utopian and dystopian fiction from an evolutionary perspective, see Cooke, *Human Nature in Utopia;* Swirski, "Skinner's Behaviorist Utopia."

2. Brown, *Human Universals;* Brown, "Human Universals"; Brown, "Human Culture."
3. For a canonical philosophical argument to this effect, see Tooby and Cosmides, "Psychological Foundations."
4. Boehm, *Hierarchy in the Forest;* Cochran and Harpending, *10,000 Year Explosion;* Klein, *Dawn of Human Culture;* Lumsden and Wilson, *Promethean Fire;* Boyd and Richerson, "Cultural Adaptation"; Mithen, *Prehistory of the Mind;* Sterelny, *Thought;* Wade, *Before the Dawn;* Wrangham, *Catching Fire.*
5. Miller, *Novel and the Police,* xi, xiii.
6. Atran, *Cognitive Foundations;* Brown, *Human Universals;* Pinker, *Stuff of Thought;* Lakoff and Johnson, *Philosophy in the Flesh.*
7. Baron-Cohen, "Empathizing System"; Gopnik, *Philosophical Baby.*
8. Brown, *Human Universals;* McClelland, *Human Motivation;* Ekman, *Emotions Revealed;* Plutchik, *Emotions and Life.*
9. Tanaka, "What Is Copernican?"
10. Freud, "Creative Writers."
11. Daly and Wilson, *Homicide,* 107–21; Degler, *Decline and Revival,* 245–69; Easterlin, "Psychoanalysis"; Sugiyama, "New Science."
12. Jung, "Analytical Psychology."
13. Tinbergen, "Aims and Methods."
14. For efforts to revise Freud in line with evolutionary principles, see Bowlby, *Attachment and Loss;* Kennair, "Evolutionary Psychology." For an effort to assimilate Jung to evolutionary psychology, see Stevens, *Archetype Revisited.*
15. See for instance Hart, "Cognitive Literary Studies"; Hogan, *Cognitive Science;* Hogan, *Mind and Its Stories;* Oatley, "Story Worlds"; Oatley, "Taxonomy of the Emotions," Oatley and Gholamain, "Emotions and Identification"; Richardson and Spolsky, *Work of Fiction;* Spolsky, *Gaps in Nature;* Turner, *Artful Mind;* Turner, *The Literary Mind;* Turner, *Reading Minds,* Zunshine, *Why We Read Fiction.*
16. Carroll, *Literary Darwinism,* 104–14; Carroll, *Reading Human Nature,* 6–9.
17. In film studies, David Bordwell (*Poetics of Cinema*) and Joseph Anderson (*Reality of Illusion*) have taken important steps toward integrating evolutionary and cognitive approaches.
18. Cacioppo and Patrick, *Loneliness;* Damasio, *Self Comes to Mind;* Goleman, *Emotional Intelligence;* Goleman, *Social Intelligence;* Kozbelt, "Neuroaesthetics"; Linden, *Accidental Mind;* Hawkins and Blakeslee, *On Intelligence;* Panksepp, *Affective Neuroscience;* Panksepp, "BrainMind"; Panksepp and Panksepp, "Seven Sins."
19. See for instance Burrows, *Computation into Criticism;* Martindale, *The Clockwork Muse;* Miall; *Literary Reading;* Moretti, *Graphs;* Oatley, "Emotions"; Özyürek and Trabasso, "Evaluation"; Rabkin, "Science Fiction"; Van Peer, *Muses and Measures;* website for the International

Society for the Empirical Study of Literature and Media: http://www.arts.ualberta.ca/igel/, accessed January 11, 2007.

20. Jameson, "Symptoms of Theory," 404.
21. Darwin, Origin of Species, 493.
22. Carroll, Introduction to *On the Origin of Species,* 17–24, 31, 54–57.
23. For evolutionary approaches to myths, epics, and folk tales, See Easterlin, "Fish out of Water"; Fox, "Male Bonding"; Gottschall, *New Humanities;* Gottschall, "Patterns of Characterization"; Gottschall, "Quantitative Literary Study"; Gottschall, *Rape of Troy.* On genre, see Ellis and Symons, "Sex Differences in Sexual Fantasy"; Nettle, "What Happens in *Hamlet?";* Nettle, "Wheel of Fire"; Salmon, *Warrior Lovers;* Salmon and Symons, "Slash Fiction"; Storey, *Mimesis.* For interpretive essays offering evolutionary alternatives to Freudian depth psychology, see Carroll, *Reading Human Nature,* 109–22; Easterlin, "Psychoanalysis"; Sugiyama, "New Science." For evolutionary approaches to the analysis of formal structures and symbolic figurations, see Anderson, *Reality of Illusion;* Bordwell, *Poetics of Cinema;* Boyd, "Spiegelman's *The Narrative Corpse*"; Boyd, *Origin of Stories;* Carroll, *Literary Darwinism,* 18–22; Carroll, *Reading Human Nature,* 91–108.
24. Ellis and Symons, "Sex Differences in Sexual Fantasy."
25. Carroll, *Evolution and Literary Theory,* 187–91, 200–15; Schmidt, "Balkanization of Science."
26. Deresiewicz, "On Literary Darwinism," 30; Crews, "Apriorism for Empiricists," 159, 157; Goodheart, "Literary Darwinism," 182. For similar formulations, see Goodheart, *Darwinian Misadventures;* Seamon, "Literary Darwinism"; Smee, "Natural-Born Thrillers"; Spolsky, "Centrality of the Exceptional."
27. For descriptive surveys, see Carroll, "An Evolutionary Paradigm"; Carroll, "Three Scenarios." For examples, see Andrews and Carroll, *The Evolutionary Review* 1; Boyd, *On the Origin;* Boyd, Carroll, and Gottschall, *Evolution, Literature, and Film;* Carroll, "Intentional Meaning"; Carroll, *Literary Darwinism;* Carroll, *Reading Human Nature;* Cooke, *Human Nature in Utopia;* Gottschall, *The Rape of Troy;* Easterlin, "Fish"; Easterlin, "Psychoanalysis"; Nordlund, *Shakespeare;* Saunders, "Male Reproductive Strategies"; Saunders, "Paternal Confidence"; Saunders, *Reading Edith Wharton.*
28. Abrams, "Transformation of English Studies," 119; Culler, *Literary Theory,* 4.

Bibliography

Abrams, Meyer H. *Doing Things with Texts: Essays in Criticism and Critical Theory*. Edited by Michael Fischer. New York: Norton, 1989.

———. "The Transformation of English Studies: 1930–1995." *Daedalus: Journal of the American Academy of Arts and Sciences* 126, no. 1 (1997): 105–31.

Ahearn, Edward J. *Marx and Modern Fiction*. New Haven, CT: Yale University Press, 1989.

Alexander, Richard D. *The Biology of Moral Systems*. Foundations of Human Behavior. Hawthorne, NY: A. de Gruyter, 1987.

———. "Evolution of the Human Psyche." In *The Human Revolution: Behavioural and Biological Perspectives on the Origins of Modern Humans*, edited by Paul Mellars and Christopher B. Stringer, 455–513. Princeton, NJ: Princeton University Press, 1989.

Amodio, David M., John T. Jost, Sarah L. Master, and Cindy M. Yee. "Neurocognitive Correlates of Liberalism and Conservatism." *Nature Neuroscience* 10, no. 10 (Oct 2007): 1246–47.

Anderson, Craig A., Nobuko Ihori, Brad J. Bushman, Hannah R. Rothstein, Akiko Shibuya, Edward L. Swing, Akira Sakamoto, and Muniba Saleem. "Supplemental Material for Violent Video Game Effects on Aggression, Empathy, and Prosocial Behavior in Eastern and Western Countries: A Meta-Analytic Review." *Psychological Bulletin* 136, no. 2 (2010): 151–73.

Anderson, Joseph. *The Reality of Illusion: An Ecological Approach to Cognitive Film Theory*. Carbondale: Southern Illinois University Press, 1996.

Andrews, Alice, and Joseph Carroll, eds. *The Evolutionary Review: Art, Science, Culture* 1 (2010).

———. *The Evolutionary Review: Art, Science, Culture* 2 (2011).

Armbruster, Karla. "Feminism and Ecology." *NWSA Journal* 12, no. 1 (2000): 210–16.

Armstrong, Isobel. Introduction to *Pride and Prejudice*, by Jane Austen. Edited by James Kingsley. New York: Oxford University Press, 1990.

Armstrong, Nancy. *Desire and Domestic Fiction: A Political History of the Novel*. New York: Oxford University Press, 1987.

Armstrong, Nancy. "Inside Greimas's Square: Literary Characters and Cultural Constraints." In *The Sign in Music and Literature*, edited by Wendy Steiner, 52–66. Austin: University of Texas Press, 1987.

Aronowitz, Stanley. "The Politics of the Science Wars." *Social Text*, no. 46/47 (1996): 177–97.

Atran, Scott. *Cognitive Foundations of Natural History: Towards an Anthropology of Science.* Cambridge: Cambridge University Press, 1990.

Auerbach, Nina. *Communities of Women: An Idea in Fiction.* Cambridge, MA: Harvard University Press, 1978.

Austen, Jane. *Emma: An Authoritative Text, Backgrounds, Reviews and Criticism.* Edited by Stephen M. Parrish. 3rd ed. New York: Norton, 2000.

———. *Mansfield Park: Authoritative Text, Contexts, Criticism.* Edited by Claudia L. Johnson. New York: Norton, 1998.

———. *Persuasion: Authoritative Text, Backgrounds, and Contexts Criticism.* Edited by Patricia Meyer Spacks. New York: Norton, 1995.

———. *Pride and Prejudice: An Authoritative Text.* Edited by Donald J. Gray. 3rd ed. New York: Norton, 2001.

———. *Sense and Sensibility: Authoritative Text, Contexts, Crticisim.* Edited by Claudia L. Johnson. New York: Norton, 2001.

Axelrod, Robert, and William D. Hamilton. "The Evolution of Cooperation." *Science* 211, no. 4489 (1981): 1390–96.

Bakhtin, Mikhail M. *The Dialogic Imagination: Four Essays.* Translated by Kenneth Brostrom. Edited by Michael Holquist and Vadim Liapunov. Austin: University of Texas Press, 1982.

Baron-Cohen, Simon. "The Empathizing System: A Revision of the 1994 Model of the Mindreading System." In *Origins of the Social Mind: Evolutionary Psychology and Child Development*, edited by Bruce J. Ellis and David F. Bjorklund, 468–92. New York: Guilford, 2005.

———. *The Essential Difference: The Truth about the Male And Female Brain.* New York: Basic Books, 2003.

Baron-Cohen, Simon, Svetlana Lutchmaya, and Rebecca Knickmeyer. *Prenatal Testosterone in Mind: Amniotic Fluid Studies.* Cambridge, MA: MIT Press, 2004.

Barrett, Louise, Robin I. M. Dunbar, and John Lycett. *Human Evolutionary Psychology.* Princeton, NJ: Princeton University Press, 2002.

Barthes, Roland. *Image, Music, Text.* Translated by Stephen Heath. New York: Noonday, 1988.

Baumeister, Roy F. *The Cultural Animal: Human Nature, Meaning, and Social Life.* Oxford: Oxford University Press, 2005.

Bellow, Adam. *In Praise of Nepotism: A Natural History.* New York: Doubleday, 2003.

Belsey, Catherine. "Making Space: Perspective Vision and the Lacanian Real." *Textual Practice* 16, no. 1 (2002): 31–55.

Bérubé, Michael, and Cary Nelson. *Higher Education under Fire: Politics, Economics, and the Crisis of the Humanities.* New York: Routledge, 1995.

Bingham, P. M. "Human Uniqueness: A General Theory." *Quarterly Review of Biology* 74 (1999): 133–69.

Bjorklund, David F. "You've Come a Long Way, Baby: Evolutionary Developmental Psychology." *The Evolutionary Review: Art, Science, Culture* 2 (2011): 10–20.

Bjorklund, David F., and Anthony D. Pellegrini. *The Origins of Human Nature: Evolutionary Developmental Psychology.* Washington, DC: American Psychological Association, 2002.

Block, Jack. *The Q-Sort Method in Personality Assessment and Psychiatric Research.* Springfield, IL: Thomas, 1961.

Blum, Deborah. *Sex on the Brain: The Biological Differences between Men and Women.* New York: Viking, 1997.

Boehm, Christopher. *Hierarchy in the Forest: The Evolution of Egalitarian Behavior.* Cambridge, MA: Harvard University Press, 1999.

Boghossian, Paul. *Fear of Knowledge: Against Relativism and Constructivism.* Oxford: Oxford University Press, 2006.

Bordwell, David. *Poetics of Cinema.* New York: Routledge, 2008.

Bower, Gordon H., and Daniel G. Morrow. "Mental Models in Narrative Comprehension." *Science* 247, no. 4938 (1990): 44–48.

Bowlby, John. *Attachment and Loss.* 2nd ed. 3 vols. New York: Basic Books, 1999.

Boyd, Brian. "Art and Evolution: Spiegelman's *The Narrative Corpse.*" *Philosophy and Literature* 32, no. 1 (2008): 31–57.

———. "Evolutionary Theories of Art." In *The Literary Animal: Evolution and the Nature of Narrative*, edited by Jonathan Gottschall and David Sloan Wilson, 147–76. Evanston, IL: Northwestern University Press, 2005.

———. "Getting It All Wrong: Bioculture Critiques Cultural Critique." *American Scholar* 75, no. 4 (2006): 18–30.

———. *On the Origin of Stories: Evolution, Cognition, and Fiction.* Cambridge, MA: Harvard University Press, 2010.

Boyd, Brian, Joseph Carroll, and Jonathan Gottschall, eds. *Evolution, Literature, and Film: A Reader.* New York: Columbia University Press, 2010.

Boyd, Robert, and Peter J. Richerson. "Cultural Adaptation and Maladaptation: Of Kayaks and Commissars." In *The Evolution of Mind: Fundamental Questions and Controversies*, edited by Steven W. Gangestad and Jeffry A. Simpson, 327–31. New York: Guilford, 2007.

Boyer, Pascal. "Specialised Inference Engines as Precursors of Creative Imagination?" In *Imaginative Minds*, edited by Ilona Roth, 239–58. Oxford: Oxford University Press, 2008.

Bradley, Andrew Cecil. "Jane Austen." In *A Miscellany*, 32–72. London: Macmillan, 1929.

Brooks, David. *The Social Animal: The Hidden Sources of Love, Character, and Achievement*. New York: Random House, 2011.

Brooks, Jean R. *Thomas Hardy: The Poetic Structure*. Ithaca, NY: Cornell University Press, 1971.

Brown, Donald E. *Human Universals*. Philadelphia: Temple University Press, 1991.

———. "Human Universals and Their Implications." In *Being Humans: Anthropological Universality and Particularity in Transdisciplinary Perspectives*, edited by Neil Roughley, 156–74. Berlin: de Gruyter, 2000.

———. "Human Universals, Human Nature and Human Culture." *Daedalus* 133, no. 4 (2004): 47–54.

Brown, James Robert. *Who Rules in Science? An Opinionated Guide to the Wars*. Cambridge, MA: Harvard University Press, 2001.

Brownstein, Rachel M. "Jane Austen: Irony and Authority." *Women's Studies: An Interdisciplinary Journal* 15, no. 1–3 (1988): 57–70.

Bullen, J. B. *The Expressive Eye: Fiction and Perception in the Work of Thomas Hardy*. Oxford: Oxford University Press, 1986.

Burrows, J. F. *Computation into Criticism: A Study of Jane Austen's Novels and an Experiment in Method*. Oxford: Oxford University Press, 1987.

Buss, Arnold. "Evolutionary Perspectives on Personality Traits." In *Handbook of Personality Psychology*, edited by Robert Hogan, John A. Johnson, and Stephen Briggs, 346–66. San Diego: Academic, 1997.

Buss, David M. *The Dangerous Passion: Why Jealousy Is as Necessary as Love and Sex*. New York: Free Press, 2000.

———. *The Evolution of Desire: Strategies of Human Mating*. Revised ed. New York: Basic Books, 2003.

———. "Evolutionary Psychology: A New Paradigm for Psychological Science." *Psychological Inquiry* 6, no. 1 (1995): 1–30.

———. *Evolutionary Psychology: The New Science of the Mind*. 3rd ed. Boston: Pearson, Allyn & Bacon, 2008.

———, ed. *The Handbook of Evolutionary Psychology*. Hoboken, NJ: Wiley, 2005.

———. "Social Adaptation and Five Major Factors of Personality." In *The Five-Factor Model of Personality: Theoretical Perspectives*, edited by Jerry S. Wiggins, 180–207. New York: Guilford, 1996.

Buss, David M., and Neil M. Malamuth, eds. *Sex, Power, Conflict: Evolutionary and Feminist Perspectives*. New York: Oxford University Press, 1996.

Butler, Judith. *Gender Trouble: Feminism and the Subversion of Identity*. Thinking Gender. New York: Routledge, 1990.

Butler, Marilyn. *Jane Austen and the War of Ideas*. Oxford: Oxford University Press, 1975.

Cacioppo, John T., and William Patrick. *Loneliness: Human Nature and the Need for Social Connection*. New York: Norton, 2008.

Campbell, Anne. *A Mind of Her Own: The Evolutionary Psychology of Women*. Oxford: Oxford University Press, 2002.

Carroll, Joseph. "The Adaptive Function of Literature." In *Evolutionary and Neurocognitive Approaches to Aesthetics, Creativity and the Arts*, edited by Colin Martindale, Paul Locher, and Vladimir M. Petrov, 31–45. Amityville, NY: Baywood, 2007.

———. "Aestheticism, Homoeroticism, and Christian Guilt in *The Picture of Dorian Gray*." In *Reading Human Nature: Literary Darwinism in Theory and Practice*, 91–108. Albany: State University of New York Press. First published in *Philosophy and Literature* 29 (2005): 286–304, 2011.

———. *Evolution and Literary Theory*. Columbia: University of Missouri Press, 1995.

———. "Evolutionary Approaches to Literature and Drama." In *The Oxford Handbook of Evolutionary Psychology*, edited by Robin I. M. Dunbar and Louise Barrett, 637–48. Oxford: Oxford University Press, 2007.

———. "An Evolutionary Paradigm for Literary Study." *Style* 42, no. 2–3 (2008): 103–35.

———. "Human Life History and Gene-Culture Co-Evolution: An Emerging Paradigm." *The Evolutionary Review: Art, Science, Culture* 2 (2011): 23–37.

———. "The Human Revolution and the Adaptive Function of Literature." *Philosophy and Literature* 30, no. 1 (April 2006): 33–49.

———. "Intentional Meaning in *Hamlet:* An Evolutionary Perspective." In *Reading Human Nature: Literary Darwinism in Theory and Practice*, 123–47. Albany: State University of New York Press, 2011. Originally published in *Style* 44, no. 1–2 (2010): 230–60.

———. Introduction to *On the Origin of Species by Means of Natural Selection,* by Charles Darwin. Edited by Joseph Carroll, 9–75. Peterborough, UK: Broadview, 2003.

———. *Literary Darwinism: Evolution, Human Nature, and Literature*. New York: Routledge, 2004.

———. "Pater's Figures of Perplexity." *Modern Language Quarterly* 52, no. 3 (1991): 319–40.

———. *Reading Human Nature: Literary Darwinism in Theory and Practice*. Albany: State University of New York Press, 2011.

———. "Rejoinder to the Responses." *Style* 42, no. 2–3 (2008): 308–411.

———. "Three Scenarios for Literary Darwinism." In *Reading Human Nature: Literary Darwinism in Theory and Practice*, 71–87. Albany: State University of New York Press, 2011.

———. "*Vanity Fair* by William Makepeace Thackeray." In *Encyclopedia of the Novel*, edited by Paul E. Schlesinger, 1397–98. Chicago: Fitzroy Dearborn, 1999.

Carroll, Joseph, and Jonathan Gottschall. "Human Nature and Agonistic Structure in Canonical British Novels of the Nineteenth and Early Twentieth Centuries: A Content Analysis." In *Anthropologie Und Sozialgeschichte Der Literatur Heuristiken Der Literaturwissenschaft*, edited by Uta Klein, Katja Mellmann, and Stephanie Metzger, 473–87. Paderborn, Germany: Mentis, 2006.

Cecil, Lord David. *Hardy the Novelist: An Essay in Criticism.* Indianapolis, IN: Bobbs, 1943.

Cixous, Hélène. "The Laugh of the Medusa." Translated by Keith Cohen and Paula Cohen. *Signs: Journal of Women in Culture and Society* 1, no. 4 (1976): 875–93.

Cochran, Gregory, and Henry Harpending. *The 10,000 Year Explosion: How Civilization Accelerated Human Evolution.* New York: Basic Books, 2009.

Coe, Kathryn. *The Ancestress Hypothesis: Visual Art as Adaptation.* New Brunswick, NJ: Rutgers University Press, 2003.

Cooke, Brett. *Human Nature in Utopia: Zamyatin's We.* Evanston, IL: Northwestern University Press, 2002.

Cooke, Brett, and Frederick Turner, eds. *Biopoetics: Evolutionary Explorations in the Arts.* Lexington, KY: ICUS, 1999.

Cosmides, Leda, and John Tooby. "Consider the Source: The Evolution of Adaptations for Decoupling and Metarepresentations." In *Metarepresentations: A Multidisciplinary Perspective*, edited by Dan Sperber, 53–115. New York: Oxford University Press, 2000.

Costa, Paul T., Jr., and Robert R. McCrae. "Personality Trait Structure as a Human Universal." *American psychologist* 52, no. 5 (1997): 509–16.

Costa, Paul T., Jr., Antonio Terracciano, and Robert R. McCrae. "Gender Differences in Personality Traits across Cultures: Robust and Surprising Findings." *Journal of Personality and Social Psychology* 81, no. 2 (2001): 322–31.

Crews, Frederick. "Apriorism for Empiricists." *Style* 42, no. 2–3 (2008): 155–60.

Critical Inquiry 30, No. 2 (2004). (Special Issue: A Symposium on "the Future of Criticism").

Culler, Jonathan D. *Literary Theory: A Very Short Introduction.* New York: Oxford University Press, 1997.

Cummins, Denise. "Dominance, Status, and Social Hierarchies." In *The Handbook of Evolutionary Psychology*, edited by David M. Buss, 676–97. Hoboken, NJ: Wiley, 2005.

Dabbs, James M., and Mary Godwin Dabbs. *Heroes, Rogues, and Lovers: Testosterone and Behavior.* New York: McGraw-Hill, 2000.

Daly, Martin, and Margo Wilson. *Homicide.* New York: Aldine de Gruyter, 1988.

Dalziel, Pamela. Introduction to *The Mayor of Casterbridge*, by Thomas Hardy. Edited by Dale Kramer, New ed., xiii–xxxiv. Oxford: Oxford University Press, 2004.

———. "Whatever Happened to Elizabeth-Jane? Revisioning Gender in *The Mayor of Casterbridge.*" In *Thomas Hardy: Texts and Contexts*, edited by Phillip Mallett, 64–86. Houndmills, UK: Palgrave, 2006.

Damasio, Antonio R. *Descartes' Error: Emotion, Reason, and the Human Brain*. New York: Putnam, 1994.
———. *Self Comes to Mind: Constructing the Conscious Brain*. New York: Pantheon Books, 2010.
Darwin, Charles. *The Descent of Man, and Selection in Relation to Sex*. Edited by John Tyler Bonner and Robert M. May Princeton, NJ: Princeton University Press, 1981.
———. *On the Origin of Species by Means of Natural Selection*. Edited by Joseph Carroll. Peterborough, UK: Broadview Press, 2003.
Davis, W. Eugene. "Comparatively Modern Skeletons in the Garden: A Reconsideration of *The Mayor of Casterbridge*." *English Literature in Transition: 1880–1920*. Special series 3 (1985): 108–20.
Dawkins, Richard. *The Blind Watchmaker*. New York: Norton, 1986.
———. *The Selfish Gene*. New York: Oxford University Press, 1976.
Dawson, Gowan. "Literature and Science under the Microscope." *Journal of Victorian Culture* 11, no. 2 (2006): 301–15.
de Waal, Frans. *Our Inner Ape: A Leading Primatologist Explains Why We Are Who We Are*. New York: Riverhead Books, 2005.
Deacon, Terrence William. *The Symbolic Species: The Co-Evolution of Language and the Brain*. New York: Norton, 1997.
Degler, Carl N. *In Search of Human Nature: The Decline and Revival of Darwinism in American Social Thought*. New York: Oxford University Press, 1991.
Deresiewicz, William. "Adaptation: On Literary Darwinism." *Nation*, June 8, 2009, 26–31.
Dietz, Mary G. "Current Controversies in Feminist Theory." *Annual Review of Political Science* 6, no. 1 (2003): 399–431.
Digman, John M. "Higher-Order Factors of the Big Five." *Journal of Personality and Social Psychology* 73, no. 6 (1997): 1246–56.
Dike, D. A. "A Modern Oedipus: *The Mayor of Casterbridge*." *Essays in Criticism* 2, no. 2 (1952): 169–79.
Dissanayake, Ellen. *Art and Intimacy: How the Arts Began*. Seattle: University of Washington Press, 2000.
Dixon, Thomas. *The Invention of Altruism: Making Moral Meanings in Victorian Britain*. Oxford: Oxford University Press, 2008.
Donovan, R.A. "The Mind of Jane Austen." In *Jane Austen Today*, edited by Joel Weinsheimer, 109–27. Athens: University of Georgia Press, 1975.
Draper, R. P. "*The Mayor of Casterbridge*." *Critical Quarterly* 25, no. 1 (1983): 57–70.
Dryden, John. *John Dryden: Selected Criticism*. Edited by James Kinsley and George A. E. Parfitt. Oxford: Oxford University Press, 1970.
Duckworth, Alistair M. *The Improvement of the Estate: A Study of Jane Austen's Novels*. Baltimore, MD: Johns Hopkins University Press, 1971.
Dunbar, R. I. M. *The Human Story: A New History of Mankind's Evolution*. London: Faber and Faber, 2004.

Dunbar, Robin I. M. "Why Are Good Writers So Rare? An Evolutionary Perspective on Literature." *Journal of Cultural and Evolutionary Psychology* 3, no. 1 (2005): 7–21.

Dunbar, Robin I. M, and Louise Barrett. "Evolutionary Psychology in the Round." In *Oxford Handbook of Evolutionary Psychology*, edited by Robin I. M Dunbar and Louise Barrett, 3–9. Oxford: Oxford University Press, 2007.

Dunbar, R. I. M., and Louise Barrett, eds. *Oxford Handbook of Evolutionary Psychology*. Oxford: Oxford University Press, 2007.

Dutton, Denis. *The Art Instinct: Beauty, Pleasure, and Human Evolution*. New York: Bloomsbury Press, 2009.

Dworkin, Ronald. "My Reply to Stanley Fish (and Walter Benn Michaels): Please Don't Talk about Objectivity Any More." In *The Politics of Interpretation*, edited by W. J. T. Mitchell, 278–313. Chicago: University of Chicago Press, 1983.

Eagleton, Terry. *After Theory*. New York: Basic Books, 2003.

———. *Myths of Power: A Marxist Study of the Brontës*. Anniversary ed. Houndmills, UK: Palgrave Macmillan, 2005.

Easterlin, Nancy. "Hans Christian Andersen's Fish out of Water." *Philosophy and Literature* 25, no. 2 (2001): 251–77.

———. "Psychoanalysis and 'the Discipline of Love.'" *Philosophy and Literature* 24, no. 2 (2000): 261–79.

Edwards, Duane D. "*The Mayor of Casterbridge* as Aeschylean Tragedy." *Studies in the Novel* 4 (1972): 608–18.

Eibl-Eibesfeldt, Irenäus. *Human Ethology*. New York: Aldine De Gruyter, 1989.

———. "Us and the Others: The Familial Roots of Ethnonationalism." In *Ethnic Conflict and Indoctrination: Altruism and Identity in Evolutionary Perspective*, edited by Irenäus Eibl-Eibesfeldt and Frank K. Salter, 21–53. New York: Berghahn, 1998.

Ekman, Paul. "Basic Emotions." In *Handbook of Cognition and Emotion*, edited by Mick J. Power, 45–60. Chichester, UK: Wiley, 1999.

———. *Emotions Revealed: Recognizing Faces and Feelings to Improve Communication and Emotional Life*. 2nd ed. New York: Owl Books, 2007.

Elliott, Jane, and Derek Attridge, eds. *Theory after "Theory."* New York: Routledge, 2011.

Ellis, Bruce J., and Donald Symons. "Sex Differences in Sexual Fantasy: An Evolutionary Psychological Approach." *The Journal of Sex Research* 27, no. 4 (1990): 527–55.

Eysenck, Hans J. "Structure of Social Attitudes." *Psychological Reports* 39, no. 2 (1976): 463–66.

Eysenck, Hans J., and Glenn D. Wilson, eds. *The Psychological Basis of Ideology*. Baltimore, MD: University Park, 1978.

Feagin, Susan L. "Imagining Emotions and Appreciating Fiction." In *Emotion and the Arts*, edited by Mette Hjort and Sue Laver, 50–62. New York: Oxford University Press, 1997.

Feal, Rosemary G., ed. *Profession 2005*. New York: The Modern Language Association of America, 2005.

Feyerabend, Paul. *Farewell to Reason*. London; New York: Verso, 1987.

Fish, Stanley Eugene. *Is There a Text in This Class? The Authority of Interpretive Communities*. Cambridge, MA: Harvard University Press, 1980.

Fisher, Helen E. *Why We Love: The Nature and Chemistry of Romantic Love*. New York: Henry Holt, 2004.

Flesch, William. *Comeuppance: Costly Signaling, Altruistic Punishment, and Other Biological Components of Fiction*. Cambridge, MA: Harvard University Press, 2007.

Flinn, Mark V., David C. Geary, and Carol V. Ward. "Ecological Dominance, Social Competition, and Coalitionary Arms Races: Why Humans Evolved Extraordinary Intelligence." *Evolution and Human Behavior* 26, no. 1 (2005): 10–46.

Flinn, Mark V., and Carol V. Ward. "Ontogeny and Evolution of the Social Child." In *Origins of the Social Mind: Evolutionary Psychology and Child Development.*, edited by Bruce J. Ellis and David F. Bjorklund, 19–44. New York: Guilford, 2005.

Focquaert, Farah, and Steven M. Platek. "Social Cognition and the Evolution of Self-Awareness." In *Evolutionary Cognitive Neuroscience*, edited by Steven M. Platek, Julian Paul Keenan and T. K. Shackelford, 457–97. Cambridge, MA: MIT Press, 2007.

Foucault, Michel. *Language, Counter-Memory, Practice: Selected Essays and Interviews*. Translated by Donald F. Bouchard and Sherry Simon. Edited by Donald F. Bouchard. Ithaca, NY: Cornell University Press, 1977.

Fox, Robin. "Male Bonding in the Epics and Romances." In *The Literary Animal: Evolution and the Nature of Narrative*, edited by Jonathan Gottschall and David Sloan Wilson, 126–44. Evanston, IL: Northwestern University Press, 2005.

Fraiman, Susan. "The Humiliation of Elizabeth Bennet." In *Refiguring the Father: New Feminist Readings of Patriarchy*, edited by Patricia Yaeger and Beth Kowaleski-Wallace, 168–87. Carbondale: Southern Illinois University Press, 1989.

Freud, Sigmund. "Creative Writers and Daydreaming." Translated by James Strachey. In *Writings on Art and Literature*, edited by James Strachey, 142–53. London: Hogarth, 1959.

Fromm, Harold. "My Science Wars." *The Hudson Review* 49, no. 4 (1997): 599–609.

———. *The Nature of Being Human: From Environmentalism to Consciousness*. Baltimore, MD: Johns Hopkins University Press, 2009.

———. "Science Wars and Beyond." *Philosophy and Literature* 30, no. 2 (2006): 580–89.

Frye, Northrop. *Anatomy of Criticism: Four Essays*. Princeton, NJ: Princeton University Press, 1957.

Gaard, Greta. "Ecofeminism Revisited: Rejecting Essentialism and Re-Placing Species in a Material Feminist Environmentalism." *Feminist Formations* 23, no. 2 (2011): 26–53.

Gallop, Jane, Marianne Hirsch, and Nancy K. Miller. "Criticizing Feminist Criticism." In *Conflicts in Feminism*, edited by Marianne Hirsch and Evelyn Fox Keller, 349–69. New York: Routledge, 1990.

Gangestad, Steven W. "Reproductive Strategies and Tactics." In *Oxford Handbook of Evolutionary Psychology*, edited by Robin I. M Dunbar and Louise Barrett, 321–32. Oxford: Oxford University Press, 2007.

Gangestad, Steven W., and Jeffry A. Simpson. "An Introduction to *The Evolution of Mind*: Why We Developed This Book." In *The Evolution of Mind: Fundamental Questions and Controversies*, edited by Steven W. Gangestad and Jeffry A. Simpson, 1–21. New York: Guilford, 2007.

Gangestad, Steven W., and Jeffry A. Simpson, eds. *The Evolution of Mind: Fundamental Questions and Controversies.* New York: Guilford, 2007.

Garson, Marjorie. *Hardy's Fables of Integrity: Woman, Body, Text.* Oxford: Oxford University Press, 1991.

Gatrell, Simon. *Thomas Hardy and the Proper Study of Mankind.* Charlottesville: University Press of Virginia, 1993.

Geary, David C. "Evolution of Paternal Investment." In *The Handbook of Evolutionary Psychology*, edited by David M. Buss, 483–505. Hoboken, NJ: Wiley, 2005.

———. *Male, Female: The Evolution of Human Sex Differences.* 2nd ed. Washington, DC: American Psychological Association, 2010.

———. *The Origin of Mind: Evolution of Brain, Cognition, and General Intelligence.* Washington, DC: American Psychological Association, 2005.

Geary, David C., and Mark V. Flinn. "Evolution of Human Parental Behavior and the Human Family." *Parenting: Science and Practice* 1, no. 1–2 (2001): 5–61.

Gigerenzer, Gerd. *Gut Feelings: The Intelligence of the Unconscious.* New York: Viking, 2007.

Gilbert, Sandra M., and Susan Gubar. *The Madwoman in the Attic: The Woman Writer and the Nineteenth-Century Literary Imagination.* 2nd ed. New Haven, CT: Yale University Press, 2000.

Giordano, Frank R. *"I'd Have My Life Unbe": Thomas Hardy's Self-Destructive Characters.* University: University of Alabama Press, 1984.

Goldberg, Steven. *Why Men Rule: A Theory of Male Dominance.* Chicago: Open Court, 1993.

Goleman, Daniel. *Emotional Intelligence.* New York: Bantam Books, 1995.

———. *Social Intelligence: The New Science of Human Relationships.* New York: Bantam, 2006.

Goode, John. *Thomas Hardy: The Offensive Truth.* Oxford: Blackwell, 1988.

Goodheart, Eugene. *Darwinian Misadventures in the Humanities.* New Brunswick, NJ: Transaction, 2007.

———. "Do We Need Literary Darwinism?" *Style* 42, no. 2–3 (2009): 181–85.

Gopnik, Alison. *The Philosophical Baby: What Children's Minds Tell Us about Truth, Love, and the Meaning of Life*. New York: Farrar, Straus & Giroux, 2009.

Gosling, Sam, and John A. Johnson, eds. *Advanced Methods for Conducting Online Behavioral Research*. Washington, DC: American Psychological Association, 2010.

Gosling, Samuel D., Peter J. Rentfrow, and William B. Swann. "A Very Brief Measure of the Big-Five Personality Domains." *Journal of Research in Personality* 37, no. 6 (2003): 504–28.

Gottschall, Jonathan. "Greater Emphasis on Female Attractiveness in *Homo Sapiens:* A Revised Solution to an Old Evolutionary Riddle." *Evolutionary Psychology* 5, no. 2 (2007): 347–57.

———. *Literature, Science, and a New Humanities*. New York: Palgrave Macmillan, 2008.

———. "Patterns of Characterization in Folk Tales across Geographic Regions and Levels of Cultural Complexity: Literature as a Neglected Source of Quantitative Data." *Human Nature* 14, no. 4 (2003): 365–82.

———. "Quantitative Literary Study: A Modest Manifesto and Testing the Hypotheses of Feminist Fairy Tale Studies." In *The Literary Animal: Evolution and the Nature of Narrative*, edited by Jonathan Gottschall and David Sloan Wilson, 199–224. Evanston, IL: Northwestern University Press, 2005.

———. *The Rape of Troy: Evolution, Violence, and the World of Homer*. Cambridge: Cambridge University Press, 2008.

———. "The Tree of Knowledge and Darwinian Literary Study." *Philosophy and Literature* 27, no. 2 (2003): 255–68.

Gottschall, Jonathan, and David Sloan Wilson, eds. *The Literary Animal: Evolution and the Nature of Narrative*. Evanston, IL: Northwestern University Press, 2005.

Gottschall, Jonathan, and Marcus Nordlund. "Romantic Love: A Literary Universal?" *Philosophy and Literature* 30, no. 2 (2006): 450–70.

Gottschall, Jonathan, C. Callanan, N. Casamento, N. Gladd, K. Manganini, T. Milan-Robertson, P. O'Connell, K. Parker, N. Riley, V. Stucker, A. Tapply, C. Wall, and A. Webb. "Are the Beautiful Good in Western Literature? A Simple Illustration of the Necessity of Literary Quantification." *Journal of Literary Studies* 23, no. 1 (2007): 41–62.

Gottschall, Jonathan, Elizabeth Allison, Jay De Rosa, and Kaia Klockeman. "Can Literary Study Be Scientific? Results of an Empirical Search for the Virgin/Whore Dichotomy." *Interdisciplinary Literary Studies* 7, no. 2 (2006): 1–17.

Gottschall, Jonathan, Jonathan Martin, Hadley Quish, and Jon Rea. "Sex Differences in Mate Choice Criteria Are Reflected in Folktales from around the World and in Historical European Literature." *Evolution and Human Behavior* 25, no. 2 (2004): 102–12.

Gottschall, Jonathan, K. Anderson, C. Burbank, J. Burch, C. Byrnes, C. Callanan, N. Casamento, A. Gardiner, N. Gladd, A. Hartnett, E. Henry, E. Hilarides, C. Lemke, K. Manganini, S. Merrihew, T. Milan-Robinson, P. O'Connell, J. Mott, K. Parker, K. Revoir, N. Riley, D. Robinson, S. Rodriguez, C. Sauve, A. Spearance, V. Stucker, A. Tapply, A. Unser, C. Wall, A. Webb, and M. Zocco. "The 'Beauty Myth' Is No Myth: Emphasis on Male-Female Attractiveness in World Folk Tales." *Human Nature* 19, no. 2 (2008): 174–88.

Gowaty, Patricia Adair, ed. *Feminism and Evolutionary Biology: Boundaries, Intersections, and Frontiers.* New York: Chapman & Hall, 1997.

Grabes, Herbert. "Turning Words on the Page into 'Real' People." *Style* 38, no. 2 (2004): 221–35.

Graham, Jesse, Jonathan Haidt, and Brian A. Nosek. "Liberals and Conservatives Rely on Different Sets of Moral Foundations." *Journal of Personality and Social Psychology* 96, no. 5 (2009): 1029–46.

Gray, Peter B., and Kermyt G. Anderson. *Fatherhood: Evolution and Human Paternal Behavior.* Cambridge, MA: Harvard University Press, 2010.

Gregor, Ian. *The Great Web: The Form of Hardy's Major Fiction.* Totowa, NJ: Rowman & Littlefield, 1974.

Gross, Paul R., and N. Levitt. *Higher Superstition: The Academic Left and Its Quarrels with Science.* Baltimore, MD: Johns Hopkins University Press, 1994.

Gross, Paul R., N. Levitt, and Martin W. Lewis, eds. *The Flight from Science and Reason.* New York: The New York Academy of Sciences, 1996.

Grossman, Julie. "Thomas Hardy and the Role of Observer." *ELH* 56, no. 3 (1989): 619–38.

Guérard, Albert J. *Thomas Hardy: The Novels and Stories.* Cambridge: Harvard University Press, 1949.

Hagen, Edward H., and Donald Symons. "Natural Psychology: The Environment of Evolutionary Adaptedness and the Structure of Cognition." In *The Evolution of Mind: Fundamental Questions and Controversies*, edited by Steven W. Gangestad and Jeffry A. Simpson, 38–44. New York: Guilford, 2007.

Haidt, Jonathan. *The Happiness Hypothesis: Finding Modern Truth in Ancient Wisdom.* New York: Basic Books, 2006.

———. "The New Synthesis in Moral Psychology." *Science* 316, no. 5827 (2007): 998–1002.

Handler, Richard, and Daniel Alan Segal. *Jane Austen and the Fiction of Culture: An Essay on the Narration of Social Realities.* Tucson: University of Arizona Press, 1990.

Hardy, Thomas. *The Life and Work of Thomas Hardy.* Edited by Michael Millgate. London: Macmillan, 1984.

———. *The Mayor of Casterbridge: An Authoritative Text, Backgrounds and Contexts, Criticism.* Edited by Phillip Mallett. 2nd ed. New York: Norton, 2001.

Hart, F. Elizabeth. "The Epistemology of Cognitive Literary Studies." *Philosophy and Literature* 25, no. 2 (2001): 314–34.

Hartveit, Lars. *The Art of Persuasion: A Study of Six Novels*. Bergen, Norway: Universitetsforlaget, 1977.

Hawkins, Jeff, with Sandra Blakeslee. *On Intelligence*. New York: Times Books, 2004.

Heider, Fritz, and Marianne Simmel. "An Experimental Study of Apparent Behavior." *The American Journal of Psychology* 57, no. 2 (1944): 243–59.

Heilman, Robert B. "Hardy's Mayor and the Problem of Intention." In *The Workings of Fiction: Essays by Robert Bechtold Heilman*. Columbia: University of Missouri Press, 1991. Originally published in *Criticism* 5 (1963): 199–213.

Heyes, Cressida J. *Line Drawings: Defining Women through Feminist Practice*. Ithaca, NY: Cornell University Press, 2000.

Hill, Kim. "Evolutionary Biology, Cognitive Adaptations, and Human Culture." In *The Evolution of Mind: Fundamental Questions and Controversies.*, edited by Steven W. Gangestad and Jeffry A. Simpson, 348–56. New York: Guilford, 2007.

Hill, Kim, and Hillard Kaplan. "Life History Traits in Humans: Theory and Empirical Studies." *Annual Review of Anthropology* 28, no. 1 (1999): 397–430.

Hinnant, Charles H. "Jane Austen's 'Wild Imagination': Romance and the Courtship Plot in the Six Canonical Novels." *Narrative* 14, no. 3 (2006): 294–310.

Hirsch, E. D. *The Aims of Interpretation*. Chicago: University of Chicago Press, 1976.

———. *Validity in Interpretation*. New Haven, CT: Yale University Press, 1967.

Hogan, Patrick Colm. *Cognitive Science, Literature, and the Arts: A Guide for Humanists*. New York: Routledge, 2003.

———. *The Mind and Its Stories: Narrative Universals and Human Emotion*. Cambridge: Cambridge University Press, 2003.

Hogan, Robert. "A Socioanalytic Perspective on the Five-Factor Model." In *The Five-Factor Model of Personality: Theoretical Perspectives*, edited by Jerry S. Wiggins, 163–79. New York: Guilford, 1996.

———. "A Socioanalytic Theory of Personality." In *Nebraska Symposium on Motivation*, edited by Monte M. Page, 55–89. Lincoln: University of Nebraska Press, 1982.

Hogan, Robert, and Brent W. Roberts. "A Socioanalytic Model of Maturity." *Journal of Career Assessment* 12, no. 2 (2004): 207–17.

Hornback, Bert G. *The Metaphor of Chance: Vision and Technique in the Works of Thomas Hardy*. Athens: Ohio University Press, 1971.

Houghton, Walter. *The Victorian Frame of Mind: 1830–1870*. New Haven: Yale University Press, 1957.

Howe, Irving. *Thomas Hardy*. New York: Macmillan, 1967.

Hrdy, Sarah Blaffer. *Mother Nature: A History of Mothers, Infants, and Natural Selection*. New York: Pantheon Books, 1999.

Hutton, Richard Holt. Review of *The Mayor of Casterbridge*, by Thomas Hardy. In *Thomas Hardy: The Critical Heritage*, edited by R. G. Cox, new ed., 136–40. London: Routledge, 1995. Originally published in Spectator, June 5, 1886, 752–53.

Iacoboni, Marco. *Mirroring People: The New Science of How We Connect with Others*. New York: Farrar, Straus and Giroux, 2008.

Jacobus, Mary. "The Difference of View." In *Women Writing and Writing about Women*, edited by Mary Jacobus, 10–21. London: Croom Helm, 1979.

Jameson, Fredric. *Postmodernism, or, the Cultural Logic of Late Capitalism*. Durham, NC: Duke University Press, 1991.

———. "Symptoms of Theory or Symptoms for Theory?" *Critical Inquiry* 30, no. 2 (2004): 403–08.

Jekel, Pamela. *Thomas Hardy's Heroines: A Chorus of Priorities*. Troy, NY: Whitston, 1986.

Jellema, Tjeerd, and David I. Perrett. "Neural Pathways of Social Cognition." In *Oxford Handbook of Evolutionary Psychology*, edited by Robin I. M. Dunbar and Louise Barrett, 163–77. Oxford: Oxford University Press, 2007.

Jobling, Ian. "Personal Justice and Homicide in Scott's *Ivanhoe*: An Evolutionary Psychological Perspective." *Interdisciplinary Literary Studies* 2, no. 2 (2001): 29–43.

John, Oliver P., Alois Angleitner, and Fritz Ostendorf. "The Lexical Approach to Personality: A Historical Review of Trait Taxonomic Research." *European Journal of Personality* 2, no. 3 (1988): 171–203.

Johnson, Bruce. *True Correspondence: A Phenomenology of Thomas Hardy's Novels*. Tallahassee: University Presses of Florida, 1983.

Johnson, Claudia L. *Jane Austen: Women, Politics, and the Novel*. Chicago: University of Chicago Press, 1988.

Johnson, John A. "Criminality, Creativity, and Craziness: Structural Similarities in Three Types of Nonconformity." In *Personality Theory, Moral Development, and Criminal Behavior*, edited by William S. Lauffer and James M. Day, 81–105. Lexington, MA: D. C. Heath, 1983.

Johnson, John A., and Fritz Ostendorf. "Clarification of the Five-Factor Model with the Abridged Big Five Dimensional Circumplex." *Journal of Personality and Social Psychology* 65, no. 3 (1993): 563–76.

Johnson, John A., Joseph Carroll, Jonathan Gottschall, and Daniel J. Kruger. "Hierarchy in the Library: Egalitarian Dynamics in Victorian Novels." *Evolutionary Psychology* 6, no. 4 (2008): 715–38.

———. "Portrayal of Personality in Victorian Novels Reflects Modern Research Findings but Amplifies the Significance of Agreeableness." *Journal of Research in Personality* 45, no. 1 (2011): 50–58.

Jones, Steve. *Y: The Descent of Men*. Boston: Houghton Mifflin, 2003.

Jung, Carl G. "On the Relation of Analytical Psychology to Poetry." Translated by R. F. C. Hull. In *The Collected Works of C. G. Jung*, edited by Sir Herbert Read, Michael Fordham, Gerhard Adler, and William McGuire, 65–83: Princeton, NJ: Princeton University Press, 1966.

Kaplan, Hillard S., and Steven W. Gangestad. "Life History Theory and Evolutionary Psychology." In *The Handbook of Evolutionary Psychology*, edited by David M. Buss, 68–95. Hoboken, NJ: Wiley, 2005.

Kaplan, Hillard S., Kim Hill, Jane Lancaster, and A. Magdalena Hurtado. "A Theory of Human Life History Evolution: Diet, Intelligence, and Longevity." *Evolutionary Anthropology* 9, no. 4 (2000): 156–85.

Kaplan, Hillard S., Michael Gurven, and Jane B. Lancaster. "Brain Evolution and the Human Adaptive Complex: An Ecological and Social Theory." In *The Evolution of Mind: Fundamental Questions and Controversies*, edited by Steven W. Gangestad and Jeffry A. Simpson, 269–79. New York: Guilford, 2007.

Karl, Frederick R. "*The Mayor of Casterbridge:* A New Fiction Defined." *Modern Fiction Studies* 6, no. 3 (1960): 195–213.

Katz, Leonard D. *Evolutionary Origins of Morality: Cross-Disciplinary Perspectives*. Thorverton, UK: Imprint Academic, 2000.

Keltner, Dacher. *Born to Be Good: The Science of a Meaningful Life*. New York: Norton, 2009.

Keltner, Dacher, and Paul Ekman. "Facial Expression of Emotion." In *Handbook of Emotions*, edited by Michael Lewis and Jeanette M. Haviland-Jones, 2nd ed., 236–49. New York: Guilford, 2000.

Kennair, Leif Edward Ottesen. "Evolutionary Psychology: An Emerging Integrative Perspective within the Science and Practice of Psychology." *Human Nature Review* 2 (2002): 17–61. http://www.human-nature.com/nibbs/02/ep.html.

Kenrick, Douglas T., Jon K. Maner, and Norman P. Li. "Evolutionary Social Psychology: From Selfish Genes to Collective Selves." In *The Handbook of Evolutionary Psychology*, edited by David M. Buss, 803–27. Hoboken, NJ: Wiley, 2005.

Kimura, Doreen. *Sex and Cognition*. Cambridge, MA: MIT Press, 1999.

King, Jeannette. *Tragedy in the Victorian Novel: Theory and Practice in the Novels of George Eliot, Thomas Hardy, and Henry James*. Cambridge: Cambridge University Press, 1978.

Klein, Richard G., with Blake Edgar. *The Dawn of Human Culture*. New York: Wiley, 2002.

Koertge, Noretta. *A House Built on Sand: Exposing Postmodernist Myths about Science*. New York: Oxford University Press, 1998.

Kolodny, Annette. "Dancing through the Minefield: Some Observations on the Theory, Practice and Politics of a Feminist Literary Criticism." *Feminist Studies* 6, no. 1 (1980): 1–25.

Kozbelt, Aaron. "Neuroaesthetics: Where Things Stand Now." *The Evolutionary Review: Art, Science, Culture* 2 (2011): 137–46.

Krebs, Dennis. "The Evolution of Morality." In *Handbook of Evolutionary Psychology*, edited by David M. Buss, 747–71. Hoboken, NJ: Wiley, 2005.

Krentz, Jayne Ann. *Dangerous Men and Adventurous Women: Romance Writers on the Appeal of the Romance.* Philadelphia: University of Pennsylvania Press, 1992.

Kristeva, Julia. "Women's Time." Translated by Alice Jardine and Harry Blake. *Signs: Journal of Women in Culture and Society* 7, no. 1 (1981): 13–35.

Kruger, Daniel, Maryanne Fisher, and Ian Jobling. "Proper and Dark Heroes as Dads and Cads: Alternative Mating Strategies in British and Romantic Literature." *Human nature* 14, no. 3 (2003): 305–17.

Kuhn, Thomas S. *The Structure of Scientific Revolutions.* 2nd ed. Chicago: University of Chicago Press, 1970.

Kurzban, Robert, and Steven Neuberg. "Managing Ingroup and Outgroup Relationships." In *The Handbook of Evolutionary Psychology*, edited by David M. Buss, 653–75. Hoboken, NJ: Wiley, 2005.

Lakoff, George, and Mark Johnson. *Philosophy in the Flesh: The Embodied Mind and Its Challenge to Western Thought.* New York: Basic Books, 1999.

Laland, Kevin N., and Gillian R. Brown. *Sense and Nonsense: Evolutionary Perspectives on Human Behaviour.* New York: Oxford University Press, 2002.

Lancaster, Jane B., and Hillard S. Kaplan. "Chimpanzee and Human Intelligence: Life History, Diet, and the Mind." In *The Evolution of Mind: Fundamental Questions and Controversies*, edited by Steven W. Gangestad and Jeffry A. Simpson, 111–18. New York: Guilford, 2007.

Lane, Christopher. *The Burdens of Intimacy: Psychoanalysis and Victorian Masculinity.* Chicago: University of Chicago Press, 1999.

Langbaum, Robert Woodrow. *Thomas Hardy in Our Time.* New York: St. Martin's Press, 1995.

Latour, Bruno, and Steve Woolgar. *Laboratory Life: The Social Construction of Scientific Facts.* Beverly Hills, CA: Sage, 1979.

Leavis, F. R. *The Great Tradition: George Eliot, Henry James, Joseph Conrad.* London: Chatto & Windus, 1948. New York: New York University Press, 1973.

Lerner, Laurence. *Thomas Hardy's "The Mayor of Casterbridge": Tragedy or Social History?* London: Sussex University Press, 1975.

Levine, George. *The Realistic Imagination: English Fiction from Frankenstein to Lady Chatterley.* Chicago: University of Chicago Press, 1981.

Levine, George Lewis, and Alan Rauch, eds. *One Culture: Essays in Science and Literature.* Madison: University of Wisconsin Press, 1987.

Lewis, Michael. "Self-Conscious Emotions: Embarrassment, Pride, Shame and Guilt." In *Handbook of Emotions*, edited by Michael Lewis and Jeanette M. Haviland-Jones, 2nd ed., 623–36. New York: Guildford, 2000.

Linden, David J. *The Accidental Mind*. Cambridge, MA: Harvard University Press, 2007.

Liou, Liang-ya. "The Politics of a Transgressive Desire: Oscar Wilde's *The Picture of Dorian Gray*." *Studies in Language and Literature* 6 (1994): 101–25.

Lippa, Richard A. *Gender, Nature, and Nurture*. 2nd ed. Mahwah, NJ: Lawrence Erlbaum, 2005.

Litvak, Joseph. "Delicacy and Disgust, Mourning and Melancholia, Privilege and Perversity: *Pride and Prejudice*." *Qui Parle* 6, no. 1 (1992): 35–51.

Litz, A. Walton. *Jane Austen: A Study of Her Artistic Development*. New York: Oxford University Press, 1965.

López, José, and Garry Potter, eds. *After Postmodernism: An Introduction to Critical Realism*. London: Continuum, 2005.

Low, Bobbi S. "The Evolution of Human Life Histories." In *Handbook of Evolutionary Psychology: Ideas, Issues, and Applications*, edited by Charles Crawford and Dennis L. Krebs, 131–61. Mahway, NJ: Lawrence Erlbaum, 1998.

———. *Why Sex Matters: A Darwinian Look at Human Behavior*. Princeton, NJ: Princeton University Press, 2000.

Lumsden, Charles J., and Edward O. Wilson. *Genes, Mind, and Culture: The Coevolutionary Process*. 25th anniversary ed. Hackensack, NJ: World Scientific, 2005.

———. *Promethean Fire: Reflections on the Origin of Mind*. Cambridge, MA: Harvard University Press, 1983.

MacDonald, Kevin. B. "Evolution and a Dual Processing Theory of Culture: Applications to Moral Idealism and Political Philosophy." *Politics and Culture*, no. 1 (2010). http://www.politicsandculture.org/2010/04/28/contents-2/.

———. "Evolution, Culture, and the Five-Factor Model." *Journal of Cross-Cultural Psychology* 29, no. 1 (1998): 119–49.

———. "Evolution, the Five-Factor Model, and Levels of Personality." *Journal of Personality* 63, no. 3 (1995): 525–67.

———. "Life History Theory and Human Reproductive Behavior." *Human Nature* 8, no. 4 (1997): 327–59.

———. "A Perspective on Darwinian Psychology: The Importance of Domain-General Mechanisms, Plasticity, and Individual Differences." *Ethology and Sociobiology* 12, no. 6 (1991): 449–80.

———. "Evolution, Psychology, and a Conflict Theory of Culture." *Evolutionary Psychology* 7, no. 2 (2009): 208–33.

Mallett, Philip. "A Note on the Text." In *The Mayor of Casterbridge: An Authoritative Text, Backgrounds and Contexts, Criticism*, by Thomas Hardy. Edited by Phillip Mallet xiii–xvii. 2nd ed. New York: Norton, 2001.

Mameli, Matteo. "Evolution and Psychology in Philosophical Perspective." In *Oxford Handbook of Evolutionary Psychology*, edited by Robin I. M.

Dunbar and Louise Barrett, 21–34. Oxford: Oxford University Press, 2007.

Mar, Raymond A. "The Neuropsychology of Narrative: Story Comprehension, Story Production and Their Interrelation." *Neuropsychologia* 42, no. 10 (2004): 1414–34.

Martin, Jane Roland. "Methodological Essentialism, False Difference, and Other Dangerous Traps." *Signs* 19, no. 3 (1994): 630–57.

Martindale, Colin. *The Clockwork Muse: The Predictability of Artistic Change.* New York: Basic Books, 1990.

Martindale, Colin, Paul Locher, and V. M. Petrov, eds. *Evolutionary and Neurocognitive Approaches to Aesthetics, Creativity, and the Arts.* Amityville, NY: Baywood, 2007.

Matravers, Derek. "The Paradox of Fiction: The Report Versus the Perceptual Model." In *Emotion and the Arts*, edited by Mette Hjort and Sue Laver, 78–92. New York: Oxford University Press, 1997.

McAdams, Dan P. *The Person: An Introduction to Personality Psychology.* 4th ed. Hoboken, NJ: Wiley, 2009.

McClelland, David C. *Human Motivation.* Glenview, IL: Scott, Foresman, 1985.

McEwan, Ian. "Literature, Science, and Human Nature." In *The Literary Animal: Evolution and the Nature of Narrative*, edited by Jonathan Gottschall and David Sloan Wilson, 5–19. Evanston, IL: Northwestern University Press, 2005.

McQuillan, Martin, Robin Purves, Graeme Macdonald, and Steven Thomson, eds. *Post-Theory: New Directions in Criticism.* Edinburgh: Edinburgh University Press, 2000.

Mellars, Paul. *The Neanderthal Legacy: An Archaeological Perspective from Western Europe.* Princeton, NJ: Princeton University Press, 1996.

Mellars, Paul, and Christopher B. Stringer, eds. *The Human Revolution: Behavioural and Biological Perspectives on the Origins of Modern Humans.* Princeton, NJ: Princeton University Press, 1989.

Mellars, Paul, Katie Boyle, Ofer Bar-Yosef, and C. Stringer. *Rethinking the Human Revolution: New Behavioural and Biological Perspectives on the Origin and Dispersal of Modern Humans.* Cambridge, UK: McDonald Institute for Archaeological Research, 2007.

Menand, Louis. "Dangers Within and Without." In *Profession 2005*, edited by Rosemary G. Feal, 10–17. New York: Modern Language Association of America, 2005.

Miall, David S. *Literary Reading: Empirical and Theoretical Studies.* New York: Peter Lang, 2006.

Miller, D. A. *Jane Austen, or the Secret of Style.* Princeton, NJ: Princeton University Press, 2003.

———. *The Novel and the Police.* Berkeley: University of California Press, 1988.

Miller, Geoffrey F. *The Mating Mind: How Sexual Choice Shaped the Evolution of Human Nature.* New York: Doubleday, 2000.

Miller, J. Hillis. "Speech Acts, Decisions, and Community in *The Mayor of Casterbridge*." In *Thomas Hardy and Contemporary Literary Studies*, edited by Tim Dolin and Peter Widdowson, 36–53. Houndmills, UK: Palgrave, 2004.

———. *Thomas Hardy: Distance and Desire*. Cambridge, MA: Harvard University Press, 1970.

Millgate, Michael. *Thomas Hardy: His Career as a Novelist*. New York: St. Martin's Press, 1994.

Mithen, Steven J. *The Prehistory of the Mind: A Search for the Origins of Art, Religion, and Science*. London: Thames and Hudson, 1996.

Mock, Douglas W. *More Than Kin and Less Than Kind: The Evolution of Family Conflict*. Cambridge, MA: Harvard University Press, 2004.

Mondak, Jeffery J., Matthew V. Hibbing, Damarys Canache, Mitchell A. Seligson, and Mary R. Anderson. "Personality and Civic Engagement: An Integrative Framework for the Study of Trait Effects on Political Behavior." *American Political Science Review* 104, no. 1 (2010): 85–110.

Moore, Kevin Z. "Death against Life: Hardy's Mortified and Mortifying 'Man of Character' in *The Mayor of Casterbridge*." *Ball State University Forum* 24, no. 3 (1983): 13–25.

———. *The Descent of the Imagination: Postromantic Culture in the Later Novels of Thomas Hardy*. New York: New York University Press, 1990.

Moretti, Franco. *Atlas of the European Novel: 1800–1900*. London: Verso, 1999.

———. *Graphs, Maps, Trees: Abstract Models for a Literary History*. London: Verso, 2005.

Moses, Michael Valdez. "Agon in the Marketplace: *The Mayor of Casterbridge* as Bourgeois Tragedy." *South Atlantic Quarterly* 87, no. 2 (1988): 219–51.

"Most Cited Authors of Books in the Humanities, 2007." *Times Higher Education Supplement*, March 26, 2009. Data provided by Thomson Reuters' ISI Web of Science, 2007. http://www.timeshighereducation.co.uk/story.asp?sectioncode=26&storycode=405956

Muehlenbein, Michael P., and Mark V. Flinn. "Patterns and Processes of Human Life History Evolution." In *Mechanisms of Life History Evolution: The Genetics and Physiology of Life History Traits and Trade-Offs*, edited by Thomas Flatt and Andreas Heyland, 153–68. Oxford: Oxford University Press, 2011.

Musselwhite, David. *Social Transformation in Hardy's Tragic Novels: Megamachines and Phantasms*. Houndmills, UK: Palgrave Macmillan, 2003.

Neill, Edward. *The Secret Life of Thomas Hardy: "Retaliatory Fiction."* Aldershot: Ashgate, 2004.

Nesse, Randolph M. *Evolution and the Capacity for Commitment*. New York: Russell Sage Foundation, 2001.

Nettle, Daniel. "The Evolution of Personality Variation in Humans and Other Animals." *American Psychologist* 61, no. 6 (2006): 622–31.

Nettle, Daniel. "Individual Differences." In *Oxford Handbook of Evolutionary Psychology*, edited by Robin I. M. Dunbar and Louise Barrett, 479–90. Oxford: Oxford University Press, 2007.

———. *Personality: What Makes You the Way You Are*. Oxford: Oxford University Press, 2007.

———. "What Happens in *Hamlet*? Exploring the Psychological Foundations of Drama." In *The Literary Animal: Evolution and the Nature of Narrative*, edited by Jonathan Gottschall and David Sloan Wilson, 56–75. Evanston, IL: Northwestern University Press, 2005.

———. "The Wheel of Fire and the Mating Game: Explaining the Origins of Tragedy and Comedy." *Journal of Cultural and Evolutionary Psychology* 3, no. 1 (2005): 39–56.

Nettle, Daniel, and Lars Penke. "Personality: Bridging the Literatures from Human Psychology and Behavioural Ecology." *Philosophical Transactions of the Royal Society B: Biological Sciences* 365, no. 1560 (2010): 4043–50.

New Literary History 36, no. 1 (2005). (Special Issue on the Crisis in the Humanities).

Newman, Karen. "Can This Marriage Be Saved? Jane Austen Makes Sense of an Ending." *ELH* 50, no. 4 (1983): 693–710.

Newton, Judith Lowder. *Women, Power, and Subversion: Social Strategies in British Fiction, 1778–1860*. Athens: University of Georgia Press, 1981.

Nietzsche, Friedrich Wilhelm. *On the Genealogy of Morals: A Polemic by Way of Clarification and Supplement to My Last Book, "Beyond Good and Evil."* Translated by Douglas Smith. Oxford: Oxford University Press, 1996.

Nixon, Cheryl L. "Balancing the Courtship Hero: Masculine Emotional Display in Film Adaptations of Austen's Novels." In *Jane Austen in Hollywood*, edited by Linda Troost and Sayre Greenfield, 22–43. Lexington: University of Kentucky Press, 2001.

Nordlund, Marcus. "The Problem of Romantic Love: Shakespeare and Evolutionary Psychology." In *The Literary Animal: Evolution and the Nature of Narrative*, edited by Jonathan Gottschall and David Sloan Wilson, 107–25. Evanston, IL: Northwestern University Press, 2005.

———. *Shakespeare and the Nature of Love: Literature, Culture, Evolution*. Evanston, IL: Northwestern University Press, 2007.

Oatley, Keith. "Emotions and the Story Worlds of Fiction." In *Narrative Impact: Social and Cognitive Foundations*, edited by Melanie C. Green, Jeffrey J. Strange, and Timothy C. Brock, 39–69. Mahwah, NJ: Lawrence Erlbaum, 2002.

———. "A Taxonomy of the Emotions of Literary Response and a Theory of Identification in Fictional Narrative." *Poetics* 23, no. 1–2 (1995): 53–74.

———. "Why Fiction May Be Twice as True as Fact: Fiction as Cognitive and Emotional Simulation." *Review of General Psychology* 3, no. 2 (1999): 101.

Oatley, Keith, and M. Gholamain. "Emotions and Identification: Connections between Readers and Fiction." In *Emotion and the Arts*, edited by Mette Hjort and Sue Laver, 263–81. New York: Oxford University Press, 1997.

Özyürek, Asli, and Tom Trabasso. "Evaluation during the Understanding of Narratives." *Discourse Processes* 23, no. 3 (1997): 305–36.

Panksepp, Jaak. *Affective Neuroscience: The Foundations of Human and Animal Emotions*. New York: Oxford University Press, 1998.

———. "Brainmind, Mirror Neurons, Empathy, and Morality: What to Believe about the Evolution of the Social Mind." *The Evolutionary Review: Art, Science, Culture* 2 (2011): 38–49.

Panksepp, Jaak, and Jules B. Panksepp. "The Seven Sins of Evolutionary Psychology." *Evolution and Cognition* 6, no. 2 (2000): 108–31.

Paris, Bernard J. *Imagined Human Beings: A Psychological Approach to Character and Conflict in Literature*. New York: New York University Press, 1997.

Parsons, Keith M. *The Science Wars: Debating Scientific Knowledge and Technology*. Amherst, NY: Prometheus Books, 2003.

Paterson, John. "*The Mayor of Casterbridge* as Tragedy." *Victorian Studies* 3, no. 2 (1959): 151–72.

Paulhus, Delroy L., and Oliver P. John. "Egoistic and Moralistic Biases in Self-Perception: The Interplay of Self-Deceptive Styles with Basic Traits and Motives." *Journal of Personality* 66, no. 6 (1998): 1025–60.

Payne, Michael, and John Schad, eds. *Life after Theory*. London: Continuum, 2003.

Peterfreund, Stuart, ed. *Literature and Science: Theory and Practice*. Boston: Northeastern University Press, 1990.

Pinker, Steven. *The Blank Slate: The Modern Denial of Human Nature*. New York: Viking, 2002.

———. Foreword to *The Handbook of Evolutionary Psychology*, edited by David M. Buss. xi–xvi. Hoboken, NJ: Wiley, 2005.

———. *How the Mind Works*. New York: Norton, 1997.

———. *The Stuff of Thought: Language as a Window into Human Nature*. New York: Viking, 2007.

———. "Toward a Consilient Study of Literature." *Philosophy and Literature* 31, no. 1 (2007): 162–78.

Plutchik, Robert. *Emotions and Life: Perspectives from Psychology, Biology, and Evolution*. Washington, DC: American Psychological Association, 2003.

Poovey, Mary. *The Proper Lady and the Woman Writer: Ideology as Style in the Works of Mary Wollstonecraft, Mary Shelley, and Jane Austen*. Chicago: University of Chicago Press, 1984.

Posner, Michael I., and Marcus E. Raichle. *Images of Mind*. New York: Scientific American Library, 1994.

Potts, Malcolm, and Roger V. Short. *Ever since Adam and Eve: The Evolution of Human Sexuality*. Cambridge: Cambridge University Press, 1999.

Premack, David, and Ann James Premack. "Origins of Human Social Competence." In *The Cognitive Neurosciences*, edited by Michael S. Gazzaniga, 205–18. Cambridge, MA: MIT Press, 1995.

Rabkin, Eric S. "Science Fiction and the Future of Criticism." *PMLA* 119, no. 3 (2004): 457–73.

Raine, Craig. "Conscious Artistry in *The Mayor of Casterbridge*." In *New Perspectives on Thomas Hardy*, edited by Charles Pettit, 156–71. New York: Knopf, 1994.

Ramel, Annie. "The Crevice in the Canvas: A Study of *The Mayor of Casterbridge*." *Victorian Literature and Culture* 26, no. 2 (1998): 259–72.

Register, Cheri. "American Feminist Literary Criticism: A Bibliographical Introduction." In *Feminist Literary Criticism: Explorations in Theory*, edited by Josephine Donovan, 1–28. Lexington: University of Kentucky Press, 1975.

Review of *The Mayor of Casterbridge*, by Thomas Hardy. *Saturday Review*, May 29, 1886, 757. Reprint in *Thomas Hardy: The Critical Heritage*, edited by R. G. Cox, 134–36, New ed. London: Routledge, 1995. 134–36.

Richardson, Alan, and Ellen Spolsky, eds. *The Work of Fiction: Cognition, Culture, and Complexity*. Aldershot, England: Ashgate, 2004.

Richerson, Peter J., and Robert Boyd. "The Evolution of Human Ultrasociality." In *Ethnic Conflict and Indoctrination: Altruism and Identity in Evolutionary Perspective*, edited by Irenäus Eibl-Eibesfeldt and Frank K. Salter, 71–95. New York: Berghahn, 1998.

———. *Not by Genes Alone: How Culture Transformed Human Evolution*. Chicago: University of Chicago Press, 2005.

Ridley, Matt. *The Origins of Virtue*. London: Viking, 1996.

Ridout, Alice. Review of *Third Wave Feminism: A Critical Exploration*. *Contemporary Women's Writing* 1, no. 1–2 (2007): 208–09.

Rizzolatti, Giacomo, and Leonardo Fogassi. "Mirror Neurons and Social Cognition." In *Oxford Handbook of Evolutionary Psychology*, edited by Robin I. M. Dunbar and Louise Barrett, 179–95. Oxford: Oxford University Press, 2007.

Rorty, Richard. *Consequences of Pragmatism: Essays, 1972–1980*. Minneapolis: University of Minnesota Press, 1982.

Said, Edward W. *Culture and Imperialism*. New York: Knopf, 1993.

Salmon, Catherine. *Warrior Lovers: Erotic Fiction, Evolution and Female Sexuality*. Darwinism Today. New Haven, CT: Yale University Press, 2003.

Salmon, Catherine, and Don Symons. "Slash Fiction and Human Mating Psychology." *Journal of Sex Research* 41, no. 1 (2004): 94–100.

Salmon, Catherine, and Todd K. Shackelford, eds. *Family Relationships: An Evolutionary Perspective*. Oxford: Oxford University Press, 2008.

———. *The Oxford Handbook of Evolutionary Family Psychology*. New York: Oxford University Press, 2011.

Salter, Frank K. *Emotions in Command: Biology, Bureaucracy, and Cultural Evolution*. New Brunswick, NJ: Transaction Publishers, 2008.

Saucier, Gerard, and Louis R. Goldberg. “Lexical Studies of Indigenous Personality Factors: Premises, Products, and Prospects.” *Journal of Personality* 69, no. 6 (2001): 847–79.

Saucier, Gerard, Stelios Georgiades, Ionnas Tsaousis, and Louis R. Goldberg. “The Factor Structure of Greek Personality Adjectives.” *Journal of Personality and Social Psychology* 88, no. 5 (2005): 856–75.

Saunders, Judith P. “Male Reproductive Strategies in Sherwood Anderson’s ‘The Untold Lie.’” *Philosophy and Literature* 31, no. 2 (2007): 311–22.

———. “Paternal Confidence in Hurston’s ‘the Gilded Six-Bits’.” In *Evolution, Literature, and Film: A Reader*, edited by Brian Boyd, Joseph Carroll, and Jonathan Gottschall, 392–408. New York: Columbia University Press, 2010.

———. *Reading Edith Wharton through a Darwinian Lens: Evolutionary Biological Issues in Her Fiction.* Jefferson, NC: McFarland, 2009.

Schaller, Mark, Justin H. Park, and Douglas T. Kenrick. “Human Evolution and Social Cognition.” In *Oxford Handbook of Evolutionary Psychology*, edited by Robin I. M. Dunbar and Louise Barrett, 491–504. Oxford: Oxford University Press, 2007.

Schmidt, Gavin. “Why Hasn’t Specialization Led to the Balkanization of Science?” In *What’s Next: Dispatches on the Future of Science*, edited by Max Brockman, 224–37. New York: Vintage Books, 2009.

Schmitt, David P. “Fundamentals of Human Mating Strategies.” In *The Handbook of Evolutionary Psychology*, edited by David M. Buss, 258–91. Hoboken: Wiley, 2005.

Schor, Naomi. “The Essentialism Which Is Not One: Coming to Grips with Irigaray.” *Differences* 1, no. 1–2 (1989): 38–58.

Schweik, Robert C. “Character and Fate in Hardy’s *The Mayor of Casterbridge*.” *Nineteenth-Century Fiction* 21, no. 3 (1966): 249–62.

Seamon, Roger. “Literary Darwinism as Science and Myth.” *Style* 42, no. 2–3 (2009): 261–65.

Sedgwick, Eve Kosofsky. *Epistemology of the Closet.* Berkeley: University of California Press, 1990.

Showalter, Elaine. “The Unmanning of the Mayor of Casterbridge.” In *Critical Approaches to the Fiction of Thomas Hardy*, edited by Dale Kramer, 99–115. London: Macmillan, 1979.

Sims, Gregory E., Se-Ran Jun, Guohong A. Wu, and Sung-Hou Kim. “Alignment-Free Genome Comparison with Feature Frequency Profiles (Ffp) and Optimal Resolutions.” *Proceedings of the National Academy of Sciences* 106, no. 8 (2009): 2677–82.

Slingerland, Edward G. *What Science Offers the Humanities: Integrating Body and Culture.* Cambridge: Cambridge University Press, 2008.

Smee, Sebastian. “Natural-Born Thrillers.” *Australian Literary Review* (May 2009): 17.

Smith, Barbara Herrnstein. *Scandalous Knowledge: Science, Truth and the Human.* Durham, NC: Duke University Press, 2006.

Smith, David Livingston. *The Most Dangerous Animal: Human Nature and the Origins of War*. New York: St. Martin's Press, 2007.

Smith, Johanna M. "'I Am a Gentleman's Daughter': A Marxist-Feminist Reading of *Pride and Prejudice*." In *Approaches to Teaching Austen's "Pride and Prejudice,"* edited by Martha McClintock Folsom, 27–40. New York: Modern Language Association of America, 1993.

———. "The Oppositional Reader and *Pride and Prejudice*." In *A Companion to Jane Austen Studies*, edited by Laura Cooner Lambdin and Robert Thomas Lambdin, 27–40. Westport, CT: Greenwood, 2000.

Snitow, Anne B. "Mass Market Romance: Pornography for Women Is Different." *Radical History Review*, no. 20 (1979): 141–61.

Snow, C. P. *The Two Cultures*. Cambridge: Cambridge University Press, 1993.

Sober, Elliott, and David Sloan Wilson. *Unto Others: The Evolution and Psychology of Unselfish Behavior*. Cambridge, MA: Harvard University Press, 1998.

Sokal, Alan D. "Transgressing the Boundaries: Toward a Transformative Hermeneutics of Quantum Gravity." *Social Text* 14, no. 46–47 (1996): 217–52.

Sokal, Alan D., and Jean Bricmont. *Fashionable Nonsense: Postmodern Intellectuals' Abuse of Science*. New York: Picador, 1998.

Spacks, Patricia Ann Meyer. *The Female Imagination*. New York: Knopf, 1975.

Spivey, Ted R. "Thomas Hardy's Tragic Hero." *Nineteenth-Century Fiction* 9, no. 3 (1954): 179–91.

Spolsky, Ellen. "The Centrality of the Exceptional in Literary Study." *Style* 42, no. 2–3 (2009): 285–89.

———. *Gaps in Nature: Literary Interpretation and the Modular Mind*. Albany: State University of New York Press, 1993.

Stanford, Craig B. *Significant Others: The Ape-Human Continuum and the Quest for Human Nature*. New York: Basic Books, 2001.

Starzyk, Lawrence J. "Hardy's *Mayor:* The Antitraditional Basis of Tragedy." *Studies in the Novel* 4, no. 4 (1972): 592–607.

Sterelny, Kim. *Thought in a Hostile World: The Evolution of Human Cognition*. Malden, MA: Blackwell, 2003.

Sternberg, Robert J. "Triangulating Love." In *The Psychology of Love*, edited by Robert J. Sternberg and Michael L. Barnes, 119–38. New Haven, CT: Yale University Press, 1988.

Stevens, Anthony. *Archetype Revisited: An Updated Natural History of the Self*. Toronto: Inner City Books, 2003.

Stone, Alison. "On the Genealogy of Women: A Defense of Anti-Essentialism." In *Third Wave Feminism: A Critical Exploration*, edited by Stacy Gillis, Gillian Howe, and Rebecca Munford, 85–96. Houndmills, UK: Palgrave, 2004.

Storey, Robert F. *Mimesis and the Human Animal: On the Biogenetic Foundations of Literary Representation.* Evanston, IL: Northwestern University Press, 1996.

Stringer, Chris, and Clive Gamble. *In Search of the Neanderthals: Solving the Puzzle of Human Origins.* New York: Thames and Hudson, 1993.

Sugiyama, Michelle Scalise. "Food, Foragers, and Folklore: The Role of Narrative in Human Subsistence." *Evolution and Human Behavior* 22, no. 4 (2001): 221–40.

———. "Narrative Theory and Function: Why Evolution Matters." *Philosophy and Literature* 25, no. 2 (2001): 233–50.

———. "New Science, Old Myth: An Evolutionary Critique of the Oedipal Paradigm." *Mosaic* 34, no. 1 (2001): 121–36.

———. "Reverse-Engineering Narrative: Evidence of Special Design." In *The Literary Animal: Evolution and the Nature of Narrative*, edited by Jonathan Gottschall and David Sloan Wilson, 177–96. Evanston, IL: Northwestern University Press, 2005.

Swirski, Peter. *Of Literature and Knowledge: Explorations in Narrative Thought Experiments, Evolution, and Game Theory.* Abingdon, UK: Routledge, 2006.

———. "When Biological Evolution and Social Revolution Clash: Skinner's Behaviorist Utopia." *The Evolutionary Review: Art, Science, Culture* 1 (2010): 18–23.

Symons, Donald. *The Evolution of Human Sexuality.* New York: Oxford University Press, 1979.

Tan, Ed S. *Emotion and the Structure of Narrative Film: Film as an Emotion Machine.* Mahwah, NJ: Lawrence Erlbaum, 1996.

Tanaka, Jiro. "What Is Copernican? A Few Common Barriers to Darwinian Thinking about the Mind." *The Evolutionary Review: Art, Science, Culture* 1 (2010): 6–12.

Tanner, Tony. *Jane Austen.* Cambridge, MA: Harvard University Press, 1986.

Thagard, Paul. *The Brain and the Meaning of Life.* Princeton, NJ: Princeton University Press, 2010.

Tinbergen, Niko. "On Aims and Methods of Ethology." *Zeitschrift für Tierpsychologie* 20, no. 4 (1963): 410–33.

Tomasello, Michael, Malinda Carpenter, Josep Call, Tanya Behne, and Henrike Moll. "Understanding and Sharing Intentions: The Origins of Cultural Cognition." *Behavioral and Brain Sciences* 28, no. 5 (2005): 675–90.

Tooby, John, and Leda Cosmides. "Does Beauty Build Adapted Minds? Toward an Evolutionary Theory of Aesthetics, Fiction and the Arts." *Substance: A Review of Theory & Literary Criticism* 30, no. 1–2 (2001): 6–27.

———. "The Psychological Foundations of Culture." In *The Adapted Mind: Evolutionary Psychology and the Generation of Culture.*, edited by Jerome

H. Barkow, Leda Cosmides, and John Tooby, 19–136. New York: Oxford University Press, 1992.

Trilling, Lionel. "*Mansfield Park*." In *The Opposing Self: Nine Essays in Criticism, 208–30*. New York: Viking, 1955.

Trivers, Robert L. "Parental Investment and Sexual Selection." In *Sexual Selection and the Descent of Man 1871–1971*, edited by Bernard Campbell, 136–79. Chicago: Aldine, 1972.

Turchin, Peter. *War and Peace and War: The Life Cycles of Imperial Nations*. New York: Pi, 2006.

Turner, Mark. *The Artful Mind: Cognitive Science and the Riddle of Human Creativity*. Oxford: Oxford University Press, 2006.

———. *The Literary Mind*. New York: Oxford University Press, 1996.

———. *Reading Minds: The Study of English in the Age of Cognitive Science*. Princeton, NJ: Princeton University Press, 1991.

Van Peer, Willie. *Muses and Measures: Empirical Research Methods for the Humanities*. Newcastle upon Tyne: Cambridge Scholars, 2007.

———. "Toward a Poetics of Emotion." In *Emotion and the Arts*, edited by Mette Hjort and Sue Laver, 215–24. New York: Oxford University Press, 1997.

Vandermassen, Griet. *Who's Afraid of Charles Darwin? Debating Feminism and Evolutionary Theory*. Lanham, MD: Rowman & Littlefield, 2005.

Vigar, Penelope. *The Novels of Thomas Hardy: Illusion and Reality*. London: Athlone, 1974.

Voland, Eckart. "Aesthetic Preferences in the World of Artifacts: Adaptations for the Evaluation of Honest Signals." In *Evolutionary Aesthetics*, edited by Eckart Voland and Karl Grammer, 239–60. Berlin: Springer, 2003.

Wade, Nicholas. *Before the Dawn: Recovering the Lost History of Our Ancestors*. New York: Penguin Press, 2006.

Weinberg, Steven. *Dreams of a Final Theory*. New York: Pantheon Books, 1992.

———. *Facing Up: Science and Its Cultural Adversaries*. Cambridge, MA: Harvard University Press, 2001.

Wells, Robin Headlam, and Johnjoe McFadden, eds. *Human Nature: Fact and Fiction*. London: Continuum, 2006.

Whissel, Cynthia. "Mate Selection in Popular Women's Fiction." *Human Nature* 7, no. 4 (1996): 427–47.

Whiten, Andrew, and Richard W. Byrne, eds. *Machiavellian Intelligence II: Extensions and Evaluations*. Cambridge: Cambridge University Press, 1997.

Wilson, David Sloan. *Darwin's Cathedral: Evolution, Religion, and the Nature of Society*. Chicago: University of Chicago Press, 2002.

———. *Evolution for Everyone: How Darwin's Theory Can Change the Way We Think about Our Lives*. New York: Delacorte, 2007.

———. "Evolutionary Social Constructivism." In *The Literary Animal: Evolution and the Nature of Narrative*, edited by Jonathan Gottschall and David Sloan Wilson, 20–37. Evanston, IL: Northwestern University Press, 2005.

———. "Group-Level Evolutionary Processes." In *Oxford Handbook of Evolutionary Psychology*, edited by Robin I. M. Dunbar and Louise Barrett, 49–55. Oxford: Oxford University Press, 2007.

———. "Human Groups as Adaptive Units: Toward a Permanent Consensus." In *Culture and Cognition*, edited by Peter Carruthers, Stephen Laurence, and Stephen Stich, 78–90. Oxford: Oxford University Press, 2006.

———. "The Role of Group Selection in Human Psychological Evolution." In *The Evolution of Mind: Fundamental Questions and Controversies*, edited by Steven W. Gangestad and Jeffry A. Simpson, 213–20. New York: Guilford, 2007.

Wilson, David Sloan, and Edward O. Wilson. "Rethinking the Theoretical Foundations of Sociobiology." *Quarterly Review of Biology* 82, no. 4 (2007): 327–48.

Wilson, Edward O. *Consilience: The Unity of Knowledge*. New York: Knopf, 1998.

———. *Sociobiology: The New Synthesis*. 25th anniversary ed. Cambridge, MA: Harvard University Press, 2000.

Wilson, Keith. Introduction to *The Mayor of Casterbridge*, by Thomas Hardy. Edited by Keith Wilson, xxi–xli. London: Penguin, 1997.

Wiltshire, John. "*Mansfield Park*, *Emma*, *Persuasion*." In *The Cambridge Companion to Jane Austen*, edited by Edward Copeland and Juliet McMaster, 58–83. Cambridge: Cambridge University Press, 1997.

Wimsatt, William K., Jr., and Monroe K. Beardsley. "The Intentional Fallacy." In *The Verbal Icon: Studies in the Meaning of Poetry*. By William K. Wimsatt, 3–18. Lexington: University of Kentucky Press, 1954.

Woloch, Alex. *The One vs. The Many: Minor Characters and the Space of the Protagonist in the Novel*. Princeton, NJ: Princeton University Press, 2003.

Woolf, Virginia. "The Novels of Thomas Hardy." In *The Second Common Reader*. 1932. New York: Harcourt, 1960.

Woolgar, Steve. *Science: The Very Idea*. Chichester, UK: Ellis Horwood, 1988.

Wrangham, Richard W. *Catching Fire: How Cooking Made Us Human*. New York: Basic Books, 2009.

Wright, T. R. *Hardy and the Erotic*. New York: St. Martin's Press, 1989.

Wylie, Judith. "Dancing in Chains: Feminist Satire in *Pride and Prejudice*." *Persuasions: Journal of the Jane Austen Society of North America*, no. 22 (2000): 62–69.

Zunshine, Lisa. *Why We Read Fiction: Theory of Mind and the Novel*. Columbus: Ohio State University Press, 2006.

Index

Note on how character names and titles of books are listed in the index.

Characters in novels by Jane Austen and Thomas Hardy are listed under the names of Austen and Hardy.

Characters in novels by novelists other than Austen and Hardy are listed under the names of the characters.

Each time a character's name is listed, the page number for that entry is duplicated in the entry for the title of the novel in which the character appears.

Titles of books that are mentioned in the main body of this study are listed under the names of their authors.

Titles of books that are mentioned only in the endnotes or in appendices 2 and 3 are not included in the index.

Characters whose names appear only in appendices 2 and 3 are not included in the index.